TALES OF SEDUCTION

IN MEMORY OF
STELLA WRIGHT (1942–2006)

TALES OF SEDUCTION
The Figure of Don Juan in Spanish Culture

Sarah Wright

Tauris Academic Studies
London & New York

Published in 2007 by Tauris Academic Studies, an imprint of
I.B.Tauris & Co Ltd
6 Salem Road, London W2 4BU
175 Fifth Avenue, New York NY 10010
www.ibtauris.com

Copyright © 2007, Sarah Wright

The right of Sarah Wright to be identified as the author of this work has been asserted by the author in accordance with the Copyright, Design and Patents Act 1988.

All rights reserved. Except for brief quotations in a review, this book, or any part thereof, may not be reproduced, stored in or introduced into a retrieval system, or transmitted, in any form or by any means, electronic, mechanical, photocopying, recording or otherwise, without the prior written permission of the publisher.

ISBN   978 1 84511 477 0 (hb)
ISBN   978 1 84885 975 3 (pb)
eISBN 978 0 75569 629 1
ePDF 978 0 85771 727 6

A full CIP record for this book is available from the British Library
A full CIP record is available from the Library of Congress

Library of Congress Catalog card: available

Copy edited and typeset by Oxford Publishing Services, Oxford

CONTENTS

List of Illustrations	vi
Acknowledgements	ix
Foreword by Juliet Mitchell	xiii
Introduction: In Search of Don Juan	1
1. Opposites Attract: An Intellectual, Don Juan and Nation in Early Twentieth-century Spain	23
2. Performance Anxieties: Don Juan in the Consulting Room	52
3. Screen Seductions: Negotiating Theatricality in Don Juan Films	84
4. Repetition Compulsion: Redoing the Tenorio	122
5. Empty Promises: Opera and the Aesthetics of Cultural Consumption	157
Conclusion: Between Limits	187
Notes	195
Bibliography	250
Index	275

LIST OF ILLUSTRATIONS

1. 'The "Effeminate" Don Juan Tenorio en el panteón' by Elías Salaverría (1883–1952). Oil on canvas, 1927. Courtesy Museo Nacional del Teatro (Almagro).   74

2. Pamphlet from *Don Juan Tenorio*. Ricardo de Baños. Courtesy of Fototeca, Filmoteca Española.   87

3. Don Juan as masquerade. *Don Juan* by José Luis Sáenz de Heredia, 1950. Courtesy of Fototeca, Filmoteca Española.   104

4. The sword-fight shot/reverse shot recalls the cinematic model for the conversation. *Don Juan*, by José Luis Sáenz de Heredia. Courtesy of Fototeca, Filmoteca Española.   107

5. Lady Ontiveros confronted by Don Juan. *Don Juan*, by José Luis Sáenz de Heredia. Courtesy of Fototeca, Filmoteca Española.   109

6. The maid's reaction recalls stereotypical depictions from postwar Hollywood. *Don Juan*, by José Luis Sáenz de Heredia. Courtesy of Fototeca, Filmoteca Española.   109

List of Illustrations

7. Cover of publicity pamphlet distributed during screenings. Courtesy Biblioteca Nacional, Madrid.   111
8. An attempt at the de-eroticization of the gaze. Doña Inés. *Don Juan*, by José Luis Sáenz de Heredia. Courtesy of Fototeca, Filmoteca Española.   116
9. Ciutti's tears provide an emotional cue. *Don Juan*, by José Luis Sáenz de Heredia. Courtesy of Fototeca, Filmoteca Española.   118
10. *Última escena de Don Juan Tenorio*, 1922 by Antonio Muñoz Degrain (1840–1924). Courtesy Museo de Bellas Artes (Granada).   134
11. Scene from the Luis Escobar production of *Don Juan Tenorio*, with scenography by Salvador Dalí, 1949. Courtesy Centro Dramático Nacional, Madrid.   152
12. Backdrop designed by Salvador Dalí for Luis Escobar's production of *Don Juan Tenorio*, 1949. Courtesy Centro Dramático Nacional, Madrid.   153
13. The Wedding Feast. Bieito's Barcelona production of *Don Giovanni*. Photograph by Antonio Bofill. Courtesy Fotos Bofill.   161
14. An evening of wrecked stagecraft. Bieito's Barcelona production of *Don Giovanni*. Photograph by Antonio Bofill. Courtesy Fotos Bofill.   162
15. A reinterpretation of the 'escena del sofá'. Bieito's production of *Don Giovanni*. Photograph by Antonio Bofill. Courtesy Fotos Bofill.   163
16. The Commendatore stuffs food into the mouth of Don Giovanni. Bieito's production of *Don Giovanni*. Photograph by Antonio Bofill. Courtesy Fotos Bofill.   176

17. An evening of hell-fire and damnation. A poster to accompany Calixto Bieto's production of *Don Giovanni* at the London Coliseum. Featuring Gary Magee as Don Giovanni. Photograph by Andy Whale. Courtesy of Andy Whale.   178

18. Barbie: postmodern diva. A poster to accompany Calixto Bieito's production of *Don Giovanni* at the Gran Teatre del Liceu, Barcelona. Designed by Joseph Bagà Associates. Photo by Hugo Menduiña. Courtesy of Hugo Menduiña.   179

19. *Seductor*, Naia del Castillo, 2002. Fotografia Luxachrome, 2002. Courtesy of Naia del Castillo.   189

ACKNOWLEDGEMENTS

A Scottish Stevenson Exchange Scholarship as an undergraduate enabled me to attend a wide variety of theatrical performances while on a year abroad in Madrid. These included an outing on 2 November, my birthday, with friends who insisted that the only play to see on the feast of All Souls' was José Zorrilla's *Don Juan Tenorio*. It is almost certainly impossible to thank all of the many people who have helped with this book, whether in generously giving their time and efforts with practical help, information or materials, or else offering emotional encouragement when it was needed most.

They include the following: Victoria Africano, Mark Allinson, José Luis Alonso de Santos, Antonia Andúgar, George Biddlecombe, Calixto Bieito, Wolfgang Burmann, Richard Cardwell, Naia del Castillo, Pilar del Castillo, Richard Cleminson, Carmen Dakin, Ann Davies, Jennifer Duffy, Geraint Evans, Peter Evans, Simon Frith, David Thatcher Gies, Andrew Ginger, Nigel Glendinning, Jack Goody, Jennifer Green, Graeme Hayes, Kirsty Hooper, Fiona Huggett, José Manuel Ibarrola, Valerie Lobban, Anja Louis, José de la Mano, Guillermo Martínez Correcher, Peter Martland, Patricia McDermott, Sir Brian McMaster, Manuel Montesinos Fernández, Pilar Nieva de la Paz,

Tales of Seduction

Eàmonn O'Ciardha, Catherine O'Leary, Rosario Olóndriz, Luisa Passerini, Ángeles Quesada, Francesca Parsons, Alicia Potes, Eamon Rodgers, Jesús Rubio, Nick Sinclair-Brown, Christopher Soufas, George Talbot, Sandra Toval, María Francisca Vilches de Frutos, Isabel Valcárcel, Dagmar Vandebosch, Eduardo Vasco, Ruth Van Velsen, James Williams, Alejandro Yarza. I also thank Jennifer Batchelor (English National Opera), José Luis Díez (Museo del Prado), James Gilbert (ENO), Cristina Jutge (Fundación Gala-Salvador Dalí), Ana Gutiérrez Márquez (Museo del Prado), Carmen Ibáñez (Fundación Gregorio Marañón), María Ángeles Langa Langa (Fundación Santiago Ramón y Cajal), Concha Largo (Centro Dramático Nacional), Tony Legge (ENO), Marga Lobo (Filmoteca Española), Berta Muñoz (Centro de Documentación Teatral), Trinidad del Río (Filmoteca Española), Adela Rocha (Gran Teatre del Liceu), Emma Sadler (ENO), Marta Serrano Vélez (Institut del Teatre), Julia Siburn (ENO), Juan Antonio Somoza (Compañía Nacional de Teatro Clásico).

My colleagues in the Departments of Hispanic Studies at the Universities of London, Royal Holloway College (Miriam Haddu, Richard Pym, Abigail Lee Six, David Vilaseca, Allsa Chaparro and Javier Muñoz-Basols) and Hull (Ruth Aedo-Richmond, Peter Beardsell, John Jones, Brian Powell, Jenny Rumble) deserve special thanks, as does Neil Sinyard. Carmen Gutiérrez Olóndriz, apart from being a great friend, carried out tireless detective work to locate some of the visual material. Her work as a ghost-writer to Spain's rich and famous means that she is not acknowledged nearly enough. María Delgado was extremely generous in sharing contacts and materials and reading parts of the manuscript. Tom Glick generously shared his materials with me. Luis Fernández Cifuentes and Paul Julian Smith have offered solid support over time. I am very grateful to Alison Sinclair for mulling over the

Acknowledgements

project with me in the early stages and for later support. Michael Black very kindly looked at the project early on and offered perceptive advice. Juliet Mitchell has been extraordinarily generous with her time and expertise.

I would like to thank the following for inviting me to present parts of this book in seminars and conferences: Alison Sinclair and Richard Cleminson for 'Alternative Discourses of Mind and Body', University of Cambridge, and also for their careful attention to detail with regards to a paper on Marañón. Ruby Reid Thompson and Lisa Salje invited me to present a paper on Bieito's opera at Clare Hall, University of Cambridge. I am grateful to David Brading and Gillian Beer for their interest while I was Visiting Fellow at Clare Hall during 2002–3. Lisa Clughen arranged for me to speak at Nottingham Trent University. I am grateful to Luisa Passerini for inviting me to present a paper at the Kulturwissensschaftliches Institut, Essen, Germany, as part of their investigations into love in Europe. Pilar Nieva de la Paz and Francisca Vilches de Frutos kindly invited me to teach seminars on women writers and Don Juan at the Consejo Superior de Investigaciones Científicas in 2006 as part of a Ministerio de Cultura project to examine the work of women writers in the Second Republic. I am grateful to them and to the students at those events for their learned comments. I am very pleased to have been the recipient of an AHRC award which granted a term's leave to conduct research. I am grateful to the research committees at the University of Hull and Royal Holloway respectively for granting me research leave. Parts of the book have been published elsewhere: 'Dropping the mask: theatricality and absorption in Sáenz de Heredia's *Don Juan*', *Screen*, 46 (4) Winter 2005, pp. 415–31; 'Gregorio Marañón and "the cult of sex": effeminacy and intersexuality in 'the psychopathology of Don Juan' (1924)', *Bulletin of Spanish Studies*,

81 (6) 2004, pp. 717–38; 'Consuming passions: the aesthetics of cultural consumption in Calixto Bieito's Don Giovanni (2001)', *Journal of Spanish Cultural Studies*, 5 (3) 2004, pp. 317–39. I gratefully acknowledge the permission granted to republish parts of these here. All attempts have been made to locate the copyright holders for the visual material reproduced here.

I owe an enormous debt of gratitude to Professor Jo Labanyi and Professor Dru Dougherty for their careful comments on the final draft. I am very grateful to Elizabeth Munns at I.B.Tauris, Jason Cohen for his expertise with the visual material and Selina Cohen for her expert editorial assistance. Finally, I offer thanks to my sister, Isabel Wright, whose career as a playwright means that she always has perceptive comments to offer, to the Smalls, particularly Chris and Stella, the Escobars (Carmen Luz, Loreto, Alejandro, Fernando) especially my son, Tomás, who was born in time to see the book completed, and in particular my husband Alejandro Escobar for his love and support. This book is dedicated to the memory of my mother, Stella Wright, whose passion for ideas, determination and love of life stays with me.

FOREWORD

There is something odd about Don Juan. An oddness wonderfully captured in the conflicting differences and endless samenesses of the portraits chosen by Sarah Wright to convey his persistence as a relevant icon of twentieth and twenty-first century Spain. There is virtually nothing to Don Juan except the peregrinations of his seductions. The frozen Statue of Liberty, the melodramatic snapshot of Marianne, the grandiosity of Britannia are icons of nationhood. But Don Juan is his story, and it is a repetitious one at that. Indeed, it is only the compulsive repetition that gives the narrative fixity – makes it, and with it him, an icon.

Don Juan is a representation of Wright's title – tales of seduction. Because it is a story, it is infinitely flexible within the constraints of its framework: seduction and conquest claim variety as their rationale. However, because whom you rape, whom you bomb, are necessarily objects of indifference, part of a shopping list (as Wright's discussion of the cannibalism and waste at the heart of conspicuous consumption brings out so interestingly) then so too must the stories themselves with all their derring-do be merely variations on a theme.

Why then the enduring interest – why so much to be said

Tales of Seduction

and thought about, as this book exemplifies? Is Don Juan all of us? Certainly, we forget he is a fictional representation and not a human being whom we meet everyday. The heroic, the infantile, the redeemed, the outrageous, the condemned – each variation will seem contemporaneously appropriate. For us today he is ourselves in the chat room, or drugged and abusive-abused in the gender-equal street, as once he was the portrait of the rake. Yet, he is not Everyman/woman. It is then not that he is us and we are him but that his story is all of ours – fulfilled or suppressed. Therefore, rather than ask 'who is this seducer/conquistador?' we should wonder first 'what does seduction/conquest effect?'

The general human story can have particular renditions that make it feel appropriate only to its specific time. Thus, when I opened on the description of Internet chat rooms and ended with Wright's fascinating depiction of Bieito's 2001 opera, it seemed as though the story had found its true home only today. But that is what it will have seemed like to enthralled fascists staring at Dalí's sets in Francoist Spain or the seventeenth century audience still wondering about the New World. For modernism, an Oedipal explanation can fit, for postmodernism, one centred on 'nameless dread', an observation of the psychoanalyst Wilfed Bion, deployed by Kristeva and re-examined here.

If we follow Wright and use the anthropologist's name for a role – a trickster – then we can see that the seducer/conqueror, androgyne who exemplifies the male is an inhabitant of the border country (Wright) because he hovers on the borders of human sociality itself. According to time and place, that sociality will be expressed predominantly in terms of religion, politics, culture, kinship.

If, despite the fact that it is the story that is ours, we nevertheless always think in terms of its exponent (even if it is only to castigate him as 'empty') this, I think, is

Foreword

because the story is about each person's survival – this may be as an individual as in Mozart's *Don Giovanni* or as a collective as in Bieito's 'street' opera. Whether it is a collective or isolated aloneness, such a condition necessitates what, using today's idiom, we can call our narcissism (Wright is open-minded about its use). Narcissism explains why, when it is the story not the character that matters, we still think in terms of the single character – that is the point of the seduction.

When I tried to think of why I dislike Don Juan in terms of my own Don Juanism, I found it represents a lot of what I dislike in myself but also that I would be bored if it were not there! One end of the seducer's progress is violence and violation, the other is play. Even if multiplied into many alonenesses, the narcissist is always, definitionally, the centre of his own world and like the small child's or the cat's self-absorption, Don Juan's narcissism invokes our own. It is horrible in the adult world of responsibility and delightful in the bisexual childhood one of play – and we all continue to move across that asocial–social border.

The seducer, the conqueror (in their narcissism) is not interested in the object of the seductions or conquests. The story, the performance (which, developing Felman's earlier work, Wright so interestingly evokes and analyses) is designed to keep the seducer always in mind even (perhaps especially) when he is not there. If he leaves, someone else must remember him because without this he has no surety of his continued existence. For this reason, it is at least as important that he breaks as makes endless promises. A promise makes a claim on the future but a promise that will be honoured is a promise taken for granted (like a marriage promise), whereas a promise broken is a promise never forgotten.

In the analyses of the performative, the role of pain is too often ignored. Because pleasure has been given, the breaking of the promise to continue this in the future hurts. Giving pain is the certainty of a powerful memorial. It is this living memorial, this statement that he exists, that the seducer, the conqueror, the narcissist needs. And sex is a powerful medium for the production of memorable pain.

In her stunning analysis of Bieito's 2001 *Don Giovanni*, Wright points out that where offstage rape united earlier versions of the Don's women, today's are sexually active. A case for the courts: can a sexually active person be seduced? Or, is seduction about sex? And if it is, is sex ever just sex? I learnt from this book, that some versions give Don Juan a daughter; but it would seem this is not for inheritance, descent and, of course, not for love and comfort. The daughters are there for incest or to indicate the decadence – no sons – of the blood line. Seductive sex must be transgressive: forbidden daughters and sisters, celibate nuns, other men's wives. They 'belong' to someone/thing else.

Wright pays tribute to the claims as to how this *enfant terrible* flouts the Law of the Commendatore/Father. And he does; but in Bieito's rendering it is not the Father who avenges but the Don's peers who arbitrarily and pointlessly murder him. Here there is gender equality in sex and peer group equity in violence. The pain, I suggest, is everyone's – but everyone is utterly alone. Don Juan's pointlessly murdering peers are each and everyone, Don Juan – they repeat his act of killing. Transgressive sex and murder are two sides of the same coin. Sex promised a rose garden of belonging to the other; the broken promise kills, it is the terrain of murder.

When Tirso de Molina penned Don Juan's introduction in the early sixteen hundreds, the Spanish conquistadors of the previous century could well have been imagined as heroic seducers. They had not known where they were going, or whom or what they would find. They had found

Foreword

land and 'no one', no one that is, who counted. Seduction takes place in an ecstatic vacuum: it takes place somewhere but there is nobody there. Donna Anna, Donna Luisa, Zerlinda and the rest of Leporello's list are metonymically replaceable, displacing each other endlessly because there is no one there who will recognize one and the conqueror is terrified.

Transgression incarnates a nameless dread – if there were to be anyone there, they would always belong to someone else. The Don is tilting at non-existent rivals – the fellow thugs whom Bieito makes murder him; he stays alive by having sex with all and every 'non-existent' woman – thereby ensuring nothing more than our, the audiences', attention.

The seductive sex keeps him alive – for centuries. But his end in a violent death is there in his beginning. Seductions ensure one is alive because the imaginary someone/anyone else wants one and they therefore do not want anyone or someone else. Endlessly new sex with its deadly broken promises replaces an old death – a death whose future is in the past, in the fear that there is nobody there to tell you that you are there too.

Juliet Mitchell
Bouzigues
January 2007

INTRODUCTION: IN SEARCH OF DON JUAN

> *gigolotenorio* ♂ 39:
>
> *Soy: un casanova*
> *Indumentaria: elegante*
> *Ocupación: buscar un desafío*
> *Intereses: comidas y bebidas*
> *Escucho: clásica y ópera*
> *Busco: una cita en la vida real.*
>
> Anon[1]

Don Juan figures populate the Spanish chat rooms of online virtual realities. In a sense, their presence in the *salas de chat* is prefigured: the descriptions provided in the epigraph above, from a personal advertisement on a web page that invites one to *flirtear en internet*, are selected from a series of pull-down tabs. After posting a profile online, and receiving messages from interested *internautas*, participants are invited to enter a chat room, for synchronous, dual or multi-party conversation in real-time,[2] or, in this case, cyber-flirting, 'an enjoyable, frivolous form of sexual communication with no serious intent'.[3]

Antonio Piedra, searching for Don Juan at the end of the millennium, also finds him in cyberspace: '*ave rapaz de todos los valores tecnológicos ... por haber*' (preying rapaciously on all the new technologies), with their '*nuevo diseño del erotismo*' (new type of eroticism), Don Juan is the very essence of *electronic eros*.[4] David Crystal, musing on the liminal nature of the language of chat, 'speech or writing?' notes that 'we "write" e-mails, not speak them. But chat groups are for "chat" and people certainly "speak" to each other there – as do people involved in virtual worlds'.[5] Tantalizingly poised between writing and speaking, virtual chat is difficult to classify, but Shoshana Felman's work on 'speech-acts', in her book *The Scandal of the Speaking Body: Don Juan with J. L. Austin, or Seduction in Two Languages* can help us to understand the peculiar brand of electronic eros at work in the virtual world of chat.[6]

Felman defines a speech-act as a 'performative'; an expression that functions to carry out a performance, to accomplish an act through the very process of its enunciation. The most obvious example of such a 'performative' is the marriage ceremony, where the promise, 'I do', accomplishes the act of marriage through its utterance.

Felman shows how Molière's *Don Juan* (1665) is the play of promises *par excellence*.[7] The scandal of Don Juan, his heresy, lies in the fact that his discourse of seduction is based on the repetition of promises he continually violates. Yet Felman shows how Don Juan operates outside the realm of truth. Don Juanian seduction is a discourse of rhetoric that cannot be judged on its truth or falsity, merely on how successful or unsuccessful it is at performing the acts (the act of promising, the act of pledging troth) it utters. It is up to the other characters to ascertain the truth or falsity of Don Juan's convictions. Don Juanian seduction is, then, a discourse that operates entirely in the present. For Felman, Don Juan's seduction demonstrates that speech is the true realm of eroticism, and not merely a means of access to that realm. To seduce is to produce language that enjoys, language that takes pleasure in having 'no more to say'. To seduce is thus to prolong, within desiring speech, the pleasure-taking performance of the very production of that speech.[8]

For Felman, the trap of seduction consists of producing a '*referential illusion* through an utterance that is by its very nature *self-referential*: the illusion of a real or extra-linguistic act of commitment created by an utterance that refers only to itself'.[9]

While not corresponding to speech-acts *per se* (although promises and pledges are undoubtedly found in online interactions), the language of chat shares characteristics with Felman's 'performative' utterances, defined with recourse to Don Juan. Felman writes that Don Juanian discourse dramatizes the three meanings of the word 'act': 'the erotic connotation, the theatrical connotation and the linguistic connotation'.[10]

At its most extreme, chat can take the form of cybersex in a textual reality in which sexual 'acts' must be rendered through language and may even be uttered in the third person. Two people describe to each other 'in a dramaturgical manner, what they are "doing" to each other and to themselves', in a fusion of sex, performance and language.[11] These are 'speech-acts' in the most literal of senses. The aspect of role-playing within cybersex only adds to the theme of performativity, but chat relies on the textual expression of gestures and actions in other ways too. For instance, non-verbal communication (like body language or facial expressions) is expressed in chat through a range of paralanguage techniques. As Stella Koh notes, 'there are three ways by which nuances in messages are conveyed: the use of "emoticons", the use of "actions" and the use of textual emphasis and word variations'.[12]

While an emoticon is a pictorial expression of the emotions of the moment, a combination of keyboard symbols that form facial expressions, other keyboard combinations present the description of 'actions' in the third person. Chat is performative in other senses too. Chat shares with speech its synchronicity, informality and its 'real-time' transience. With the written form it shares reflectivity, distance and the opportunity for self-representation. But while this hybrid form, like speech, is spontaneous and dynamic, a chat-log (the textual transcript of chat sessions) mimics the dramaturgical nature of a theatre script. Language is 'heightened', while the disguise of a *nick* (alias) or avatar, lends chat a ludic quality that permits *usuarios* (users) to masquerade in character, turning the chat channel into a liminal space, and chat into a meta-discourse.

Like Don Juanian discourse, chat produces language that 'enjoys', involving, if not the 'deletion of the body', then certainly a form of 'disembodiment', revelling in the 'pleasure of the interface',[13] producing language that enjoys 'having no more to say'. Like Don Juan's rhetoric of seduction, this type of cyber-flirting offers a promise (from the Latin *promittere*, to send forth) in the sense that it conjures up new worlds, new vistas beyond the *channel* of the chat room, that rely on an 'orchestration of potentials'[14] for their power, but that burst like empty bubbles beyond the virtual realm. Like Don Juan's discourse of seduction, chat produces the illusion of a real or extra-linguistic act of commitment (the *'cita en la vida real'* (date in real life), the meeting of two lovers who exist in their imagined form only in the minds of the participants),[15] while by its very nature it is nothing other than self-referential.

Operating, like Don Juan, outside the realm of the

Introduction: In Search of Don Juan

truth/falsity criterion, within its enclosed world, chat is complete unto itself, the very definition of the 'virtual'. For even in the rare cases that the '*maridajes y guiños virtuales*' (virtual marriages and flirtations)[16] lead to a '*cita en la vida real*', we move out of the realm of this heightened performative space, the realm of electronic eros.

Masquerade is a defining characteristic of serial *ligues virtuales* (virtual pick-ups). The participants disguise their identities under one or a range of imaginative or clichéd pen-names and Don Juan types, both male and female, cruise cyberspace like virtual *flaněurs*, disguising their gender, sexual orientation, class and background. Don Juan in the chat room resides at the limits between speech and the written word, between language and the body, and between gender divisions and sexual orientation. Don Juan is at home in new technology, a site for the projection of fantasy and identification, which offers electronic promiscuity without responsibility.

While the myth of Don Juan has been modified over the years, brought down to size, shown up and, post-feminism, renamed ageing lothario, skirt-chaser, cad and debaucher, nevertheless, for some at least, in a Spanish chat room and however ironically expressed he remains an icon to represent the thrill, allure and promise of seduction (indeed the thrill, allure and promise of seduction constitutes the seduction itself). With his masquerade, serial seductions and lack of personal responsibility, Don Juan is the perfect icon for the peculiar language of electronic eros. The spirit of Don Juan, it seems, lives on in the twenty-first century.

Don Juan exists in the popular imagination as the legendary seducer of women, charismatic rogue, trickster and transgressor of sacred boundaries. A potent icon of uncontained male sexual energy, he promiscuously crosses cultures, from east to west, while at times it appears that his only constancy is his continued presence in a global cultural heritage that links the past to the present. Don Juan's appeal and presence is transnational and he lays claim to the status of myth. He flits through different media, from painting to photography, from opera to theatre, from novel to film, Internet to essay. His greatest constancy is his infidelity. This means that he is dedicated to the perpetual crossing of limits, never content to remain wedded to any particular medium, genre, ideology or time frame. His infidelity endows him with rejuvenatory powers, allowing him to reappear in different guises, perpetually, throughout time. Intellectually promiscuous, he finds his way into a range of Western theories, from semiotics to medicine, eugenics and degeneration to psychoanalysis or consumerism, aesthetics to spectatorship, from the performative to the visual and the haptic, and may be pressed into service for opposing ideologies or pedagogical aims. Don Juan can represent a variety of debates, whether about nation, sexuality, or consumption – he is a figure of excess in all these realms.

Don Juan is often employed as a scapegoat to allow the reader or public to test the limits of culture (be they of gender, class, religion, nationhood, sexual orientation, ethics or a host of other cultural and ideological manifestations). We send Don Juan before us as a substitute to test the waters. These exercises in testing the limit slip effortlessly into scenarios for the exploration of vicarious pleasures through fantasy. Such is the case with the Internet, the perfect realm for fantasy relations.

A Spanish publication of 1919, the *Manual del perfecto mujeriego* (Manual for the Perfect Womanizer), provides another interesting example. It tells the adventures of a Don Juan who becomes involved in lesbian affairs, and who enjoys prostitutes and sordid erotica. It purportedly offers advice to those men who want to '*estudiar nuestro curso*' (study our course), including insisting that they have a lot of money, maintain good health and, most importantly, are '*muy cuidadoso de su ropa interior*' (very fastidious about their underwear), but simultaneously the book provides a flight of fantasy, allowing the reader to test the limits of sexual orientation, erotic fantasy, treatment of women and social acceptability.[17]

Only once one is nearing the end of the book, however, does it become clear that this is, in fact, a morality tale that ends in death and destruction. This purported self-help book concludes not by teaching men how to become Don Juans, but the opposite: '*entrando como los gladiadores romanos en el estadio de las lascivias y haciendo desempeñar a nuestros novelescos muñecos diversos papeles en la tragicomedia del amor sensual, para que nuestros lectores lo aborrezcan y lo aparten de sus almas*' (entering like Roman gladiators into the arena of lasciviousness and having our novelistic dolls play out diverse roles in the tragicomedy of sensual love, so that our readers learn to abhor it and separate it from their souls). The salacious text collapses into a warning about the dangers of indulging in lascivious behaviour and the importance of religious instruction.

Don Juan is a trickster-figure,[18] following the tradition of the study of tricksters borrowed from anthropology.[19] Doty and Hynes note the first use of the term 'trickster' in English in the eighteenth century, not as an anthropological category, but 'to designate morally one who deceives or cheats'.[20] Don Juan's designation since the seventeenth century as a *burlador*[21] aligns him with the eponymous trickster figure. Despite the myriad versions of trickster tales, there is an understanding of what constitutes a trickster figure.[22] C. W. Spinks suggests, moreover, that the trickster can be understood as a sign.[23] As Spinks, points out, the

> Trickster can best be understood as a semiotic creature because Trickster is the lord of the boundaries,

Tales of Seduction

> the hinge, the road, the edge, and most of the other marginalities of culture – the sibling of semiosis ... [he] constantly tries the boundaries between the known and the unknown, between the signed and the unsigned, between the legitimate and the outlaw, between the domesticated and the wild; that is, between culture and non-culture.[24]

Don Juan as a sign shares characteristics with trickster semiotics. Don Juan, too, as we shall see, is a cultural icon, continually testing the limits of culture, perpetually shifting between cultural worlds.

It is his edgy nature, and the ambivalence of his marginal dance, that allows one to discuss a trickster in terms of dualities. This dualistic sign 'divides the wholeness of space into a continual polarity of things, with this on one side of the mark, and that on the other'.[25] The trickster as a sign allows us to make sense of the world in terms of 'this' or 'not-this'. 'We use negation to digitally mark an analogue world, to structure a continuum into a comprehensibility, and to weave the narrative of culture.'[26] Don Juan also has the capacity to unite opposites within his figure. Both the trickster and Don Juan are figures with narrative origins and their complexity often derives from their narrative role. The Don Juan story, which is seen to be traced to Tirso de Molina's *El burlador de Sevilla y convidado de piedra* (The Trickster of Seville and the Stone Guest, c.1630) is perceived as an amalgam of two separate plot devices, the dissolute libertine (sustained by the *burla* or trick), fused with the double invitation (Don Juan invites a stone statue to dinner and is rewarded with an invitation to join the ranks of the dead).

Tirso de Molina's Don Juan in some ways seems to be diametrically opposed to the protagonist of his earlier play *El vergonzoso en palacio* (The Bashful Man at Court) where

Introduction: In Search of Don Juan

marriage is seen to triumph over unlicensed sexuality.[27] In Tirso de Molina's *El burlador de Sevilla*, the eponymous bragging anti-hero scorns marriage and social convention and meets his end in hell, the punishment for a life lived in sin. Meanwhile, in his nineteenth-century revision of the story, *Don Juan Tenorio* (1844), José Zorrilla rewrites the ending to have Don Juan repent for his sins and be rewarded with a reservation in heaven. Zorrilla's version is the one that holds sway in Spain. Thus, within Don Juan's narrative origins, we find not just the articulation of dualisms (exemplified by the division between heaven and hell), but also the perpetual threat that opposites can collapse into one another. An ending in hell is neatly transposed into heavenly rewards. Under the law of 'self-cancellation', a dissolute life is counterbalanced by a glorious afterlife.[28] Thus, Don Juan as a sign explores the contingency of our cultural systems, as well as revealing their constructed nature.

It is this characteristic of dualistic signs to unite opposites within the same figure that makes Don Juan such an unstable icon. The extremes contained within Don Juan as a sign threaten constantly to cave into their opposite. The cancelling out of dualisms gives way to a plurality of meanings, an inability to pin Don Juan down, to fix any one meaning. Don Juan as a sign here becomes understood as a cultural icon – a site for the projection of a variety of (often shifting) meanings and national obsessions.

Don Juan has over the years been pressed into service for a variety of ideological programmes, but his dualism makes him volatile as an ideological weapon. We have seen how the *Manual del mujeriego* starts out as a self-help course for would-be womanizers, but quickly collapses into warning its reader against the evils of Don Juanesque ways. Similarly, while the Internet offers the *usuario* the allure of electronic *jouissance*, of freedom from the boundaries

Tales of Seduction

separating genders, sexual orientations, or language and the body, its pleasures can nevertheless seem as empty as *'el cibersexo como metáfora recurrente de cuerpos deshabitados, solitarios y hasta ridículos'* (cybersex as a recurrent metaphor for bodies that are uninhabited, solitary or even ridiculous), while the Internet, with its promiscuity without responsibility, sustained by the metaphor of deception, can be seen as merely the latest resting place for the prototype for the most *inconfesable* (unspeakable) type of masculinity.[29]

A genealogy of Don Juan would contain countless variations on the Don Juan theme. One has only to glance at José Manuel Losada's *Bibliography of the Myth of Don Juan in Literary History* to see evidence of his appeal in English, French, German, Italian, Portuguese and Spanish-speaking countries.[30] Leo Weinstein includes a section on versions of Don Juan that have Dutch, Flemish, Swedish, Danish, Norwegian, Russian, Ukrainian, Hungarian, Romanian and Croatian variations.[31] Takayuki Yokota-Murakami explores points of contact between the Western Don Juan and some key Japanese premodern literary figures.[32] Molière, Byron, Mozart, Dumas, Goldoni, John Berger, Lenau, Max Frisch, George Bernard Shaw, Kierkegaard and E. T. A. Hoffman are just some of the many artists who have been provoked to produce their own versions on a theme.

Nevertheless, it is generally acknowledged that Don Juan's roots are Spanish. Moreover, Ramiro de Maeztu noted in his *Don Quijote, Don Juan y la Celestina* (Don Quixote, Don Juan and Celestina) of 1926 that there seems to be a difference between the European Don Juan, a figure driven by love and given to searching endlessly and dreamily for a lost feminine ideal, and the Spanish Don Juan, a man of appetites and lacking in ideals who is driven by power.[33] The Spanish Don Juan story, which may have its origins in oral folk tradition,[34] can be traced to Tirso de Molina's *El burlador de Sevilla y convidado de piedra* (The

Introduction: In Search of Don Juan

Trickster of Seville and the Stone Guest) (*c*.1630). But there are difficulties here. Tirso de Molina is believed to be the pseudonym of a Spanish monk, Gabriel Téllez.

Ian Watt suggests that even if it is attributable to him, 'it is unlikely that *El burlador de Sevilla* as it has come down to us is exclusively by Tirso – it may well have been revised by a second, less gifted playwright'.[35] There are also two versions of Tirso's *comedia*, *El burlador de Sevilla y convidado de piedra* and *¿Tan largo me lo fiáis?* (What a long time you give me, God!) both of which are thought to date from the seventeenth century.[36] The play consists of four *burlas*, or deceptions, by which Don Juan seduces four women: two of noble blood and two peasants. The play opens to find Don Juan in the palace of the King of Naples, his face shrouded in darkness, pretending to be the fiancé of Isabela, a countess, in order to seduce her. Later, on the coast, he seduces Tisbea, a humble fisher-girl, while his faithful servant, Catalinón, chastizes him for his unscrupulous ways: '*Tan largo me lo fiáis*' (death is a long way off yet), is Don Juan's response.

Trusted to deliver a note to the Marqués de la Mota from his fiancée, the Countess Doña Ana, Don Juan tells the *marqués* to arrive later than the designated hour and takes his place in the lovers' tryst. When Ana discovers the deception, she sounds the alarm and her father, Don Gonzalo, challenges Don Juan but is killed. The *marqués*, wearing the cloak Don Juan has just returned to him, arrives at the scene in time to be arrested for Don Gonzalo's murder. Don Juan flees to Lebrija where he seduces a young bride at her wedding. When walking through a cemetery, he comes across a statue in memory of Don Gonzalo. Playfully, he invites the statue to dine with him. Later that evening, Don Gonzalo's ghost arrives at Don Juan's house to accept the invitation and drags Don Juan down to hell.

Tales of Seduction

Written against the backdrop of the Council of Trent, Tirso's play can be read as a morality tale to shore up Catholic values. In Spain it was followed by another variation on a theme, Antonio de Zamora's *No hay plazo que no se cumpla ni deuda que no se pague o El convidado de piedra* (Every Deadline shall be Met and No Debt Remain Unpaid, or the Stone Guest) (1713), whose scene of the Stone Guest was captured by Francisco de Goya in a painting of 1797-8.[37] But it is José Zorrilla's nineteenth-century Romantic version that is now most well-known in Spain. *Don Juan Tenorio* (1844) opens in a local hostelry at carnival time. Don Juan and Don Luis, overheard by Don Gonzalo, all wearing masks, are totting up the results of a bet they have undertaken to seduce as many women as possible. Don Luis, after losing the bet, accepts Don Juan's challenge that he will manage to seduce Don Luis's fiancée Doña Ana de Pantoja. Don Juan accomplishes this, but Don Gonzalo, on hearing the tale later, refuses to offer consent for Don Juan to marry his daughter, Doña Inés. Don Juan kidnaps Inés and kills both Don Luis and Don Gonzalo in duels. Don Juan flees the scene. Returning five years later, he discovers that his beloved Inés has died. Don Gonzalo's ghost appears to him and is about to take him to hell, but Doña Inés's ghost persuades Don Juan to repent for his sins. The couple ascend to heaven and celestial paradise.

We have seen how within the history of the literary Don Juan, the figure deconstructs before our eyes. Don Juan the dissolute libertine, who flouts God's law, turns into Don Juan the pious observer of faith, in a radical *volte face*. This unification of extremes within the same figure will be taken up by Spanish writers and cultural practitioners. To take just a couple of examples, Miguel de Unamuno, for example, in his 1929 play *El hermano Juan o el mundo es teatro* (Brother Juan or the World is a Theatre) explored the relationship between Don Juan and Hermano Juan (Brother

Introduction: In Search of Don Juan

Juan), conceived as not-Don Juan, diametrically opposed, and yet contained within the same being. In a similar vein, Rafael María Liern's *Doña Juana Tenorio*, of 1874, allows the arch womanizer to collapse into his opposite, a *femme fatale*, in order to explore gender relations. There are as many studies of variations of Don Juan, parodies, reworkings and opposites, as there are studies of the originary mythical figure and the creation by his founding fathers Tirso and Zorrilla.

As guardian of the limit, Don Juan can take on a seemingly endless variety of other connotations (adopting myriad disguises), and has been subject to thousands of different readings. Julia Kristeva describes him as the 'most perfectly ambiguous figure ... pertaining to masculine sexuality that western legend has passed on to us'.[38] Jesús Rubio Jiménez writes that Don Juan has been the '*pretexto de ensayos y objeto de variaciones sin fin*' (pretext for essays and the object of endless variations); furthermore, '*don Juan Tenorio llena millares de páginas donde conviven las ideas más atrabiliarias con otras más sensatas*' (Don Juan Tenorio fills thousands of pages where the most peevish ideas coexist with the most sensible ones).[39] David T. Gies compares him with Woody Allen's cinematic *Zelig* (1983), all things to all people, who transforms himself into different characters in order to reflect those around him.[40] Ann Davies notes that his main characteristic is his ability to change over time.[41] But if Don Juan's constancy is his unfaithfulness, it is still possible to talk about 'the Don Juan figure', a character drawn in part from the myriad of literary variations on a theme, and in part from the potency of our attraction to the womanizing (anti-)hero.

'How can so many Don Juans be dealt with systematically, synthetically and exhaustively?' wonders James Mandrell. 'Obviously, one way to introduce unity is by means of a synthetic taxonomy, by creating a hypothetical unity.'[42] This is Don Juan as transcendant myth. While some scholars find it fruitful to see Don Juan as a myth (Ian Watt, for example, sees him as representative of the myth of individualism),[43] others, such as Davies, warn against 'suggesting that there is some "essential" Don Juan against which all literary renditions of the figure can be measured'.[44] Moyra Haslett puts forward Claude Lévi-Strauss's structuralist approach to myth as a way out of this conundrum. For Haslett, Lévi-Strauss, 'counters the rigidity of semantic interpretation by accepting a more generous understanding of what constitutes a "myth"'.[45]

Opposing Jung's transcendant 'archetypes', Lévi-Strauss applies the semiological approach of Saussure to propose that the 'meaning' of mythology resides not in isolated elements, but in the way these elements are combined. 'Every version as it emerges diachronically in history is a sort of mythic *parole* which unfolds within a synchronic system of the mythic *langue*.' Thus, Lévi-Strauss is able to combine a historicist approach (that recognizes particular versions) with the more essentialist versions of mythology (that consider all versions).[46] Davies, meanwhile, prefers to dispense with Don Juan as myth altogether, and discuss him as discourse.[47] Mandrell prefers to treat Don Juan not as literature, but rather as 'text'. Mandrell cautions that the term 'Don Juan' 'has frequently been used as a convenience – as a sort of methodological shorthand'[48] that can prevent critical engagement. He reminds us that Don Juan is a synecdoche that represents the whole of a story that has been 'told and retold in wildly disparate manners'.[49]

At the same time, given the weight of the literary and cultural baggage Don Juan carries, it is impossible to approach him afresh, as if seeing him or his cultural manifestations for the first time. But it is interesting to note how Don Juan is bolstered by the myriad of variations that proliferate in his name, the way that Don Juan as a sign

Introduction: In Search of Don Juan

gains potency from the satellites it attracts into its force-field.[50] Thus, 'every manifestation of the character of Don Juan gains access to the larger domain of his cult and transcends the specificity and therefore the limitations of any single text',[51] while at the same time, each variation, however it may work to deflate the icon, to send Don Juan up or bring him down to size, or to change his gender, sexuality, or national and cultural context, only serves to contribute to the cult in his name. A genealogy of Don Juan (an impossible task, due to its enormity) would have to track not just the myriad tiny transformations carried out in his name, but also the large, gradual modifications to Don Juan as a sign.

Over time, the associations of Don Juan arguably have changed: in the seventeenth and nineteenth centuries he was a figure associated with the transgression of or adherence to God's law; by the twentieth he had come largely to represent the sexual sphere.[52] However, such a tracing would have to track the way Don Juan moves fluidly, staging encounters between the literary and the popular, between culture and its reception by a public. Don Juan is a tool of exchange between artists and public. Aristocratic, belonging to high literature, he is simultaneously a man of the people. As the avatar for a flight of fantasy, he can become a figure of remarkable intimacy for some.

Don Juan arrives at the twenty-first century as a sign loaded with the connotations of the legendary attractive and charismatic hero who is loved by women and aspired to by men. His status as a dualistic trickster sign means that he is simultaneously the cad and chauvinist who ought, at all costs, to be avoided. At once 'diabolic and heroic, seductive and sleazy', a figure who inspires the ambivalence of our attraction to or repulsion from him:[53] Don Juan as a sign has come to stand in the popular imagination for seduction with its attendant ambivalent connotations. The cult of Don Juan shows no sign of dissipating as we move into the twenty-first century.

There is a vast body of literature on the significance of (pan-European) Don Juan figures from the seventeenth, eighteenth and nineteenth centuries, but relatively few works address Spanish Don Juan figures from the twentieth century. In *Don Juan and the Point of Honour: Seduction, Patriarchal Society and Literary Tradition* James Mandrell presents a far-reaching discussion on the 'mythography' (the discourse about discourse) of the Don Juan myth and provides fascinating concrete literary examples, but his study is restricted to textual accounts of Don Juan,[54] as is Carlos Feal's *En nombre de Don Juan: estructura de un mito literario*.[55]

In *Caballero de novela: ensayo sobre el donjuanismo en la novela española moderna 1880–1930*, Ignacio-Javier López shows how the Don Juan figure is degraded and parodied in nineteenth-century novels (Galdós and others), but then gradually becomes an object of discourse in early twentieth-century texts (Unamuno, Valle-Inclán and Pérez de Ayala).[56] In the edited book by Andrew Ginger, Huw Lewis and John Hobbs, *Selected Interdisciplinary Essays on the Representation of the Don Juan Archetype in Myth and Culture*, there are a plethora of essays spanning the seventeenth to the twentieth centuries, but they only briefly intrude into the twentieth century.[57]

Ana Sofía Pérez-Bustamante's excellent collection of essays in *Don Juan Tenorio en la España del siglo XX* presents penetrating studies of many different aspects of Don Juan in the twentieth century.[58] Luis Miguel Fernández, in his *Don Juan en el cine español: hacia una teoría de la recreación fílmica*, uses Don Juan filmic texts to address the theory of adaptation.[59] In *Don Juan: East/West: On the Problematics of Comparative Literature*, Takayuki Yokota-Murukami explores Don Juan's potential to cross cultures, but its specialized focus provides few references to the Spanish context.[60]

Introduction: In Search of Don Juan

Elena Soriano's wide-ranging *El donjuanismo femenino* considers female Don Juans and *femme fatales* from the Bible and Antiquity to cinema.[61] Richard Cardwell's analysis of Zorrilla's Don Juan shows how women are traffic in the exchange commodities that pervade the play.[62] Women are likewise the subject of Ann Davies's *The Metamorphoses of Don Juan's Women: Early Parity to Late Modern Pathology*, but this time she tracks the changing attitudes and gender paradigms attached to Don Juan's female victims.[63] Roberta Johnson's illuminating *Gender and Nation in the Spanish Modernist Novel* pays much needed attention to the works of neglected women writers in the early part of the twentieth century, and the ways they 'domesticated' the myth of Don Juan for their own national, social or private ends.[64] Jo Labanyi's recent articles on shifting sands of Don Juan and nation are excellent contributions to the corpus.[65]

While I am indebted to these studies for providing a fertile field of study and for pointing the way towards possible approaches to the myth of Don Juan, even such a wide field is far from exhaustive. I am interested in Don Juan's interdisciplinary potential, for I intersect literary, theatrical and filmic texts from a Spanish context with elements of Western intellectual history.

Given his status as 'lord of the border', it is hardly surprising that Don Juan should have found his way into a range of Western theories. From semiotics to consumerism, from the study of hormones to theories of gender, Don Juan has been in the vanguard (and, by the same token, can now seem anachronistic as theories go out of date). Is it not the duty of every theory to seduce? As the master of linguistic seduction, Don Juan presents the perfect icon for the persuasiveness of ideas, the rhetorical aspects of a text.[66] Don Juan reveals the capacities of discourse for seduction. Often the secrets apparently revealed by a text are a mere consequence of dazzling virtuosity and surface effects. Don

Juan in discourse points to the limitations of many theories, coherent only within their own terms.

For Jean Baudrillard, nowhere is this truer than of the discourse of psychoanalysis, with its claims of revelations of a 'psychic interiority'. In *Seduction*, Baudrillard situates the roots of the obsession with psychic interiority in the Romantic period. Such a view chimes with the case history of Don Juan, who arguably gains a reflective conscience only with Zorrilla's nineteenth-century incarnation. Over time, scholars have attempted to locate Don Juan's interior, to discover the motivations for his serial seductions. But Baudrillard argues that desire and sexuality belong to the sphere of production, in that they *produce* (*reproduce*) or make appear. Psychoanalysis belongs to this sphere in its creation of the unconscious and its effects.

Mandrell, for his part, in *Don Juan and the Point of Honour*, offers a critique of the intervention of psychoanalysis within the 'myth' of Don Juan as a perpetuation rather than explication of Don Juan.[67] Despite attempts to psychoanalyse the eponymous seducer, Don Juan remains a seductive absence at the very heart of psychoanalysis. Despite his drama being that of the family (he flouts the father's law, while some have seen his obsession for women as the endless search for a substitute for his mother) he is absent from the theories of Sigmund Freud, a point Juliet Mitchell makes in her *Mad Men of Medusas*.[68] Otto Rank's study from a psychoanalytic perspective (which comes under discussion in Chapter 5) does not fill this void.[69]

In Spain it was an endocrinologist, Gregorio Marañón, who would take up Don Juan's case and dominate the horizon: Marañón's ideas captured the popular imagination. He led the study of Don Juan away from the mind and into physiology. Marañón's theories aimed to substitute the scientific 'fact' offered by the body, over the

Introduction: In Search of Don Juan

more interpretative realm of the mind. His theories are riddled with inconsistencies, but they provide an illuminating glimpse into the scientific ideas circulating in Spain in the 1920s and 1930s. Marañón's theories become the focus for Chapter 2.

Don Juan is seen as owing his origins to Spain (a confluence of Catholic values during the sixteenth century resurfacing in the nineteenth). His associations with Spanish nationhood therefore make him perfect for intellectuals at the start of the twentieth century who were looking for icons within which to represent the problems facing the nation in the wake of the loss of colonies in 1898 (Chapter 1). As we move into the 1920s and 1930s (Chapter 2), other social preoccupations, such as the changing gender paradigms following shifts in rights for women and changes in, for example, the divorce law, mean that Don Juan (with his stark view of gender relations) is turned to again. At this time he enjoyed a real 'Don Juan mania', with Don Juan becoming the focus for newspaper columns, entering into debates about law, finding his way into medical tracts, focusing discussions of gender, and entering into endless literary and theatrical variations on a theme. Don Juan's relationship with the Spanish public was by now firmly established.

In a century dominated by Francoism, perhaps what ensured his survival throughout the twentieth century was his adoption by the Franco regime, surprisingly, and in different guises, as an avatar for national Catholicism. Don Juan's popularity with the Spanish public, and his ability to cross from the popular to the intellectual spheres, make him perfect for a regime wishing to spread its ideology to all sectors of the population. Don Juan as an icon for Francoism pops up continually as a subject of this book (but particularly is the focus of Chapter 3). If Don Juan's interest for the Spanish public early on was spontaneous

Tales of Seduction

and driven by competing ideologies, in Francoism it is determined by a desire to bludgeon the public with a monolithic set of ideas.

Trickster-like, Don Juan has the capacity for endless renewal. If he is conservative, he can also transgress these limits to take on a variety of different obsessions. As Don Juan enters the twenty-first century, we find him still hovering at the borders, crossing into new genres. Thus, he takes with him his history, undeniably attached to obsessions of Spanish gender and nation, but at the same time, can rework these, or push constantly into new areas, new domains, and new lands to conquer.

This book is in no way meant to be an exhaustive study of Don Juan. In offering up these chapters, I hope to present a view of some of the different uses to which Don Juan has been put throughout the twentieth century in Spain.

Chapter 1 takes as its focus the work of Blanca de los Ríos, intellectual, public speaker and writer whose *novela corta* (short novel) *Las hijas de don Juan* (Don Juan's Daughters) dates from 1907. For de los Ríos, Don Juan represents the frontier between past (the Spanish imperial Golden Age) and present (Restoration Spain). He also negotiates Spain's borders, allowing de los Ríos to consider the implications for Spain's loss of colonies in 1898 and to envisage a future for the nation. I intersect de los Ríos's *novela corta* with her speeches at public institutions, with theories of degeneration (the Spanish and European contexts) and bloodline.

In Chapter 2 I consider the writing of Spanish physician and endocrinologist, Gregorio Marañón, on the figure of the Spanish seducer. Marañón's idiosyncratic blend of the literary with the medical allows him to treat the figure from myth as if he were a man in the street. In his attempt to dent the glamorous image of Don Juan (which he sees as

Introduction: In Search of Don Juan

a negative paradigm for Spanish males) he associates him with impotence and homosexuality. Interestingly, while Marañón uses Don Juan conservatively, his discussion of the 'effeminate' Don Juan opened up a productive space for other writers to free up gender paradigms in early twentieth-century Spain.

Chapter 3, 'Screen Seductions', is focused on cinematic versions of Don Juan. In the first part of the chapter I explore theatricality and the trick-shot in Ricardo de Baños's 1922 cinematic Don Juan. The main focus of the chapter is Sáenz de Heredia's *Don Juan* of 1950, produced as a national 'superproduction' with state funds from the Franco government. I explore the ways that Don Juan seduces the audience with his suggestion of the glamour of the cinema and its star system. Using theories of spectatorship, I show how, ultimately, the film interpellates a spectator who is firmly entrenched in national–Catholic ideology.

In Chapter 4 I consider the ubiquity and repetitious nature of stagings of Zorrilla's *Don Juan Tenorio* on the Spanish stage from the late nineteenth century and into the beginning of the twenty-first. After a brief overview of the parodies that have proliferated in Don Juan's name, the rest of the chapter is given over to an examination of a landmark production of Zorrilla's *Don Juan Tenorio* from 1949, directed by Luis Escobar and with scenography and costumes by the painter Salvador Dalí.

A production of Mozart/Da Ponte's *Don Giovanni* from the start of the new millennium by Catalan theatre practitioner Calixto Bieito is the focus for Chapter 5. Using a theory of 'taste' borrowed from Pierre Bourdieu, I explore the ways that Bieito uses Don Juan to negotiate the boundaries between sound and visuals; high and low culture and good and bad taste.

Don Juan is used as an avatar, a productive site, within

which to explore borders that are of concern within culture. It is interesting to note that this 'virtual space' generally involves the reception by a public. De los Ríos and Marañón are attracted to Don Juan for his ability not only to tap into the national psyche, but also for his potential as a didactic tool. But if Don Juan may be judged on how successful or unsuccessful he is at performing acts, then it is clear that the acts he performs are not always those intended by his creator. Don Juan is volatile when pressed into service for ideology. Marañón's case is particularly interesting as it appears that the public received the Don Juan figure in a way not intended by the Spanish doctor.

The same is potentially true of the cinematic spectator theorized in Chapter 3: where the Franco state wishes to inculcate a national–Catholic ideology, the spectator may choose to read the film differently, revelling in its potential for glamour and flights of fantasy. In Chapter 4, meanwhile, the act performed by Don Juan for the theatre spectator is to mediate between different time periods and to negotiate a path between the past and the present. Chapter 5's spectator, meanwhile, follows Don Juan's trajectory as he moves fluidly between high and low culture, understanding and interpreting meanings from each in a dialectical arrangement. In a variety of ways, the chapters of this volume explore Don Juan in Spain from the beginning of the twentieth century to the present. Moving between Don Juan as myth (in the sense of idea rooted in the national psyche) and cultural manifestation, they focus on the shifting projections of meaning which centre on the figure of Don Juan.

1. OPPOSITES ATTRACT: AN INTELLECTUAL, DON JUAN AND NATION IN EARLY TWENTIETH-CENTURY SPAIN

The dawn of the twentieth century saw Spain in the grip of anxiety about the future of the nation. In the summer of 1898, imperial Spain collapsed with the loss of Cuba, Puerto Rico and the Philippines. The war against the United States had been commonly depicted as the struggle between two races, and Spaniards wondered whether the *raza española* (Spanish race) was doomed.[1] Spaniards began to look inwards at the 'problem of Spain', as well as outwards to Spain's position as a world nation.

As Christopher Britt Arredondo explains in his cogent *Quixotism: The Imaginative Denial of Spain's Loss of Empire*, Spanish intellectuals looked to literary models as imaginative metaphors to express both an understanding of what had happened to the Spanish nation and a paradigm for future regeneration.[2] Literary models such as Don Quixote, Don Juan and La Celestina were held to represent the 'essence' of Spain.[3] Britt Arredondo's example is Cervantes's *Don Quixote* and he shows how Miguel de Unamuno,

Ramiro de Maeztu and Angel Ganivet, among others, not only 'imaginatively denied' the loss of Spanish empire in the years after its demise (and beyond),[4] but also presented Quixote as alternatively a spiritual conquistador, messiah or lover in a bid to regenerate the nation.

In early twentieth-century Spain, Don Juan also became the site for the projection of a variety of national obsessions and preoccupations. In 1896, Italian hispanist Arturo Farinelli had questioned Don Juan's 'Spanishness' when he claimed that Don Juan's roots lay in Renaissance Italy. His remarks provoked scornful commentary from Víctor Saíd Armesto and Ramón Menéndez Pidal, among others.[5] Saíd Armesto traced Don Juan to oral and folk culture. He also claimed that the legend could be linked to an historical figure: the rake Miguel de Mañara whose epitaph at the Hospital de la Caridad in Seville is dedicated to 'the worst man that ever lived'. Don Juan's literary and mythological heritage was seen to lie in Spain; furthermore he could be seen to form part of the Spanish bloodline and ancestry.

In this chapter, I consider the work of intellectual and writer Blanca de los Ríos (1862–1956). De los Ríos founded the scholarly journal *Raza Española* (Spanish Race) and she was committed to exploring how to bring about the regeneration of Spain and extending Spain's links with its former colonies.[6] She was a lifelong scholar of Don Juan and her edition of Tirso de Molina's *Obras Completas* is still the definitive edition of his work. Her prose fiction was translated into French, Norwegian, Danish, German and Italian, and she gave talks at Spanish cultural institutions on topics of interest in her day.[7] Her writing absorbed and fed into the work of many writers of the so-called 'Generation of 1898' although she is never discussed alongside her male contemporaries.[8]

Recently, scholars have begun to rediscover her essays and prose fiction. Her *novela corta* (short novel), *Las hijas de don Juan* (Don Juan's Daughters) of 1907 in particular has attracted critical attention.[9] She has been reclaimed as a female intellectual from the early part of the twentieth century and also as a rare female writer on Don Juan. Her relationship with the large institutions illuminates the sexism of the age. However, while most recent scholars have seen her work as '*si no feminista, "feminocéntrica"*' (if not feminist, then feminocentric),[10] I find, rather, that it recapitulates negative stereotypes of women. I have chosen to include her work here, first because it seems unjust that first a scholar who spent so many years conducting research into Don Juan should be excluded so unilaterally in books on the figure,[11] and secondly because she provides a fascinating snapshot (albeit conservative) of the spirit of an age. Don Juan, for de los Ríos, is a symbol of Spain's decline, but by association, Don Juan can also help us to understand her vision for a rejuvenated Spain of the future.

Nation and Degeneration

On 12 April 1899, in a ceremony at the Real Academia de la Lengua, Madrid, the Duque de Rivas accepted an award on behalf of Doña Blanca de los Ríos, for a critical study of the life and work of Tirso de Molina. De los Ríos was not permitted to receive the award in person, for the rules did not allow the '*bello sexo*' (fair sex) to take part in activities at the Academia. De los Ríos had composed her extended essay in response to a competition set by the Academia to write a biographical and critical study of the author of *El burlador de Sevilla y convidado de piedra*. Her research took her to the Biblioteca Nacional in Madrid, various universities, as well as to Toledo, Alcalá de Henares and Trujillo. '*Debía de resultar ciertamente extraño que una jovencita anduviera rebuscando en los archivos*' (it must have certainly seemed strange for a young woman to go searching in the archives) as González López notes.[12]

De los Ríos submitted an interpretative study of Tirso's work, as well as revealing contentious details about his birth.[13] At the Academia, it was decreed that neither of the works submitted (the other was by Pedro Muñoz Peña, a professor at the University of Valladolid) reached the high standard warranted by the prize (of 2500 pesetas, a gold medal, a diploma and 500 copies printed of the paper). However, the judges decided to award de los Ríos's achievement with a lesser award of 1500 pesetas and a print-run of her work. Despite the outrageous sexism revealed in this incident, or perhaps in part because of it (a fierce debate had arisen in the Academia surrounding the admission of women to its ranks), de los Ríos soon gained prestige, granting her a space for her scholarly articles in the press and literary journals.[14]

In *Las hijas de don Juan*, de los Ríos begins whimsically by evoking the Don Juan of legend: Don Juanism is to be found, '*en el aire, en el clima, en la fácil vida alegre, frugal y aventurera, en la sangre ardorosa, atavismo caballeril, menosprecio de la vida, odio al trabajo, sobra de sol, prodigalidad del tiempo, mujerío irresistible y legendario fama de valor, rumbo y galantería*' (in the air, in the climate, in the happy frugal and adventurous easy life, in passionate blood, in atavistic gentle-manliness, scorn for life, hatred of work, too much sun, squandering of time, irresistible womanizing and legendary fame for valour, drive and gallantry). She reminds the reader of the great literary incarnations of the myth: '*flotaban en el aire todavía muchos efluvios donjuanescos: el gran mito de Tirso reencarnado en Molière, en Mozart, en Byron, en Espronceda, en de Musset y revivido en Zorrilla, alentaba en las estrofas de Baudelaire, en el dandyismo de Brummell*' (there were many donjuanesque creations still floating in the air: Tirso's great myth reincarnated in Molière, in Mozart, in Byron, in Espronceda, in de Musset and revived in Zorrilla, inspired in the stanzas of Baudelaire, and in Brummell's dandyism).[15]

In a paper she read at the Ateno in 1916, '*Los grandes mitos de la edad moderna*' (The great myths of the modern age), de los Ríos underlines the way Don Juan moves between myth and reality. There is something 'ultra real' about him, caused by his supernatural prestige, yet at the same time '*tiene de los hombres la pasión y el pecado*' (his passion and sin are human). He has something of the '*semidiós mitológico*' (mythological demigod) and yet he interests us because '*tiene nuestra carne*' (he has our flesh).[16] Later in the same piece she muses that, '*si Don Juan no fuera creyente, su rebeldía ante los poderes sobrehumanos perdería toda su grandeza; si Don Juan fuera un vulgar libertino, su figura perdería todo su esplendor legendario*' (if Don Juan were not a believer, his rebellion against superhuman powers would lose all its greatness; if Don Juan were a vulgar libertine, his figure would lose all its legendary splendour).[17]

Perhaps it is this tension between greatness and mediocrity encapsulated in the figure that led Emilia Pardo Bazán, in a short story of 1898, to recast Don Juan as the hero in a tale of romantic love and lost illusions between a devout child and a man whose heart overflows with feeling. Her 'La última ilusión de Don Juan' reads like an apologia for a figure who '*sólo hemos comprendido los poetas*' (only we poets have understood).[18] Blanca de los Ríos, follows, rather, in the tradition of Ortega Munilla, Pérez Galdós and others who were proffering a critiqued, debased or degraded Don Juan in their writing.[19] In *Las hijas de don Juan*, she chooses to present Don Juan as a mediocre alcoholic womanizer of Restoration Spain.

For de los Ríos, Don Juan is '*no sólo un retrato histórico, sino el símbolo de una raza*' (not just an historical portrait, but the symbol of a race).[20] She emphasizes stock (*estirpe*) in her discussions of Don Juan.[21] *Las hijas de don Juan* continues this emphasis on lineage in its focus on Don Juan's progeny. Don Juan, in both Tirso and Zorrilla, may have to do with paternal succession,[22] while Don Juan flouts the paternal law, but there is no suggestion of his producing any offspring of his own.[23]

In 1892, however, José Echegaray wrote *El hijo de don Juan* (Don Juan's Son), a play dedicated to Ibsen's *Ghosts* (1890), in which the protagonist, Lázaro, like Ibsen's Oswald, goes insane due to hereditary syphilis: Don Juan's profligate ways have cruel consequences for his son.[24] In de los Ríos's novelette, the daughters of Don Juan are likewise afflicted by the evils of heredity (a corruption of the bloodline): Lita, crossed in love, will turn to prostitution, while Dora, after turning to religious mysticism, dies of consumption. Kathleen Glenn, in her study of the work, notes that a 'key concept here is degeneration'.[25] However, she does not explore the intricate nexus of ideas evoked by the term 'degeneration', linking bloodline, heredity and social and artistic decadence present in this work.

In 1857, two years before the appearance of Darwin's *Origin of Species*, Bénédict Morel, in *Traité des dégénérescenes physiques*, claimed that both heredity and environment were causing a progressive, cumulative degeneration of humanity, as demonstrated by the high incidence of alcoholism, syphilis, tuberculosis, epilepsy, hysteria and criminality. Morel's central hypothesis was the notion of the 'individual as the epitome of the sins of the fathers'.[26]

In 1883, Francis Galton, Darwin's first cousin, coined the term 'eugenics':[27] taken from the Greek *eugenes*, eugenics meant 'good in stock'.[28] In 1908, in his autobiography, Galton defined eugenics as 'the study of agencies under social control that may improve or impair the racial qualities of future generations, either physically or mentally'.[29] In Spain, eugenics, or 'race hygiene', 'developed in the context of a heightened nationalist discourse due to growing awareness of Spanish decadence', coinciding with the loss of Spain's colonies.[30] Nordau's *Entartung* (Degeneration) (1892), dedicated to Cesare Lombroso[31] and translated into Spanish in 1902 by Nicolás Salmerón, expanded the heredity thesis to see *fin de siècle* culture as afflicted by disease, insanity, and above all fatigue. The age itself was exhausted.

Writers of finesecular Spain confronted with the loss of Spain's colonies, sought ways to regenerate their nation. Cardwell cites Unamuno, who, writing against Nordau, posits the artistic genius as a '*médico-espiritual*' (spiritual doctor) who can regenerate, rather than degenerate, the nation's spiritual strength.[32] De los Ríos's text sees Don Juan (a degenerate with profligate ways) as a symbol of the degeneration of the Spanish nation.[33] Degeneration here, (as for Nordau) is not merely biological, but also social, historical and artistic, while the theme of heredity crosses all these spheres. *Las hijas de don Juan* can be read as an attempt at national regeneration through consciousness-raising by means of literary endeavour.

Fluidity between the mythical and the vulgar Don Juan is a characteristic of *Las hijas de don Juan*. Juan Fontibre is a degenerate Don Juan, a womanizer who goes on alcoholic binges and spends nights in brothels. Yet even while the narrator lambasts Don Juanism for its evil attractions ('*llena los teatros cuando se representa el Tenorio y abastece con sus víctimas cárceles y hospitales*' (filling the theatres when the *Tenorio* is performed and supplying prisons and hospitals with its victims), as we have seen, she nevertheless evokes a glamorous history for Don Juan: '*atavismo caballeril ... legendaria fama de valor, rumbo y galantería*' (atavistic gentlemanliness, legendary fame for valour, drive and gallantry) as well as a prestigious literary heritage.[34]

The apparent contradictions cited by Reyes Lázaro in her excellent study of the work, between a Don Juan who '*vive, ha muerto y está a punto de hacerlo*' (lives, has died and is about to do so)[35] and between a Don Juan who is a drunken philanderer or a gallant nobleman can be explained with recourse to the theory of degeneration. Don Juan appears to encompass a spectrum that ranges from the noble hero of the past to the drunken womanizer of the present. De los Ríos's Don Juan comes close to the 'fallen angel' hypothesis put forward by Morel.[36] Thus, atavism, for de los Ríos, concerns not a return of primitive man, but the evocation of a 'more perfect state' from a 'less perfect state'.[37] The word '*atavismo*' is liberally sprinkled through the text, but as Lázaro points out, these atavisms are generally positive in tone, such as the endorsement of faith, pride, the Spanish nation, '*la conciencia de la propia caída y el sentido calderoniano del honor ante la prostitución de una hija*'(the consciousness of his own decline and the Calderonian sense of honour in the face of the prostitution of one of his daughters).[38]

Fontibre is degenerate, but he has moments of 'organic memory' of a distant, noble inheritance.[39] At the end of the story, when Fontibre is faced with the ruin of his family, '*sintió arder en su sangre la ira de toda una raza; el hombre, el caballero, el padre, revivieron en él; el honor, su religión atávica, sacudióle con ese impulso de héroe calderoniano que todo español lleva en el ápice del alma*' (he felt the anger of a whole race burn within his blood; the man, the gentleman, the father revived in him; honour, his atavistic religion, shook him with the impulse of the Calderonian hero that every Spaniard carries in the heart of his soul).[40]

He is contrasted with Paco Garba, the suitor who seduces Lita merely to enact revenge on Fontibre (Lita takes the consequences for a degenerate form of retribution) and who represents a more degenerate Don Juan. '*Degenerado por herencia, decadentista por oficio ... no era antiguo ni moderno, sino sencillamente detestable*' (Degenerate by inheritance, decadent by vocation, he was neither ancient nor modern, but simply detestable).[41] Fontibre represents a family stock that was once noble, but that through a bad marriage to Concha, who is cheerfully working class and goes on spending sprees to buy tasteless cloth, has become corrupted.[42] Concha is a 'fashion victim', which was a symptom of degeneracy according to Nordau.[43] Degeneration is as much to do with environment as heredity and Concha is ruined by Fontibre's philandering ways; she becomes increasingly hysterical, *'una histérica de Lavapiés'* (an hysteric from Lavapiés): hysteria is another classic sign of degeneracy for Nordau, while in turn she brings Don Juan down with her bad taste, idolatry and constant nagging.[44]

Degenerationist theories held that it was possible for the human race or stock to become weakened, until finally it would die out, what was known as 'race suicide'. It was also thought that the symptoms of degeneration could vary from generation to generation.[45] The twinning of sex and religion in the Don Juan myth becomes split in the two daughters and simultaneously degenerates. After the girls read love letters sent to their father from his lovers, 'the girls assume more mature and sexually defined identities almost overnight'.[46] Dora reads Santa Teresa of Ávila's *Interior Castle* and gives herself over to mysticism. Santa Teresa's form of mysticism, moreover, is a blend of the spiritual and the erotic.[47] Lita, meanwhile, attends clubs, becomes flirtatious, is heartbroken and finally turns to prostitution. Dora dies of tuberculosis, Lita degenerates into prostitution, while Don Juan, on seeing her moral degradation, turns to morphine before shooting himself in a church. Lita, on seeing her father's bloody body, has a convulsive fit, which is described as either epileptic or hysterical, foaming at the mouth before being carried off by her fellow revellers, reduced to a *'mísera carne de pecado'* (miserable sinner's flesh).[48] *'En Lita acabó la estirpe de don Juan'* (The Don Juan stock ends with Lita),[49] so the narrator informs us.

De los Ríos uses the motif of degeneration to explore a

range of ills in Restoration Spain. By making Fontibre into an habitual binge drinker, de los Ríos was entering into the discussion of the evils of alcoholism, a 'key sign in the degenerationism debate'.[50] Definitions of alcoholism by Restoration hygienists and social commentators vacillated between the terms *vicio* (a moral concept) and *enfermedad* (a medical concept).[51] Rafael Cervera Barat, writing in 1898, noted that, *'el bebedor no sólo hace víctima a sí mismo, sino que hace víctimas a sus hijos y a los hijos de sus hijos. Con vigor inexorable transmite el alcoholismo sus estragos de generación a generación hasta extinguir por completo las familias'* (the drinker does not only make himself into a victim, but he makes his children and the children of his children into victims too. With inexorable vigour alcoholism transmits its ravages from generation to generation until it wipes out entire families).[52] In 1903, B. González Álvarez proposed the creation of a legally binding health certificate prior to contracting marriage to be issued by a public health tribunal, as a means of alleviating the degeneration and extinction of the race.[53] Parental responsibility and parental health were key debates of the time.

In Restoration Spain, as depicted by Blanca de los Ríos, sexual relations, once the domain of gallant noblemen incarnated in the figure of the legendary Don Juan of old, are degraded into the salacious, overblown and badly written love letters describing nights of passion from the women who write to Fontibre, into womanizing and visits to brothels on the part of Don Juan and, finally, into Lita's prostitution.

Religious faith forms the backbone of Don Juan tales. Tirso's Don Juan flouts God's law to meet with loud retribution, while in Zorrilla the love of God and the love of a good woman are purifying elements. Fontibre *'rendía culto a su sola ostensible religión: su madre'* (worshipped the cult of his only ostensible religion: his mother).[54] Fontibre, who scorned his mother when he married Concha, thereby hastening her death, is now deeply remorseful. Yet, Fontibre's obsession with his mother does nothing to mitigate his womanizing (unlike some versions that render Don Juan's multiple seductions as a search for ideals stemming from a cult to his mother) and also underlines his complete lack of interest in theological questions. Indifference to God is, for de los Ríos, a far greater crime than flouting His law. But Fontibre's obsession receives none of the scorn reserved by the narrator for Concha, who worships the '*supersticioso culto de las exterioridades y ciega idolatría a la* Virgen de los Barrios' (superstitious cult of appearances and blind idolatry of the *Virgen de los barrios*),[55] in a degenerate form of religious faith.

Dora, meanwhile, is awakened to love by her reading of Don Juan's letters, just as Lita is, but where Lita turns towards flirtations and assignations, Dora's awakening is '*menos fisiológico, más lírico y espiritual*' (less physiological, more lyrical and spiritual), a love of God.[56] Attracted by the '*callado asilo semimonacal de la seráfica Doña Salesia*' (quiet semi-monastic home of the seraphic Doña Salesia), she visits her neighbour whose name recalls the Silesian order, while her home is described as a *morada* (dwelling), which recalls the title chosen by Santa Teresa for her *Interior Castle*, *Las moradas*. After reading Santa Teresa's work, '*su lectura irradiaba luz que, visiblemente, encendía el alma y el semblante de la tierna criatura, y poco a poco veíasela impregnarse en aquellos deliquios celestes como en un bálsamo precioso que parecía ungirla para existencia sobremundana*' (her reading radiated a light which, visibly, illuminated the soul and countenance of the tender creature, and little by little could be seen to become impregnated in those celestial swoons as if in a precious balsam that seemed to anoint her for supernatural existence).[57]

As Noël Valis has shown, Santa Teresa de Ávila had

become a cult figure in the late nineteenth century, with her tricentenary being celebrated in 1882 with a public event of 'scandalous proportions', while the question of whether her mysticism was deviant or pathological turned into a (politically motivated) polemic.[58] In an essay of 1911, de los Ríos praises Santa Teresa's *Interior Castle* for its shining prose and communication of spirit.[59] Just as Nordau had seen mysticism as an aesthetic (if degenerate) category, so de los Ríos believes that mysticism provides the capacity for introspection, sensitivity to aestheticism and the richness and suggestiveness of images.[60]

This view of Santa Teresa as *'puro y todo español'* (purely and wholly Spanish), and providing *'el platónico amor a Díos en la hermosura del universo'* (the platonic love of God in the beauty of the universe)[61] was very much in keeping with the ideas of most intellectuals in early twentieth-century Spain on Spanish mysticism. Miguel de Unamuno saw the essence of Spain as encompassing a twinning of the mysticism of Santa Teresa with the idealism of Don Quixote.[62] He also held up the Spanish mystic as a spiritual warrior, capable of seeing the ills of the Spanish nation and simultaneously calling for a spiritual reawakening.[63] But notwithstanding these positive images of Spanish mysticism, within *Las hijas de don Juan* we find a more equivocal attitude. Doña Salesia, for example, is *'virgen vieja que se mustiaba en la piedad como una azucena ante un sagrario'* (an old virgin who faded in piety like a lily of the valley before a tabernacle), while her home is *'pulcra, silente y perfumada por flores y esperanzas eternas'* (immaculate, silent and perfumed by flowers and eternal hopes).[64]

In addition, both Dora's mysticism and her tuberculosis are said to date from her reading of the letters: she says that ever since she has been coughing up blood.[65] In her frequent fainting fits, increasingly she seems to inhabit another world: *'sus párpados de nácar violáceo transparentaban ensueños luminosos; sentíase, parecía verse que aquel almita beata iba subiendo, peldaño por peldaño, sin pensar sobre ellos, la escala de oro del éxtasis'* (her purplish mother-of-pearl eyelids barely veiled luminous dreams; she sat down, it seemed as if that little soul were climbing, step by step, as if without thinking, the golden staircase of extasis). The question of whether Dora's illness has more to do with bad genes, or with noxious environmental factors is left open, but if her death from tuberculosis appears to make mysticism into a sickly form of faith, the insinuation is also that Dora may simply be paying for the sin that Lita is about to commit: her prostitution.[66]

Much like Nordau, de los Ríos extends the range of degenerate forms into questions of aesthetics. Fontibre is 'a literary and social decadent who prefers art to religion and is a devotee of *flamenquismo* [showy Spanish customs]'.[67] But, as Roberta Johnson notes, when faced with the choice between their mother's 'practical vulgarity and their father's tasteful disdain for contemporary reality, Don Juan's daughters, Dora and Lita, prefer the latter'.[68] Their father has *'exquisitices y refinamientos'* (niceties and refinements) while their mother is *'vulgarísima y ordinaria'* (very vulgar and common). The tasteless pieces of cloth Concha bought on her sprees are described as *'cosas de mamá'* (Mum's things).[69] Concha hangs out the washing, as well as *'toda la trapería y mobiliario de las alcobas, por roto, sucio y maltrecho que estuviese ajuar tan íntimo'* (all the rags and furniture from the alcoves, however broken, dirty or worn such an intimate trousseau may have been) on the balcony, a metaphor for her turning private domestic matters onto the street so that all the world could hear.

Scorn is also poured upon the Cordero family, *nouveau riches* ex-butchers who since they won the lottery, now attend *'sus reuniones* seleztas *–¡cómo que* salían *en los diarios! –, con su poquito de piano y de bailoteo y sus buenos* lunches, *y* *para corona, su abonito en todos los teatros donde se riera – ¡no les diera a ellos malos ratos con* dramones tristes! *– y el colmo de los colmos de la bienandanza burguesa: ¡su cochecito!'* (their *select* get-togethers, how they appeared in the newspapers! – with their little bit of piano and dancing and their fine *lunches* and to crown it all, their season ticket to all the theatres where one can have a good laugh – they didn't want to have a bad time with *sad dramas*! – and the *pièce de résistance* of their bourgeois good fortune: their little car!).[70] Yet the narrator never lets them forget the descriptions of entrails of slaughtered animals that seem to follow them even in their newfound splendour.

The Corderos introduce Lita to Paco Garba (nicknamed Larva), a bad writer who becomes a success socially because neither the couple supporting him nor Lita know enough about literature to distinguish the good from the bad. Lita has only known the *'novelones eróticos leídos a hurto en el cuarto de Don Juan'* (erotic novels read in secret in Don Juan's room), which are described as enticing the girls with their salacious content: *'Lita, con las mejillas encendidas y los ojos chispeantes, empuñaba un fajo de papeles abigarrados, que exhalaban una bufarada violenta, acre, nauseabunda, de promiscuos perfumes escandalosos,* infames, *que difundían por la atmósfera contagio sugestivo, perturbador, como de voluptuosidad respirable'* (Lita, with red cheeks and shining eyes, was brandishing a bundle of multi-coloured papers that gave off a strong, acrid, nauseating smell of promiscuous, scandalous, infamous perfumes, which spread a suggestive, perturbing contagion through the air, as if one could breathe in voluptuousness).[71]

The consequences of reading bad literature are clear: Lita is awakened sexually from her reading, which may be seen as a critique of pornographic literature, reading is also associated with the formation of identity: *'a mí los hombres me gustan a lo* Don Juan Tenorio ... *como papá'* (I like *Don*

Juan-type men, like Dad).[72] But reading bad literature also makes her unable to see Paco Garba for the bad writer he is: she is dazzled by him *'Larva era tanto como Cervantes, fuera de que para ella la literatura no era sino el nimbo y la aureola del hombre; y éste, feo y todo, gustábale de veras'* (Larva was therefore like Cervantes. To her, literature surrounded men like a halo, and, ugly as he was, she really liked this one.)[73] Paco Garba represents the degenerate form of literature that begins with Cervantes, passes through Zorrilla,[74] and ends up as literary decadentism, aligned by association with titillating literary rubbish.[75]

De los Ríos chooses the *novela corta* as the genre for her assault on the mediocre times that have produced a degenerate Don Juan. Descended 'from a marriage between the popular literature – *folletines, novelas por entregas, cuentos de la prensa* – of the nineteenth century, and the French *nouvelle'*, the *novela corta* was aimed at mass consumption by urban middle-class readers.[76] Lázaro suggests that de los Ríos was aiming at a specifically female audience, *'por su uso de la estética y temas del folletín romántico'* (through her use of the aesthetics and themes of the romantic serial),[77] interpellating a politicized female reader. Invoking Don Juan in the title undoubtedly made it of interest to both male and female readers, but any reader who was attracted by the salaciousness often attached to the name of Don Juan would have been rewarded with a tale about the dangerous consequences of society's ills.[78]

Lázaro draws attention to the radical move of de los Ríos in focusing attention on the devastating effects of the profligate on his daughters: *'incluir la situación de las hijas del héroe no es, en este sentido, menos audaz de lo que sería presenter el abandono paterno de su imaginaria progenie femenina por parte de James Bond'* (including the position of the hero's daughters is not, in this sense, any less audacious than it would be to present the father's abandonment of his imaginary feminine progeny on the part of James Bond). If not feminist, the work is, for Lázaro, certainly *'feminocéntrica'* (feminocentric) in its move to place women centre stage, a strategy also lauded by Glenn.[79] Both scholars see the work as a timely reminder that, although they were omitted from the canon of Spanish fiction in the first third of the twentieth century, 'women *did* write'.[80] These are good points, but it is difficult ultimately to extract a 'feminist' resting place for this novella, even within the limited strains of the championing of rights for women of the early years of the twentieth century.

De los Ríos's achievement is to have questioned the ribald indulgence normally reserved for an adulterous husband. She does this by comparing it with the glamour associated with the notorious figure of Don Juan, before swiftly and cleanly bringing both Don Juan and the wayward husband to their knees. There is no glamour in alcoholic binges and visits to brothels, she suggests. She then focuses on the devastating effects such behaviour can have on the women of the family. Although she does not cite venereal disease as a direct result of philandering (Ibsen, meanwhile, cites syphilis but he too prefers to concentrate on the metaphor of hereditary illness),[81] her focus on the consequences for women of men's profligate ways is nevertheless daring. Through Don Juan, male sexuality is attacked radically as a polluting force.

It is disappointing, therefore, that de los Ríos chooses to confirm such negative stereotypes of femininity. In the first place, through the theme of degeneration, the suggestion is that the feminization of the bloodline is equivalent to its irrevocable decline. It is true that in blaming Don Juan for the young women's decline, de los Ríos was introducing male sexuality as polluting and contagious, a space generally reserved for female sexuality. Nevertheless, de los Ríos does nothing to reverse the prevailing attitude that aligned female sexuality with pollution and contagion.[82] Dora's case is perhaps more interesting than that of Lita in that her form of devotion to God is blended with eroticism in a way that has the potential to be transgressive. Her ecstasy is a blend of the erotic and the religious.

At the same time, however, her consumption merely confirms the stereotype: tuberculosis was understood as a 'disease of passion' in which the victim is '"consumed" by ardor, that ardor leading to the dissolution of the body', a variant of the 'disease of love', a war between sensuality and its repression.[83] Its description encapsulates both the archaic ideas that consumption was linked to heredity and the new discovery of contagion.[84] The novella shows evidence of an attempt to control female sexuality: Dora's transgressive form of ecstasy and Lita's degraded female sexuality through prostitution are bracketed off as deviant. Dora appears afflicted as a result of her father's profligate activities; Lita, meanwhile, seems to fall into prostitution as punishment for her flirtatious ways. Both daughters ultimately find no escape from their father's sins other than death. Both daughters and their father are removed from the scene as tragic casualties on the road to a purer race.

Nation and Regeneration
In an excellent article on *Las hijas de don Juan*, Reyes Lázaro suggests that the ambivalence shown by de los Ríos towards the figure of Don Juan can be extended to her attitude towards Spanishness. She writes that in *Las hijas de don Juan*, '*se antepone al casticismo "andaluz" otro "castellano", instaurando, en el aspecto étnico, una España que se extiende entre Madrid y un Aragón Navarra castellanizados*' (Andalusian Spanishness is counterposed with Castillian Spanishness, which inscribes, in ethnic terms, a Spain that extends between Madrid and a Castillianized Aragon and Navarre.)[85] She reminds us that Fontibre comes from the

north of Spain (the border between Navarre and Aragon), thereby supplanting Don Juan's traditional roots in Seville. The narrator uses questions of taste to eschew certain elements in favour of others. Lázaro cites the negative tone used to describe any foreign elements in the congregation at church (the clothes from exotic locations) which are, she suggests, evidence of a rejection of '*la influencia del mundo postcolonial, caribeño y filipino*' (the influence of the postcolonial world, the Caribbean and Philippines).

Thus, '*en la nave se apretaba concurrencia promiscua: no faltaban guayanaveras de chulo entre blusas tiznadas de obrero, flecudos mantones de negra espumilla contorneando reales cuerpos de chulas; roídos mantoncillos pardos pendientes de angulosos hombros de viejas*' (in the nave a promiscuous gathering squeezed against one another: there was no lack of working-class men's *guayaberas* amid blackened workers' shirts, fringed, black Manila shawls contouring the bodies of working-class women; worn dull-brown shawls hanging from the angular shoulders of old women).[86] For Lázaro, both Spain's peripheries (Seville) and the ex-colonies, are rejected in favour of a Castillian-centric Spain, which, as Silver and Fox indicate, was exalted by writers during the Restoration.[87]

I suggest, however, that this passage does not so much identify a rejection of Spain's ex-colonies, as imply an inscription of them in a deferential relationship to Spain. The reference to '*promiscua*' (promiscuous, from the Latin 'to mix') suggests the blending of exotic and Spanish elements. 'Promiscuous' might also suggest Don Juan, and Jo Labanyi has shown how Don Juan was used in the first half of the twentieth century by some intellectuals in Spain to represent the colonizer of the New World.[88] De los Ríos condemns the influx of foreign elements that enter Spain through commerce in her scorn reserved for Concha, who plies the local markets for exotic cloth, but is marked by her bad taste. Yet here the promiscuous blend of foreign and domestic elements is a fertile image: '*en el presbiterio, una fila de mujeres pálidas, con sus tiernas criaturas en brazos y una vela encendida en la diestra, ofrecían a la Virgen el fruto recién desprendido, caliente aún del calor de sus entrañas, el hijo nuevo*' (in the presbytery, a row of pale women, with their tender children in their arms and a candle in their right hands, offered to the Virgin the recently plucked fruit, still warm from their intestines, the new child). She goes on:

> *en aquellas pálidas caras de madres resplandecían y se mezclaban dos luces de lo alto, dos sacras majestades: la maternidad y la fe; y aquellos rostros de chulas que en la vida tendrían gestos zaínos y picantes, allí descoloridas, convalecientes, fervorosos, alumbrados por luz de cirios y fulgores matinales, se espiritualizaban, conmovían hasta el llanto* (in those pale mothers' faces two lights shone from on high and brought together two sacred majesties: motherhood and faith; and those working-class women's faces, which would have been dark-skinned and common in daily life, were there pale, convalescent, fervent, illuminated by the light of candles and shining matins, they were spiritualized and moved to lament).[89]

The image has complex, ambivalent and not wholly coherent racial overtones: this promiscuous blend of cultures assembled in the church is seen as the product of the blending of New and Old Worlds. Reading this passage subtly, a new child is implicitly produced from the union between Don Juan the colonizer and the ('dark-skinned and common') women. But these women and children are simultaneously made paler, symbolically colonized (in an image in which fair-skin equals religious faith) by Catholicism.

Tales of Seduction

As Frederick Pike notes in his *Hispanismo, 1898–1936*, aside from seeking to cure Spain of a range of national ills, many intellectuals responded to the quest for the regeneration of Spain post-1898 in terms of 'hispanization' (looking to the ex-colonies to strengthen their national power).[90] As many intellectuals 'contemplated the Iberian "raza" not just in Spain, where it seemed weak and listless, but in the New World, where it seemed strong and dynamic, they were capable of summoning up far greater optimism than those who observed only the plight of peninsular Spaniards'.[91] Unamuno, for instance, in 1904, noted that America had erased sterile Spanish institutions and what was dead and useless of the past, leaving only *casticismo*, the pure Spanish essence.[92]

Intellectuals who had mused over the peculiarly Spanish traits that constituted the Spanish *raza* increasingly held it up as a civilizing element in the New World.[93] De los Ríos was one intellectual who debated the *'porvenir de la raza'* (future of the race) in terms of a *'porvenir hispanoamericano'* (Hispano–American future).[94] In a paper presented at the Centre for Hispano-American Culture in 1911, she began by noting the *'afinidades indestructibles, solidaridad, atracciones y mancomunidades inevitablemente necesarias, que todo: el comercio, la geografía, las relaciones internacionales, los instintos de la propia conservación, las atracciones del amor, de la sangre y de la lengua, todo contribuye a estrechar, y estrecha más y más cada día'* (indestructible affinities, solidarity, inevitable and necessary attractions and communities, in which everything: commerce, geography, international relations, instincts of self-preservation, the attractions of love, blood and language, all work every day to strengthen ties).[95]

Spain needs Latin America for its commercial power, in the face of monetary strength from the United States. *'En suma: que frente al bloque anglo-sajón se levanta el bloque hispanoamericano'* (In sum, when facing the Anglo-Saxon block the Hispano–American block rises up).[96] Links with the ex-colonies are therefore beneficial to Spain in terms of money and power. Latin America, meanwhile, is dispersed into 20 republics, without an *'alma colectiva'* (collective soul). What Latin America needs is a *'fuerza cohesiva'* (cohesive force) a *'gran energía renovadora'* (great renovating energy).[97] In an interesting parallel, Ramiro de Maeztu, writing in 1926, would later use Don Juan as a motif to exhort energy as a regenerating force for the relationship between Spain and Latin America.

In *Don Quijote, Don Juan y La Celestina*, Maeztu separates the Spanish Don Juan from the Romantic Don Juan of northern Europe (that of Byron, Molière, Lenau) who searches endlessly for his ideal woman. *'El Don Juan nuestro, el burlador, no lo conocen, y creo que si lo conocieran su primer impulso sería deportarlo por "indeseable"'* (They don't know our Don Juan, the Trickster, and I think that if they did their first impulse would be to deport him as an 'undesirable').[98] The Spanish Don Juan is the *'burlador'* (trickster), who *'carece de anhelos superiores. Es, por definición, hombre de apetitos, pero sin ideales'* (is lacking in superior desires. He is, by definition, a man of appetites, but without ideals).[99] Don Juan is a myth rather than a reality, but he represents the will to power: *'Don Juan es, ante todo, una energía bruta, instintiva, petulante, pero inagotable, triunfal y arrolladora'* (Don Juan is, above all, brute energy, instinctive, petulant, but inexhaustible, triumphal and overpowering).[100]

It is this Don Juan without ideals, pure brute energy that Maeztu recuperates for the Spanish nation. In his trio of literary giants, Spaniards should seek to combine Don Quixote's capacity for selfless love, with La Celestina's wisdom and Don Juan's brute energy as a paradigm for the regeneration of Spain through a fusion of Old World and

New. In this myth and model for the future, Maeztu vindicates Tirso's trickster even as he celebrates Zorrilla's romantic Don Juan, who discovers divine justice. As Britt Arredondo notes, Maeztu's 'redemption' of Don Juan 'thus comprehends both the violent energy of the faithless trickster of Tirso de Molina – the conquistador – and the spiritual values of the converted trickster of Zorrilla – what in his 1934 *Defensa de la hispanidad* Maeztu would formulate as the 'Hispanic Gentleman'.[101] Thus, where de los Ríos describes Latin America's need for a re-energizing force to counter the United States menace, Maeztu (admittedly, almost twenty years later) supplies that font of energy imaginatively in the form of the mythical Don Juan.

Maeztu's *hispanidad* constituted 'Spanishness', or the 'qualities of the soul, acquired through historical experiences as synthesized and integrated by Catholicism, in which all members of the Hispanic raza shared and by which they were united into a vast transatlantic community'.[102] De los Ríos shares this emphasis on Spain as the main force in the relationship between Old and New Worlds.

Can de los Ríos be said to advocate miscegenation, as Maeztu would in his *Defensa de la hispanidad*? In *Las hijas de don Juan*, in the description of the 'promiscuous' and exotic congregation at church, a result of commerce between Old and New Worlds, the image is of fecundity, of maternity, of the production of an '*hijo*' (child). In her 1911 essay she picks up the theme of maternity again, but her emphasis is on Spain as the motherland: '*España, la heroica, la excelsa madre*' (Spain, the heroic, the sublime mother) and '*España es la madre de casi todo el continente americano – dijo el Presidente de la República de Méjico – y sigue siéndolo, porque las maternidades no se prescriben*' (Spain is the mother of almost all the American continent – so said the President of the Republic of Mexico – and it continues to be so, for maternities cannot be prescribed).[103]

Opposites Attract

In spite of the Spanish disaster, therefore, de los Ríos manages to engineer the 'imaginative denial' of the loss of Spain's colonies. Like many other writers, de los Ríos focuses on the Spanish language as the link between Spain and the ex-colonies. Castilian is the symbol of Spain's colonial power. In 1911 she speaks of the need to keep the language free of all foreign, corrupting elements, a fact all the more remarkable in the face of her enjoyment of *Las hijas de don Juan*, as she imitates the language of the lower classes, plays with words borrowed from French, or English or the ex-colonies – of course she attaches a great deal of scorn to these words, even as she appears to revel in their use.[104] Language, for de los Ríos, at least officially, is the means for the dissemination of Catholicism throughout the New World.

Language has to be preserved because it is *'la geografía espiritual de una estirpe; es su historia, su psicología; es su sentencia de muerte y de olvido, o su promesa de gloria y de eternidad: porque en la lengua y en los monumentos de la lengua perduran las razas más que en los bronces eternos'* (the spiritual geography of a lineage; it is its history, its psychology, it is its death sentence or sentence to forget, or its promise of glory and eternity: because in language and the monuments of language races last longer than bronze statues).[105] Thus, rather than rejecting the colonies, de los Ríos recognizes the need for *'hispanismo'*, but at the same time, Spain must be the spiritual heartland, the locale of artistic, cultural and historical greatness. Implicit in her imagery is the threat of linguistic contagion (and with it, cultural corruption) and the motif of imperial conquest. Spain can and must maintain ties with the ex-colonies, but it must always remain superior to the colonized. The flow of culture must go only one way. In 1916 de los Ríos suggests that Don Juan was born of the negative influences brought from the New World:

Tales of Seduction

> *Si hubo medios propicios a producir donjuanes, lo fue aquella España, lo fue aquella Sevilla del Renacimiento, emporio del comercio intercontinental, cosmópolis tumultuosa, verdadera capital de la España de dos mundos, depósito del oro de las Indias, corte del ocio, del lujo y del amor, ancho asilo de aventureros y de pícaros, Chipre y Babilonia del hampa, del matonismo y de la valentonería, formas degenerativas en que bajo el influjo de aquel sol, y entre codicias del oro indiano, del vicio y del cohecho, allí imperantes, comenzaban a descomponerse el robusto valor y las virtudes de la raza'* (If there were ideal conditions to produce Don Juans, they were in that Spain, that Seville of the Renaissance, emporium of intercontinental commerce, turbulent cosmopolis, true capital of the Spain of two worlds, depositary of gold from the Indies, court of leisure, luxury and love, refuge for adventurers and tricksters, Cyprus and Babylon of the underworld, of thuggery, brutishness and degenerative forms; under the influence of that sun, that greed for Indian gold, the vice and bribes that ruled there, the robust valour and virtues of the race began to decompose).[106]

Although implicit rather than explicit, Don Juan represents the colonizer, the conquerer, symbol of the Spain of empire, of the blend of Old World and New and all its attendant dangers. In an article entitled 'Hispanismo', reprinted in 1925 from the journal *Raza Española* on the occasion of a Spanish-American exhibition on Seville and the future of the race, de los Ríos changes her position to become more forcefully in favour of miscegenation. Spain is distinguished from other empires, she declares (*'sólo España realiza el mliagro, sin par en los fastos del mundo, de crear una raza'* (only Spain achieves the miracle, without compare in the annals of world history, of creating a

Opposites Attract

race).[107] Here *raza* has changed noticeably from referring solely to the Spanish nation to embracing the concept of a mixed race. Unlike other empires who lived within their frontiers, or who exploited the colonies, writes de los Ríos, Spain created a new race through miscegenation ('*mezclar la sangre propia con la indígena*' or mixing one's own blood with indigenous blood) that shared a common culture:

> *Religión, la lengua, las leyes, el arte, la cultura, toda la vida, toda el alma nacional, en suma, con los pueblos trasatlánticos, darles a comer de nuestra carne y a beber de nuestra sangre en sublime comunión humana, sin sombra de odios étnicos, sin la desalmada codicia exterminadora de que tan espantosos ejemplos dan los pueblos que pretenden superarnos en cultura y humanitarismo; realizar la empresa incomparable de crear en la fraternidad de Cristo una nueva familia humana, esto sólo España lo ha hecho.* (Religion, language, law, art, culture, all of life, the whole national soul, in short we have the trans-Atlantic people eating our flesh and drinking our blood in sublime human communion, without a shadow of ethnic hatred, without the callous exterminating greed of the terrible examples of people who seek to overtake us in culture and humanitarianism; only Spain has achieved the incomparable enterprise of creating in the brotherhood of Christ a new human family).[108]

The image of people from the New World eating the flesh and drinking the blood of the Spaniards has racist overtones of the stereotypical cannibal 'discovered' abroad, but these nuances are overlaid with connotations of Catholicism, a performance of the Eucharist in a Holy Communion. Finally, the result is miscegenation, a blending of bloods to create a 'new human family'. '*Amor*' (love), writes de los Ríos, is the name to be given to this spirit of cohesion, strength, solidarity and union that creates the Hispanic race. Now when she cites the motherland, it is in terms of *'ser hijos de la gran Madre educadora y cristianizadora de América'* (being children of the great educating and Christianizing Mother of America) and *'dentro del nombre de la Península descubridora, HISPANIA, cabrían las dos Patrias Madres y su doble descendencia'* (within the name of the discovering Peninsula, Hispania, there are two Motherlands and their double line of descendants).[109]

These descendants should unite: *'agrupémonos, fusionémonos como si nos animara un alma sola'* (let us group together, may we fuse as if animated by a single soul), creating a new family of the hispanic race.[110] Despite her new language of 'family' and new interpretation of race, for de los Ríos this new race still acts as standard bearer for the Spanish language, for Catholicism, and celebrates the imperial history in which Spain and Spanish America are intertwined.

In 1927, fascist ideologue Ernesto Giménez Caballero underlined the link between the current *'moda de don Juan'* (fashion for Don Juan), which *'tiene una cuna nacionalista, política, localizada en España 1898'* (has a nationalistic, political birthplace, localized in Spain 1898) and the influence of Nietzsche on the writers of 1898.[111] For Giménez Caballero then, Don Juan is representative of Nietzsche's will to power. In an excellent article, Jo Labanyi traces Giménez Caballero's use of the Don Juan figure in his writing. In *Love Dialogues between Laura and Don Juan*, for example, he links his discussion of Don Juan to Spain's conquest of the American empire. Like Maeztu, he divorces Don Juan from the Petrarchan idealization of women to equate him with the violent (sexual) conquest of empire. In *Genio de España* he described Spain's imperial 'genius' as that of a nation of 'race-makers, Don Juans, magnificent virile studs', who generously 'donate' their seed to women of colour in order to create a 'new race'.[112]

'*Cuando Don Juan ... se enamoraba de una mujer, no era para convertirse en su amigo y colaborador, sino en su adversario – en el supreme éxtasis de triunfo genital, imprimirla un inolvidable beso ardiente sobre la boca.*' (When Don Juan fell in love with a woman, it was not to become her friend and partner, but her adversary. To conquer her, force her to the ground – admirable enemy! – and in the supreme ecstasy of genital triumph, stamp an unforgettable, burning kiss on her mouth.)[113] In *Love Dialogues*, he uses the motif of Don Juan to open up a space for Spain (which has shown its worth in its history of violent colonization as represented by Don Juan) within European fascism: the marriage of Don Juan and Laura is the marriage between Spain and fascist Italy.[114] De los Ríos, as we have seen, advocates a vision of Spain as the conquistador, the colonizer, a force of energy, who seduces with words. Seen in this context, it is perhaps possible to see de los Ríos's work (for all its discussion of the 'love' between Spain and Spanish America) as part of a genealogy of conservative thinking on the subject of conquest. This reasoning leads directly to national Catholicism. As Labanyi points out, Giménez Caballero exalts

> miscegenation as the major achievement of Spain's empire – as would Maeztu in his last book, *Defensa de la hispanidad*, which proposed the Spanish model of colonial relations as the basis for a new world system embracing all peoples, regardless of race, while all three are united by a belief that the miscegenation practices in Spain's early modern empire signified a political order based on love. This view has regularly been advanced under modernity to justify Spain's imperial project, by both Spanish Right and Left –

and is still heard in Spain today to argue that Spaniards are not racist.[115]

De los Ríos advances a view of miscegenation based on love. Like Maeztu, de los Ríos sees Spain and Spanish America's future to be united by the Catholic faith. As González López has noted, *Raza Española* and other writing by de los Ríos, '*constituye un momento intermedio en la evolución de dicho nacionalismo hacia la tesis de la derecha autoritaria, que terminarán sirviendo de fundamento a la Dictadura de Franco*' (constitutes an intermediate moment in the evolution of nationalism towards the authoritarian right, which would end up providing a basis for Franco's dictatorship).[116]

It is possible to find a trajectory from the conservative ideas of de los Ríos (devout, exalting motherhood, Castillian-centric) to Francoism. But unlike Giménez Caballero, and however misguided she may be about the realities, her view of colonization is of a loving, humane, 'meeting' of two continents. This is not Giménez Caballero's 'reduction of empire to a scenario of sexual violation [that] betrays a desperate need for the male to conquer the threat of formlessness figured by the feminine'.[117] At the same time, her image of the colonizer contains similarities with her image of the Don Juan of old (as seen in *Las hijas de don Juan*): both are linked to imperial power, culture, tradition, chivalry and linguistic seduction. I suggest that de los Ríos does not cite Don Juan explicitly as the standard-bearer for her vision of Spain's future (in spite of her invocation of a seductive conquistador as key to Spain's future), precisely because of his volatile nature, the negative overtones he may afford of degeneration, contagion and sexual conquest (explored in *Las hijas de don Juan*). In her thesis on miscegination, de los Ríos exalts motherhood and love as a blueprint for the future of the nation. But the seemingly benign image of motherhood (which at first appears 'feminocentric' in nature),[118] obscures implicit earlier scenarios of sexual colonization. De los Ríos's view of the future of Spain's role within Spanish America is, at root, nothing more than a partially disguised vision of sexual conquest: a rejuvenated, conquistador Don Juan.

2. PERFORMANCE ANXIETIES: DON JUAN IN THE CONSULTING ROOM

The rise of feminism in Spain in the 1920s and 1930s brought with it intense debate about the assignment of gender roles. The freshly conceived 'New Modern Woman' offered a new gender paradigm for women, challenging the *'ángel del hogar'* (angel of the house) model of domesticity that had prevailed since the nineteenth century. Political conservatism and a powerful Roman Catholic Church as a political institution were now joined by a number of social movements that aimed variously to promote sex education, feminism, prostitution reform, legal reform (in particular the divorce law), hygiene and eugenics. In the increasing secularization of cultural values in the early twentieth century, 'doctors began to supplant clergymen as male authorities on cultural norms', while biological determinism rather than religion became a core feature in the cultural construction of gender difference.[1]

Gregorio Marañón, the most famous Spanish doctor of the century, was a leading endocrinologist and champion of hygiene and sex reform in the discourse and practice of

Performance Anxieties: Don Juan in the Consulting Room

birth control, maternity and childcare.[2] Perhaps surprisingly, in his attempt to shore up pronatalism through scientific means, it was Marañón's use of the figure of Don Juan as an icon to contest received gender roles that was to capture the public's imagination. Don Juan became a site not just for the confluence of ideas surrounding pronatalism, as well as gender roles (in particular conceived of as a masculinity in crisis), but it also fed into and fostered contemporary anxieties surrounding the threat of a universal bisexuality. In this chapter I explore the confluence of ideas surrounding Don Juan as a 'medical metaphor', and show how Don Juan came, in the public imagination, to be associated with homosexuality.

Don Juan and Paternity

A champion for women's rights in the arena of maternity, Marañón was also distinguished from some other intellectuals of the time by his belief that women were in no way inferior to men (merely different). He even held progressive views on the desirability of female orgasm for the 'harmony of conjugal life'. Yet Marañón continued to maintain that childbirth was woman's biological destiny, to the exclusion of everything else. But it was to Don Juan that he would turn, in his desire to reach out to a public regarding the desirability of his pronatalist project. That he should choose to write about Don Juan is perhaps not so surprising, given that his writing on the legendary Spanish seducer fed into and drew upon a proliferation of studies on the Don Juan phenomenon from a wide range of journalists, thinkers and doctors, both within Spain and elsewhere in Europe.[3]

By writing on Don Juan, Marañón was assured a ready audience (both popular and intellectual) for his ideas. Furthermore, given Marañón's eugenic concern for the propagation of a healthy race, it is not difficult to understand why Don Juan would be chosen as the antithesis of a model for fatherhood. His view is that men should have an important role in the reproductive sphere. Debates on the question of paternal responsibility in law invoked the spectre of *'tenorios'* (Don Juans) who had fled from the scene leaving single mothers often with no option other than prostitution.[4] Demands for a change in the law on paternal responsibility would mean that *'los tenorios serían menos'* (there would be fewer Don Juans), in the words of one Spanish doctor, as men who had to pay for illegitimate children would see the consequences of their multiple seductions.[5] Promiscuous adulterers hardly fit with the model of monogamy put forward by Marañón.

Interestingly, however, Marañón chooses not to focus on the question of paternal responsibility, but rather on Don Juan's lack of offspring. Pérez de Ayala had gone so far as to classify Don Juan as a *'maldito garañón estéril'* (damned sterile stud)[6] as neither Tirso nor Zorrilla mention any descendants. We saw in the last chapter how Blanca de los Ríos's *Las hijas de don Juan* of 1907 and Echegaray's play *El hijo de don Juan* had provided exceptions to the rule. Degeneration, bad blood and heredity (what Foucault would term 'degenerescence' theories)[7] circulate in these tales of the progeny of Don Juan. Elsewhere, in reference to an exaltation of monogamy as a way of life, Marañón will claim that Don Juan's roots are not Spanish at all. Don Juan is Italian, Mediterranean, or else derives from Arabic custom (the harem) or gypsy life (the passionate tragedy) rather than the austere, Spanish eugenic paradigm. Don Juan is thus the foreign body, infiltrating the nationalist project.

Don Juan presents a view of masculinity as driven by instinctive desire. Thus Marañón writes that *'el instinto es casi siempre antieugenésico'* (instinct is almost always antieugenic). Hence:

Performance Anxieties: Don Juan in the Consulting Room

Decid a un hombre ebrio de deseo, en el momento que va a lograr la posesión de la mujer, que está enferma; que aquel beso encendido le puede contagiar; que el hijo que se va a engendrar en el minuto de la unión codiciada puede ser un degenerado o un enfermo. Nada de esto lo detendrá. (Tell a man, drunk with desire, at the moment he is about to possess the woman, that she is ill, that that burning kiss can be contagious, that the child they are about to conceive at the moment of desired union might be a degenerate or sickly. None of this will stop him.)[8]

This overflow of sexual desire works against '*el fin altruista de crear una descendencia y una raza enérgicas e inteligentes*' (the altruistic aim of creating a lively and intelligent descendancy and race).[9] Don Juan is indiscriminate in the production and dispersal of sexual fluids. As a gender paradigm for the nation, men would do well to consider sexual continence as a higher form of virility.[10] These ideals resonate with nineteenth-century concerns about the weakening of sperm through onanism. Conservation of sexual fluids leads to stronger male seed. At the same time, despite, or possibly because of, Don Juan's over-sexed drive, Marañón considers him to be sterile. Male sterility confounds the project to create a healthy race. Bad blood and weakened sperm make of Don Juan a negative prototype for Spanish paternity.

Bad blood and sexual instinct can be seen as 'pre-scientific ideas' associated with the notion of Don Juan in the early twentieth century.[11] It is perhaps no wonder, therefore, that Marañón, a prominent endocrinologist, should have found Don Juan so appealing. Endocrinology, a modern chemical science, was founded on the relationship between blood and sex. At the end of the nineteenth century, Charles Edouard Brown-Séquard set in motion a popular and scientific interest in the ductless glands as organs of 'internal secretion', organs that release chemicals into the bloodstream as a way of regulating the metabolism. Brown-Séquard emphasized the ancient folk-wisdom that femininity and virility reside in the gonad. Ernest Starling, the British doctor who coined the term 'hormone' in 1905, directed the search for these 'chemical messengers' specific to testis and ovary.[12] For Marañón, as for these early pioneers, sex morphology, function and behaviour was seen to be 'all in the glands'. Marañón labels Don Juan 'hypergonadal', and sets out to find ways to extirpate his 'abnormal' form of sexuality from the blood of the Spanish nation.

Sex and Lies
In *Mad Men and Medusas*, Juliet Mitchell notes the extraordinary absence of Don Juan in Sigmund Freud's theories, which are 'so crucially about sexuality and death in human life'.[13] Freudian psychoanalysis, after all, often draws on mythical or literary archetypes as explanatory devices for clinical cases. This lack in the theoretical foundations of the science that addresses sexuality, neurosis and lack of conscious agency is striking, given that Don Juan is often regarded as a pathological case, 'as an individual driven, in spite of himself, by the sombre madness of sex'.[14] Mitchell invites Don Juan onto the psychoanalyst's couch and diagnoses him, ('creative but seducing, lying, someone for whom death has no meaning') as a male hysteric.[15]

In 1927, Spanish doctor Gonzalo Rodríguez Lafora had likewise diagnosed Don Juan as an hysteric, noting that 'for nearly half a century now psychologists have readily acknowledged hysteria in men, and during the Great War it was shown that a number of soldiers with paralyses, contractures and other symptoms of hysteria reached a high percentage'. However, as a matter of fact, Lafora explains, hysteria in men, though frequent, is rarer than in women; the proportion is perhaps 25 per cent, as may be seen from statistics (he cites the number of people cured by suggestion after a visit to Lourdes as one man to every three women).[16] Mitchell tracks the disappearance of male hysteria from clinical work. She suggests that it was Freud's own hysteria that caused Don Juan to remain suppressed at the heart of psychoanalysis, a normalization of the male hysteric at the expense of the pathological, female 'other'.[17]

Freud's new science of psychoanalysis came to be known in Spain from 1914. Gregorio Marañón commented on the '*ausencia de alusiones concretas*' (absence of concrete allusions) to Don Juan in Freud's work '*hecho realmente extraño dada la boga actual del donjuanismo, en la literatura y en la ciencia, y dada también su indudable trascendencia social*' (a truly curious fact given the current vogue for Don Juanism in literature and science, and also given its undoubted social transcendence).[18] After noting Freud's omission, Marañón will go on to bring Don Juan into the consulting room, principally in an article of 1924, '*Notas para una biología de Don Juan*' (Notes for a biology of Don Juan) and in a series of follow-up articles and references. Furthermore, he sees Don Juan as an emblem for the fusion of lying and sex, which is psychoanalysis itself.[19]

He sees the Spain of the 1920s in the grip of a terrible problem, which is the 'cult of sex', which '*ninguna pedagogía ni religión ha alcanzado a resolver en la práctica: el problema sexual*' (no pedagogy or religion has managed to resolve in practice: the problem of sex).[20] Man (masculinity and mankind are elided) is being educated in the '*estúpido culto de su sex*' (stupid cult of his sex).[21] The myth of 'false' or 'quantitative' virility, one based on '*apuntar en un papel el número de las mujeres conquistadas*' (jotting on a piece of paper the number of female conquests)[22] is embodied in the figure of Don Juan, an image produced with the collusion

Tales of Seduction

of teachers, spiritual leaders and women alike. As soon as a young man takes his first steps in the world, a thousand suggestions, stories and half words inform him that *'ser hombre es fundamentalmente hacer de la mujer carrera de obstáculos de la propia resistencia'* (to be a man is fundamentally to make a woman into an obstacle course of her resistence).[23] How, asks Marañón, has the 'radical' and 'noble' reproductive instinct become the cause of *'tantas desdichas'* (so much misfortune)?

The myth of carnal sin, according to Marañón, ought to act as an 'hygienic aphrodisiac'.[24] But with the cult of sex, in this history of sexuality, instead of the scene of original sin, we find an ordinary locker-room discussion: *'Podemos inclinarnos a admitir que el mito de la seudovirilidad nació la primera vez que dos hombres se juntaron para hablar de sus secretos amorosos. A partir de entonces, mentira y sexo van perdurablemente unidos.* (We could be inclined to admit that the myth of pseudovirility was born the first time that two men got together to talk about their amorous secrets. Since then, lies and sex are endurably linked.)[25]

Sex, like Don Juan, becomes a seductive yet deceitful performative, it is the sexual boast, the domain of the braggart. Moreover, for Marañón, *'toda una patología y toda una terapeútica se han fundado sobre el fatal equívoco'* (both pathology and therapy are founded on this fatal error) the union between sex and lying.[26] The bragging cult of sex fuses with, accentuates and repeatedly reproduces the hyper-erotics of the age. Marañón invokes Freud in his discussion of the cult of sex:

> *Gentes que sufren de lo que sea, sin preocupaciones neurósicas* [sic] *y sin sospechar la existencia de Freud. Y sin embargo, ¡cuántas y cuántas veces, allá en lo hondo de las causas de sus males, encontramos una cosa torcida, que es siempre un vestigio de catástrofes grandes o de pequeños*

descarrilamientos de su vida sexual! (People who have all kinds of ailments, without being neurotic and without even knowing that Freud exists. And yet, how many times, in the depth of the cause of their illness, do we find something twisted, which is always a vestige of large catastrophes or small derailments in their sexual life!)[27]

Marañón attributes sexual aetiology at the root of this collective malaise. At the same time, given the ambiguity of the word *'encontramos'* (do we find what we seek?) we can also find a critique of psychoanalysis, in the allegation of a pathology and a therapeutics based on the imbrication of sex and mendacity. Marañón is suggesting implicitly that the 'talking cure' is no more than a chance for patients to act as pathologized sexual braggarts. Like Mitchell, Marañón intimates the fusion of sex and lies at the heart of psychoanalysis. For if we read the 'two men who get together to talk about their amorous secrets' as a recreation of a clinical psychoanalytic session, then the objectivity and impartiality of the analyst is placed in question (this is a man with his own sexual desires, neuroses and investments).

At the same time, Marañón puts male patients in the place of Freud's (and Charcot's) mainly female hysterics. *'No hay hombre'* (There is no man) writes Marañón *'que no mienta, en el caso más favorable, sin saber que miente, al descubrir su interior sexual'* (who does not lie, at best without even knowing that he is lying, when he discovers his sexual interior).[28] Just as in 1932 Freud was to posit femininity as a 'dark continent', in 1924 Marañón explains that at the heart of masculinity, and the whole cult of sex, is a 'penumbra', a seductive greyness, an unknowability covered over with empty performatives. Such a reading inverts the traditional metonymic chain between femininity, hysteria and lying.[29] An hysterical urge to lie is placed at

Tales of Seduction

the heart both of a modern sexual collective malaise, and at the heart of the modern science of psychoanalysis. Jacqueline Rose has noted that the birth of psychoanalysis entailed a shift in clinical neurology in the ranking of the senses: implicitly rejecting the visuality and empiricism of an earlier essentialist biologism (she cites Charcot's methods for treating female hysterics in the Paris Salpêtrière asylum) and developing therapeutic techniques based on speech and hearing.[30] Marañón implicitly advocates a turn away from listening to the (male) patient speak (which may be untrustworthy) and a return to viewing the organs, sites and causes of the body, a return to blood and away from language.[31]

Literature and Science
In March 1928, the famous Spanish histologist Santiago Ramón y Cajal wrote to Gregorio Marañón:

> *Amigo Marañón, ... si no fuera porque los periodistas no nos dejan escribir a los médicos de temas literarios – que ellos estiman de su exclusiva propiedad – también terciaría yo en el interesante debate sobre el Don Juan real y sus variedades y otros temas de actualidad. Pero hay que renunciar a tan peligrosos propósitos.* (Marañón, my friend, if it were not for the fact that journalists will not let us doctors discuss literary themes – which they view as their property – I too would enter the interesting debate on the real Don Juan and his variants and other current themes. But one must renounce such dangerous propositions.)[32]

Ramón y Cajal had, in fact, written fiction, giving an exhilarating description of lovers' kisses in terms of the microscopic detail of cellular activity and the physiological changes in the lovers' bodies in 'La casa maldita', a short-story from his *Cuentos de vacaciones* (1905), a supreme example of the fusion of science and literature. It may seem curious, therefore, that he should underwrite the rigid distinctions between the literary and medical spheres.

Marañón offers a disclaimer (*excusarme*) at the start of his 1924 text on Don Juan, 'Notas para una biología de Don Juan', for entering into the field of literary criticism in which '*no soy ducho*' (I am not an expert) and invokes Eryximachus, the doctor in Plato's *Symposium*, who was moved to speak of love. In the literary arena, Marañón claims that he is deprived of the '*lenguaje preciso de la ciencia*' (precise language of science), but he wishes to remind us that Don Juan is not merely a myth but also '*un ser de carne y hueso, con su anatomía y su fisiología peculiares; pudiéramos añadir que con su historia clínica peculiar*' (a being of flesh and bone, with his own peculiar anatomy and physiology; we could add with his own peculiar clinical history).[33] Marañón will shed light on the penumbra of masculinity by stripping Don Juan back to his '*raíces biológicas más profundas*' (deepest biological roots).[34]

He claims he is in a privileged position, having access not just to the literary myth, but also to the '*estudio personal de varios ejemplares de donjuanes auténticos y afamados que he tenido la fortuna de poder observar*' (personal study of several examples of authentic and renowned Don Juans that I have had the fortune to observe).[35] It seems clear that Marañón chose the Don Juan type as a way to reach out to his audience, but it is his desire to read the sexualized, human body of what Corpus Barga calls a '*prejuicio literario*' (literary device) that causes him difficulties in his writing.[36]

For Marañón, the internal secretion of hormones into the blood accounts for a patient's secondary sexual characteristics, including morphology. Elsewhere, Marañón describes Don Juan as a 'hypergenital' type.[37] Marañón's desire to read the sexualized, human body of Don Juan, seeing the organic root as animating the narrative, caused him difficulties in his prognosis of the pathology in 1924. Marañón writes that Don Juan, as a highly sexed individual, ought to display *'morfología hipergenital'* (hypergenital morphology), which is something very different, according to Marañón, from the canons of Donjuanesque beauty. Hypergenital morphology is disproportionate so that the chin protrudes; the beard and moustache are thick (as displayed in Velázquez's 1643 painting of Don Sebastián de Morra who exhibited stunted growth).[38] Don Juan, meanwhile, is graceful, smooth and elegant.[39]

The move between literature and science is confusing: are we supposed to assume that all the Don Juan figures who passed through Marañón's consulting room were equally beautiful, that they all displayed *'morfología hipergenital'* (hypergenital morphology)?[40] What too is one to make of his assertion that all Don Juans are sterile, that their endless seductions never once produce progeny? Don Juan may be a 'medical metaphor' (in 1926 Corpus Barga described him as such),[41] but this blend of the literary and the scientific leaves Marañón open to criticism: F. Oliver Brachfeld, a staunch critic of Marañón, writing in 1933, describes Marañón's taxonomy of Donjuanesque morphology 'wavy hair, tendency to premature baldness' as 'completely arbitrary'. Marañón is stuck, writes Brachfeld, in *'un estado de ánimo de cientifista muy siglo diez y nueve'* (a scientific state of mind from the nineteenth century).

In terms of the sheer proliferation of interest in Don Juan among medical practitioners, Don Juan seemingly bridges without effort the chasm between literature and science. As James Bono has written, literature and science are distinguished in terms of their relationship to language: as a 'mode of expression', literature cannot be disengaged from language, whereas implicit in science is the notion that language is merely a 'transparent vehicle through which it

Performance Anxieties: Don Juan in the Consulting Room

transmits to others its encounter with a lawful universe'.[42] We could add that science is aided in this task by the visual, the perceptual field. Once empirical evidence is gleaned through the visual medium, this evidence is then communicated through language.[43] Both these media (the visual and the linguistic) become invisible in science: they are regarded as merely media to reflect an apparently 'transparent reality'.

Don Juan is at once literary and scientific. In his attempts to bring the body of Don Juan to the dissecting table, Marañón re-establishes the gap between the discourses of literature and science. His 1924 article, 'Psicopatología del donjuanismo' is of a date that makes it possible for it to have been influenced by the appearance of Freud's *The Psychopathology of Everyday Life* (which, as Glick has documented, was published in Spanish in 1922).[44]

Psychoanalysis as a discipline enacts a move away from visual empiricism (which uses vision to view symptoms directly from the body), and also bases a pathology and a therapeutics on the linguistic as mediator (the 'talking cure'). Thus, psychoanalysis moves from the purely scientific, the transparent 'truth' of reality, and into the realm of the literary (an emphasis on the importance of narrative and on symptoms both psychic and somatic as signifiers to be read and interpreted).

The renaming of Marañón's first incursion into Don Juan studies in 1924 from 'Notas para una biología' to be republished as 'Psicopatología', may suggest a move from biology to psyche.[45] However, despite this apparent shift of focus, Marañón's insistence in the article is on observing Don Juan's body rather than on listening to the workings of his mind, or rather than interpreting or 'reading' somatic symptoms as displaced psychic conditions. This reliance on 'unmediated' scientific reality rather than on Don Juan implemented as analogy and metaphor produces a tension in Marañón's writings.

By using the myth of Don Juan to address his body (and blood), eliding real cases with mythical ones, Marañón gets caught in just the same linguistic short cuts (*'atajos del lenguaje'*) he so disdained earlier in the same article. Don Juan is an analogy, a metaphor and cannot be used to present the transparent 'legible face' of reality, consistent with the claims Foucault makes for the discourse of science.[46] Marañón's writing on Don Juan is at the intersection between literature and science, and it makes Don Juan into a medium of exchange between two discourses (one role of metaphor),[47] drawing attention to the constructed, linguistic bases of both discourses and disrupting the stable meaning generally attributed to science.

Sex Wars
In her book, *Beyond the Natural Body: An Archaeology of Sex Hormones*, Nelly Oudshoorn notes that the (Victorian) notion of 'sex antagonism' was present in the early endocrinological studies. According to this doctrine, women's activities were in most respects the opposite of those of men. Male and female were understood as opposite categories, not as two independent or complementary dimensions. By 1910, writes Oudshoorn, 'the prescientific idea of the gonads as agents of sex differences had been transformed into the concept of sex hormones as chemical messengers of masculinity and femininity'.[48] Studying the intersexes in cows, seemed to bear this out further.

In 1916 Frank Lillie suggested that the freemartin was genetically female, but that a 'powerful blood-borne chemical produced in the male had altered the sex that the genes intended for the freemartin'. For his part, Marañón describes a clinical session of 1928 on an intersexual, exhibited at the *'feria de Madrid'* (providing a stark glimpse of the cruelties of the age) who displayed intersexual characteristics (breasts and a small penis) and mixed gonad (a mixture of testis and ovary).[49] Chemical determinism suggested that male and female should occupy opposite ends of the spectrum.

As hormones were thought to influence behaviour, this scientific theory crossed over into the social sphere, into the realm of gender roles. Oudshoorn cites Kruif to show how cultural notions of gender difference came to inform scientific discovery: 'the chemical war between the male and female hormones is, as it were, a chemical miniature of the well-known eternal war between men and women'.[50] Marañón shared this notion of 'sex antagonism'.

Following Otto Weininger, Marañón classifies human activity into primary and secondary sexual activity. Thus, he views primary sexual activity as the fulfilment of the procreative act, common to both sexes, and in women the functions of maternity. For women, the fulfilment of that primary sexual function of motherhood is all-absorbing: she is a vessel for motherhood, chained to her biological fate ('*la naturaleza le recuerda de un modo periódico ... que está sometida a su esclavitud durante los años mejores de su vida*') (nature reminds her periodically that she is its slave during the best years of her life).[51]

Woman is not '*hecha para intervenir*' (made to intervene) in social struggles (the sphere of secondary sexual characteristics), unless by an accident of nature (generally, hirsutism).[52] The cult of sex, for Marañón, is not dangerous to women, so long as it remains linked to the role of reproduction. Men, on the other hand, have a twofold responsibility to fulfil their biological destinies. In the first place, a man can separate himself entirely from the obligations of his sex, either by living an entirely contemplative, ascetic life, or by channelling or sublimating his primary sexual energy into secondary sexual activities: the social spheres of work, science or war.

This last is related to the contemporary nationalist

preoccupation with the 'problem of Spain', and a project to combat Spain's bellic decline (the loss of colonies), and to revolutionize work and science, both intellectual and manual endeavour, which Marañón sees as central to the modernization of Spain.[53] Hence, Marañón's concern is with the global and universal condition of gender roles. At the same time, however, he views this in the context of Spanish contemporary specificity. The danger of Don Juan, as an emblem, is that he remains linked to his body, all-absorbed by sex and love and he does not care to channel his sexual desire into other, more nationally useful activities. Don Juan's hyper-eroticism creates a dangerous feminization of the age in which the cult of sex occludes other more serious occupations such as career, intellect and empire building.

Yet, endocrinology soon discovered that not only are male and female chemical hormones present in both sexes, but also, as Diana Long Hall notes, that the embryo of higher animals is initially bisexual and acquires its sexual characters during development.[54] This gives Marañón his real ammunition against Don Juan. He suggests that male and female occupy two poles of a spectrum that ranges from light to shade. Those types occupying the middle ground of the spectrum contain a blend of masculinity and femininity. Within each gender there is also the division into intellectual, emotive and instinctive. In this gender map, Don Juan is placed on the instinctive side of the masculine end of the spectrum and towards the middle, shading into the feminine.[55] Don Juan possesses feminine traits: he has a tendency to lie, is adorned with accoutrements that attract and is the passive centre of gravity, merely waiting for the female to approach him (females who are attracted to Don Juan moreover exhibit viriloid characteristics).[56] The differentiated masculine position is the reverse.[57] The blend of masculine and feminine traits is normative (the hypothesis of a universal 'bisexuality'):

> *cada hombre, o la inmensa mayoría de ellos, llevan un fantasma de mujer, no en la imaginación, que entonces tal vez sería fácil expulsarle, sino circulando en la sangre; y cada mujer un fantasma, más o menos concreto, del hombre. Y esa mujer o ese hombre en esbozo, y no los de fuera, los de carne y hueso, son los que pueden conducir al dolor y al pecado* (every man, or the vast majority, carries a phantasm of woman, not in their imaginations, which would perhaps be easy to expel, but circulating in their blood; and every woman has a phantasm of man. That man or that woman sketched within, and not those outside, those of flesh and bones, are those that may lead to pain and sin).[58]

In 1929 Marañón would write that the task of every individual is to kill '*al fantasma del otro sexo que cada cual lleváis dentro; sed hombres, sed mujeres*' (the phantasm of the other sex that every one of you carries within; be men, be women).[59] Don Juan, supreme emblem of Spanish masculinity, is, for Marañón, marked by his femininity, and, moreover, becomes symbolic of the nebulous sketch of intersexuality. Quite how one is supposed to kill the phantasm of the opposite sex, circulating within one's blood, is not made clear. Marañón appears to believe that reversing images as ideals, to influence behaviour, can then have an effect on the chemicals in one's blood. It is a sort of chemical determinism in reverse.

Performance Anxieties

Modern endocrinology is founded on the surgical and functional approach to hormones. Significantly, one of Brown-Séquard's earliest experiments involved the

Tales of Seduction

injection into his own blood of an extract of animal testis, which he believed had rejuvenated his body. By the 1920s, glandular techniques as a way of rejuvenating the aged were abounding. In 1926, Marañón and a surgeon called León Cardenal conducted a series of sensational operations that received coverage in the Madrid dailies. These operations used procedures that reabsorbed sex hormones, or made testicular transplants on an impotent man.[60] The methods, following Steinach's vasoligature to augment the production of gonadal hormones, or Voronoff's famous injections of an extract of ape testes (monkey glands), attracted enormous attention, including a host of jokes such as the vignette featured on 27 February 1926 in *El Sol*. This tells the tale of Nemesio García *'a quien la edad se le echaba encima, decidió injertarse las glándulas del mono'* (who, as old age came upon him, decided to inject himself with monkey glands). After meeting and marrying a young woman, she gives birth to *'una verdadera "monada"'* (a real cutey). This is a play on the word for monkey, *'mono'*, for the drawing shows a monkey dressed in shorts, *'que se gastaba un capital en cacahuetes'* (which cost a small fortune in peanuts).

The following year, Pedro Muñoz Seca's play *Las inyecciones o el Doctor Cleofás Uthof vale más que Voronoff* (The Injections or Doctor Uthoff is better than Voronoff), which opened at the Teatro Romea in Madrid on 28 March 1927, mercilessly satirized the operations by following the antics of a doctor (Uthof, who looks like a man of 25) who uses a variety of injections from different animals to cure a panoply of complaints, from his wife's infidelities to short-sightedness.[61]

As Tom Glick has noted, Marañón 'while repeatedly disavowing identification of endocrine dysfunction as the master factor in ageing, became identified popularly with the view that the therapeutics of ageing, if not the causes, were centred on the glands of internal secretion, particularly the gonads. In Marañón's view, human beings begin to die when they lose the capacity for love.[62] It is perhaps for this reason that Don Juan, supreme emblem of sexual function, should once again be chosen by Marañón as an emblem, this time for ageing. In a 1929 essay, 'La vejez de Don Juan' (Don Juan's old age), he writes that Don Juan is better equipped to confront senile decline than other men because he can stretch his sexual maturity to an advanced age. However, ageing Don Juans could become psychotic at the trauma of old age.

He suggests three possible outcomes for Don Juans in old age: they can marry, they can continue as Don Juans or '*viejos verdes*' (dirty old men) or they can repent and become a priest.[63] The theme also circulated in popular literature. Thus, Isaac Morales and Pablo Suero's protagonist in *La vejez de don Juan* does '*gimnasia sueca*' (Swedish gymastics) to keep fit and, despite all attempts to marry him off, at the end of the play contemplates his wrinkles in the mirror and gives way to the younger generations. Juan Ignacio Luca de Tena's *Las canas de don Juan* (Don Juan's Grey Hairs), however, ends with Don Juan as a '*viejo verde*', going off to chase yet another servant girl.

Surgeon León Cardenal noted some success with the Steinach procedure. As Tom Glick notes,

> to obviate the effects of autosuggestion Cardenal informed none of his fifty-eight patients that he was going to use the procedure on them (they were operated on for other symptoms, typically hernia) nor were his assisting personnel informed. Because of his scepticism and caution, Steinach himself deemed the results significant.[64]

Then, on 24 February 1926, Cardenal and Marañón performed a marathon session of endocrinological implants, including an adrenal implant on a patient with Addison's disease, a testicular graft on an impotent man and on an adolescent eunuch.[65] But, as E. Bonilla was to write in *El Sol*, there was little proof of the rejuvenation that had raised the hopes of '*donjuanes apolillados*' (worn-out Don Juans): a eugenic concern for male impotence became in the press a sort of male viagra for ageing Lotharios.[66]

Organotherapeutics would also be useful to Marañón in his theorization of intersexual states. As we have seen, Marañón believed in the bisexual nature of the embryo. Like Hirschfeld, he believed in the principle of sexual indeterminacy, according to which every human being was partly male and partly female (that is placed on a spectrum between the absolute male and the absolute female). Thus, the genital hermaphrodite was an intermediate form, but so was the male homosexual, who was more female than the average man, and the adolescent tomboy, who was more male than the average girl of her age.[67]

Steinach was useful in that he argued that 'masculinity and femininity were not immutable qualities that one was born with, but, rather, morphological and psychological attributes that developed under the influence of glandular secretions'.[68] In his book, *The Evolution of Sex*, Marañón documents organotherapeutic grafts that he, or on his advice a colleague, Dr Ferrero, carried out on homosexual men. In the operation he carried out, the grafting of a monkey's testicle augmented the libido, but in a homosexual direction. In the cases of Dr Ferrero, the operation completely modified the 'irresistible tendency of his libido towards the man … and [it] was still normal six months later'. In the second case, the libido was augmented, but in a homosexual direction.[69]

> The subject, however, himself recognized that this apparently abortive result might have been influenced by an event in his private life. I have latterly again had

the same operation carried out on an adult eunuch without libido and obtained the appearance of a normal libido, which persisted two months afterwards. Since then I have lost sight of the patient.[70]

In the book, Marañón makes it clear that he is strongly against the criminalization of homosexuality, a condition he sees as having an organic cause and no 'fault' of the person in question. However, he is excited at the prospect of a cure for homosexuality, which for him, as for Steinach, offered the 'restitution of masculinity, as defined traditionally by science and society'.[71] True males, for Marañón, were hard working, strong and heterosexual. 'That these were glandular phenomena, rather than immutable givens was, in the final analysis, no reason to cease believing in the categories of "male" and "female" or in the normativeness of homosexuality.'[72]

Effeminacy and Homosexuality

La plasmatoria, a bawdy vaudeville farce by Pedro Muñoz Seca, was staged in Madrid in 1935. At the end of the first act, during the play's *estreno* at the Teatro María Isabel, Rafael Somoza, playing the lead role, stepped forward beyond the proscenium arch, drew his sword from its sheath and peered menacingly into the Madrid audience. '¡¡A ver!!' he threatened, '¿Dónde vive Marañón?' (Let's see! Where does Marañón live?).[73] Gregorio Marañón, clinician and celebrated member of the medical establishment, had entered the popular imaginary.

La plasmatoria dramatizes a polemic on contemporary paradigms of masculinity that was played out over the body and figure of Don Juan. It features a pompous pseudo scientist (with a German accent), Adrión Laván, '*dominador en el espacio astral*' (dominator of astral space) and architect and creator of '*la plasmatoria*', an apparatus that can resuscitate the dead. The critic Jorge de la Cueva, reviewing the opening performance in *El Debate*, cites the psychic inventions of Thomas Alva Edison and Sir Arthur Conan Doyle as possible prototypes for Muñoz Seca's machine.[74] In his memoir, *The Diary and Sundry Observations of Thomas Alva Edison*, Edison revealed that he had been assembling a machine (a valve) that could make contact with the spirit world by recording paranormal sonic events.[75]

In 1932, two years after Conan Doyle's death, the photograph, 'Conan Doyle's Return' fashioned the writer's psychic reappearance in the form of 'ectoplasm' exuding from the nose of the medium, Mrs Mary Marshall, during a séance.[76] Muñoz Seca's fictional invention goes further than these nebulous attempts to seize the spirit world in sound and image: *'la plasmatoria'* performs the somatic materialization of the dead. The etymology of the verb *'plasmar'* derives from Latin and means to mould, reflect or make manifest (the María Moliner definition is *'dar forma concreta ostensible a una cosa inmaterial'* – give concrete form to something immaterial) and from the same root is derived 'plasma', referring to blood cells. *'La plasmatoria'* returns the dead to living flesh and blood.

'Plasmarse' is often used to refer to the way a character is brought to life on stage, and Muñoz Seca carefully exploits this ulterior meaning. The scientist, grateful to a Spanish family for its hospitality, offers to breathe life into one of its cadaverous ancestors: the family turns out to be descended from Don Juan Tenorio. Adrión Laván predicts a brilliant political career for Don Juan, his creation, whose anachronistic theories (attacks on modernity and technology) will make him a man of the future and saviour of the *patria*. At the end of the play the resuscitated Don Juan, horrified at the idea of politics, prefers to *desplasmarse* (deconstruct). The piece is a commentary on divorce (the divorce law was enacted in Spain in 1932) and sees two of the characters

Performance Anxieties: Don Juan in the Consulting Room

falling in love again post-divorce. The play also provides relief from the political ferment of republican Spain shortly before the outbreak of the Spanish Civil War.

The humour of the play derives from its main theme – the intersections and discrepancies between the biography of Don Juan provided by José Zorrilla's version of the myth (which would have been well-known to contemporary audiences) and the information Muñoz Seca mournfully provides about Don Juan's case history. The supposedly masterful swordsman and dashing rake is in fact rather a peaceful sort who is indignant at the propagation of false myths around his name; in his lifetime the legendary womanizer made no more than *'cuatro conquistas'* (four conquests). But just as Tina asks in Act Three how a *'mujer que se entusiasma con todo lo viril'* (woman who is keen on all things virile) can love *'un plasmado fungiforme'* (a fungiform creation), the question of Don Juan's virility is posed even before he appears on stage.

Bartolo explains that he wishes to summon Don Juan from the clutches death in order to settle the debate over his contested manhood. After many years of *'buena fama y de tenerlo nosotros por un gachó de lo más castizo y barbián que se encorambra'* (good fame and with us holding him to be the purest and most self-assured bloke you could hope to find), he says, *'salió un pintó de los buenos y lo pintó así… como una mijita ladeao'* (one of those fine painters came along and painted him like that … a little bit at an angle).[77] The reference is undoubtedly to a portrait that Elías Salaverría painted in 1927.[78] In the play, Bartolo continues with his coarse banter: *'¿Usté me entiende a mí? Y un médico eminente ha dicho de él que si sí, que si no, que si mira donde pongo un deíto (Postura de zape)'* (Do you understand me? And an eminent doctor has said of him that he is, that he is not, look where I am pointing (*shooing* motion).)

Tales of Seduction

1. 'The "Effeminate" Don Juan Tenorio en el panteón' by Elías Salaverría (1883–1952).

Performance Anxieties: Don Juan in the Consulting Room

As is hinted at in the words cited above, by 1935 Gregorio Marañón had been received in the popular imagination as having discovered the 'truth' about Don Juan's homosexuality. The play dramatizes a confrontation between myth and medicine that raged over Don Juan's body and figure, interrogating received notions of manliness. Different versions of the Don Juan myth are invoked in the play, from the legendary tales of a rake and womanizer to the propagation of new myths about an effeminate or homosexual Don Juan. Both sets of myth are contrasted against the apparently rather limited number of sexual conquests of women made by Don Juan, the protagonist of *La plasmatoria*. All these versions of Don Juan present shifting models of masculinity. If the audience is gathered together for a collective diagnosis of the eponymous Spanish seducer's virility, then this Don Juan enters ready to defend his manhood against the writings of the doctor: '*¡¡A ver!! ¿Dónde vive Marañón?*'[79]

After the publication of the 1924 article 'Notas para una biología de Don Juan', Marañón became famous with a mass audience. Barco Teruel writes:

> *De la noche a la mañana, Marañón se convierte en un tema nacional de polémica. Por todas partes, se hablaba de Marañón y de su versión del donjuanismo; en el casino, en la tertulia del café (donde pululaban esos grandes expertos del amor a que Marañón, irónicamente, aludía); en las reuniones cultas y en las que eran menos; se comentaba, ora con curiosidad, ora con auténtica cólera, la flamante feminidad de Don Juan.* (Overnight Marañón became a national topic of debate. Marañón and his versión of Don Juanism was talked about everywhere; in the casino, in coffee shops (where those great experts on love that Marañón ironically alluded to congregated); wherever intellectuals and those who were less intel-

lectual met, everyone was commenting, with curiosity, with real anger, on Don Juan's flagrant effeminacy.)[80]

It was Don Juan's *'feminidad'* (effeminacy), outlined in Marañón's theories that doubtless led to Elías Salaverría's portrait of Don Juan in 1927. Bernadino de Pantorba described the painting as *'inquietante, turbadora'* (disquieting, perturbing) in its depiction of an effeminate Don Juan adorned *'con todas sus galas y joyas, donjuaneando'* (with all his finery and jewels being Don Juan) and with *'una mirada de soslayo, que la penumbra hace equívoca'* (a sideways look that seems equivocal in the murky light).[81] Nerea Aresti's study of the period draws out the high level of interest generated in Spain by the painting.

On visiting an exhibition of the painting, General Primo de Rivera declared that Salaverría's portrait of Don Juan portrayed *'un castigador de moda'* (a fashionable ladykiller, literally 'punisher'), leading Teófilo Mendive to comment that in this case Don Juan *'resulta tan afeminado como ellas, casi tan "castigadora" como ellas'* (is as effeminate as they (women) are, almost as punishing as the are). Presumably Primo de Rivera was commenting on what he viewed as Salaverría's faithful representation of Don Juan, scourge of weak women, which reinforces his masculinity – the dictionary definition of *'castigar'* is *'enamorar por puro pasatiempo'* (to break hearts as a pure diversion). Teófilo Mendive turns this around into a play of words on the seductive female who turns into the nagging woman: *'castigadora'* (chastiser) may mean *'que enamora'* (to break hearts, literally to make others fall in love with one) but can also mean *'que reprende y amonesta a otro'* (to reprimand and admonish another).[82]

Bartolo, a character in *La plasmatoria* of 1935, refers to the painting as being *'una mijita ladeao'* (slightly off the vertical, not quite straight). *'Ladeao'*, from *'ladear'* (to tilt), *'inclinar y torcer una cosa hacia un lado'* (to incline and bend a thing to one side), *'dícese de las hojas, flores, espigas y demás partes de una planta cuando todas miran hacia un solo lado'* (said of leaves, flowers, ears of grain and other parts of a plant when they all face the same direction),[83] is reinforced by the eminent doctor's remark (with a shooing motion) *'que si sí, que si no'* (that he is, is not), which appears to suggest an equation of effeminacy with homosexuality.[84]

Alan Sinfield warns against reading homosexuality into history and simply equating 'effeminacy' with 'same-sex passion'.[85] He points to the existence in history of 'fops' and 'royal favourites' who were effeminate, may have indulged in same-sex passion, but were not necessarily 'homosexuals' as we understand the term.[86] Paul Julian Smith has asserted the paradox of the 'apparent transparency of García Lorca's effeminacy and the genuine surprise felt by his friends at the revelation of his homosexuality', which would suggest that effeminacy may have stood for artistry or a poetic soul rather than for sexual 'inversion'.[87] Yet in 1935 *La plasmatoria* appears to assert the equivalence of effeminacy and homosexuality, a notion reinforced by Marañón's statement in 1940 that, *'de todo esto, que yo he dicho en varias ocasiones, lo que más directamente ha llegado al público es la conclusión de que don Juan es un hombre afeminado, casi un homosexual'* (of everything I have said on several occasions, what has most directly registered with the public is the conclusion that Don Juan is an effeminate man, almost a homosexual).[88] Following Richard Cleminson, we could assert that this period and place is possibly a 'critical "faultline" where the limits of effeminacy, "sexual inversion" and a new [homosexual] subculture were being inscribed'.[89]

The notion of the period as a time of shifting interpretations and reinscriptions appears to be reinforced by Marañón's comment that *'Don Juan es un hombre afeminado, casi un homosexual'* (Don Juan is an effeminate man, almost

Tales of Seduction

a homosexual), *'no es esto, exactamente, lo que yo he querido decir'* (is not exactly what I meant to say).[90] He goes on to say that, *'Don Juan posee un instinto inmaduro, adolescente. ... Ama a las mujeres, pero es incapaz de amar a la mujer'* (Don Juan possesses an immature instinct. He loves women, but is incapable of loving *the* woman).[91] There are, however, striking correlations between his definition of femininity as an immature version of masculinity, of Don Juan as an immature, undifferentiated man, and of homosexuality as an undifferentiated state. There are other links too. In 1929, in a letter from Ramón y Cajal, we find the following observation:

> *puesto que Vd. prepara una nueva edición del mito de Don Juan, yo le aconsejaría, si decide ocuparse en los Tenorios reales, para contrastarles la verosimilitud de las creaciones literarias, la lectura de Stekel* (Onania und Homosexualismus, 1923). *En este libro se contiene una teoría del Don Juan afeminado que tiene cierto parentesco con la de Vd* (given that you are preparing a new edition of the myth of Don Juan, I would advise, if you decide to look at real Don Juans, to contrast their verosimilitude with that of literary creations, that you look at Stekel's *Onania and Homosexualismus*, 1923. This book contains a theory of the effeminate Don Juan that is quite similar to your own).[92]

In 1939, Marañón cites the case of a writer who had led a *'vida sexual borrascosa de tipo donjuanesco'* (stormy Don Juan type of sexual life) who later had homosexual relations.[93] In 1940, in his account of the Donjuanesque Conde de Villamediana, after a series of pages on the count's womanizing activities, Marañón adds, almost as a discreet afterthought, that in 1929 historians had discovered papers proving that the count was implicated in what Marañón terms *'el pecado nefando*' (people accused of homosexual practices).[94] Homosexuality haunts Marañón's texts on Don Juan.

In his analysis of the evolution of sex, Marañón sees Don Juan as perpetually in the adolescent phase, which is undifferentiated. According to his analysis, both men and women begin life in a 'feminine' phase, reaching the 'viriloid' phase in maturity (in women this masculine phase corresponds to the climacteric period). In the case of Don Juan, he remains in the adolescent, feminine, undifferentiated phase, unable to mature and progress. For Marañón this phase may, although not necessarily, produce homosexuality. Masculinity is thus portrayed as a perilous, rocky road.

Homosexuality is also present in Marañón's theories of intersexuality. Thus, in 1939 Marañón will write that '*la intersexualidad orgánica es tan frecuente, la mayoría de los seres humanos, probablemente todos, tendrían una aptitud primaria para la homosexualidad*' (organic intersexuality is so frequent, that the majority of human beings, probably all of them, would have a primary aptitude for homosexuality) that may or may not develop later.[95] Marañón's account of a male patient whom he discovered years after treatment on a mortuary slab presents homosexuality as a morality tale.[96] Moreover, the anxiety of Don Juan, as an example of the blurring of the sexes, becomes the ubiquity and 'threat' of potential universal homosexuality.

Marañón undoubtedly chose to focus his attention on Don Juan for reasons of pedagogy, for he wanted his message about the threat (to the nation) of nebulous gender to reach the masses. It was perhaps for this reason that he chose to write in a genre that is a blend of the literary and the scientific. Lyotard has written that when scientists want their theories to reach a popular audience, they couch their rhetoric in the narrative mode.[97]

La plasmatoria provides evidence of the success of the notoriety of Marañón's theories. Through Marañón, Don

Juan became a 'momentarily ubiquitous' feature of popular culture that catered 'to the public appetite for a character type that sums up the times'.[98] As a site for the projection of imaginary desires and a focus for the galvanization of current issues, however, Don Juan may become open to myriad interpretations. If Marañón's theories on him have been imperfectly interpreted (as Marañón claims), then *La plasmatoria* dramatizes the role of the public in Don Juan's dissection and diagnosis; the figure of Don Juan, as discussed in bars, casinos and clubs, takes on a life of his own, irrespective of Marañón's wishes. In *La plasmatoria* Don Juan 'talks back' to the doctor, who is metaphorically gagged in the audience, thereby resisting the clinician's pathologizing definitions. Might Don Juan's 'talking back' to his doctor also be read as an example of the homosexual resisting medical discourse, such as some gay men had begun to do in New York in the 1930s?[99]

Alternatively, we could read the play as a reinforcement of virility, with the 'story' of an effeminate Don Juan being banished for good by Don Juan brandishing his sword. Gaylin Studlar contains an interesting discussion of Douglas Fairbanks in *The Mark of Zorro* (1920) playing under the disguise of an effeminate man (which the female finds abhorrent) only later to reinforce his virile masculinity. Studlar attributes this move to anxiety about undifferentiated gender roles.[100]

There is no doubt that Marañón's theories on Don Juan touched the public imagination. If the play can be seen as a privileged moment for shifting definitions of effeminacy and homosexuality, then it also dramatizes the passage of a scientific theory into popular discourse, leaving in its wake a modified Don Juan.

La plasmatoria's stress on bloodline and ancestry (Bartolo is a descendant of Don Juan) suggests that the 'degenerescence' theories of heredity and degeneration were still prevalent in the 1930s. At the same time, the reference to blood ('plasma') reminds us that in his discussion of Don Juan, Marañón had not only reached the imagination of his Spanish audience, but his ideas were also metaphorically circulating in their blood. Thus, Ricardo Royo-Villanova wrote that, *'el donjuanismo – en potencia o en presencia – lo llevamos dentro, muy dentro de nosotros mismos, en el mismo plasma de la sangre, se encuentra íntimamente fijado en algunos tejidos imponderables de nuestra economía psíquica'* (Don Juanism – whether as potency or presence – is carried within us, deep within us, in the plasma of our blood, it is intimately fixed in some imponderable threads of our psychic economy).[101]

For Marañón, internal secretions in the blood determined all secondary sexual characteristics. In his theory of intersexual states, of which Don Juan became a symbol, Marañón exhorts his audience to *'matad al fantasma del otro sexo'* (kill the phantasm of the other sex)[102] that is *'circulando en la sangre'* (circulating in the blood).[103] The circulation of blood suggests non site-specific fluids and flows.[104] It suggests a loss of conscious agency and an individual will subject to the influence of chemical reactions in the body. It presents metaphors of invasion, of attack from the enemy within.[105] It is hardly surprising, therefore, that many male intellectuals should close ranks against Marañón's theories of Don Juan. In attacking Don Juan, Marañón seemed to have touched a raw nerve, evidence of a hurt national pride. Bloodline may, after all, suggest a preoccupation with the 'honour' of a national stereotype represented by Don Juan. In an article written in 1925, 'Para una psicología del hombre interesante', José Ortega y Gasset, for example, asserts that:

> *Todo el mundo cree tener la auténtica doctrina sobre él – sobre Don Juan, el problema más recóndito, más absurdo, más agudo de nuestro tiempo. Y es que, con pocas excepciones, los hombres pueden dividirse en tres clases: los que*

creen ser Don Juanes, los que creen haberlo sido y los que creen haberlo podido ser, pero no quisieron. Estos últimos son los que propenden, con benemérita intención, a atacar a Don Juan y tal vez a decretar su cesantía. (Everyone thinks they have the true doctrine about him – about Don Juan, the most recondite, absurd, piercing problem of our times. And with few exceptions, men can be divided into three types: those who think they are Don Juans, those who think they were Don Juans and those who think they could have been but chose not to. The last are those who propose, with good intentions, to attack Don Juan and even to decree his end.)[106]

Here we see Ortega declaring that all men are, at root, Don Juans, whether they embraced their Don Juanism or (presumably like Marañón), are Don Juan *manqués*. One of Marañón's staunchest critics, F. Oliver Brachfeld, accuses him of peddling in *'alta pornografía que viaja elegantemente empaquetada, bajo la altanera etiqueta de la "ciencia"'* (high pornography that travels in elegant packaging under the label of 'science'). For Oliver Brachfeld, Marañón has an *'interés loco por las cosas sexuales y se pasa por el mayor sabio en estas materias'* (insane interest in sexual things and he passes himself off as the greatest sage in these matters). While other countries have sexologists who are *'unos viejos barbudos, con el pelo cano'* (some old bearded types with white hair), Marañón is *'un joven y flamante sexólogo, guapo como un torero'* (a young and flagrant sexologist, as good looking as a matador). In his lengthy polemic of 1933, Oliver Brachfeld accuses Marañón of attracting notoriety for notoriety's sake, and dealing in matters about which he has little knowledge.[107]

In his polemic on Don Juan, Marañón was indicting a national Spanish emblem, the way a nation reflected itself to itself, and at the same time, he was troubling the heart of gendered identity. Carmen de Burgos's novela corta *La entrometida* (The Busybody) of 1921, had already featured an effeminate Don Juan: Pérez Blanco, is neither *'un galanteador de oficio, ni un seductor, no era más que un* despelusador, *a cuyo contacto las mujeres, sin perder la castidad, perdían la inocencia'* (a lover by trade, nor a seducer, he was no more than a hair-disheveller, in contact with whom women lost their innocence without losing their chastity), an aesthete and an effeminate dandy (in contrast with Clarisa's masculinized femininity).[108]

Meanwhile, in 1926 Pérez de Ayala, whose theories on the effeminate Don Juan first appeared in articles in *Las máscaras* in 1916 (seven years before Marañón's first essay on Don Juan, as Lozano Marco[109] points out) published *Tigre Juan y el curandero de su honra* (Tiger Juan and the Healer of his Honour) in which Vespasiano Cebón is an effeminate, sterile Don Juan.

Azorín's feminized *Don Juan* forsakes women for spirituality, while the protagonist of Unamuno's *El hermano Juan o el mundo es teatro* (1929) is a character from the theatre, a shadow, only half a man[110] who takes on the role of *nodrizo* (male wet nurse) to facilitate relations between couples.[111] Meanwhile, the protagonist of Federico García Lorca's *Así que pasen cinco años* (1929) can be read as the exploration of an Amiel-type anti-Don Juan, sensitive and effeminate in contrast to the Don Juanesque first friend.[112]

Marañón's theories therefore opened up and fed into a productive space in literature for the exploration of the freeing up of gender paradigms.[113] Don Juan, endless seducer through the ages, in the Spain of the 1920s and 1930s, largely through the writings of Gregorio Marañón, stood at the crossroads between the popular and the elite, the literary and the scientific, male and female, individual and collective: a complex and productive icon for the preoccupations of the times.

3. SCREEN SEDUCTIONS: NEGOTIATING THEATRICALITY IN DON JUAN FILMS

Julia Kristeva assembles a dream team in her conception of the perfect cinematic work: 'an impossible film: *Don Juan* by Eisenstein and Hitchcock with music by Schoenberg. Invisible. Empty hall. But what a rite of terror and seduction!'[1] Good cinema, for Kristeva, ought to evoke a place somewhere between the reassuring identification of another, and nameless dread, what she terms the 'fascinating specular', of which Don Juan, transgressive, seductive, sexy and terrifying is the emblem *par excellence*.

It is not hard to imagine Don Juan as an icon for the cinema. Like much cinematic theory, he can be seen to be wrought out of Oedipal conflict, and while Don Juan flouts the father's law he arguably is preoccupied with a search for the unattainable mother: like the cinema he searches endlessly through a series of brief but intense affairs for the perfect female image.[2]

Don Juan's favourite accoutrement is the carnival mask, which, as for Doane's *femme fatale*, aligns him with the sexy seductiveness as well as the deceptiveness of the visual medium. His endless visual tricks and masquerades make him a useful emblem for the cinema, which 'appeals to the visible as the ground of its production of truth'.[3] Conversely, it seems significant that the lover known for his virtuosity in linguistic seduction should be entwined in film history with the motion picture that first introduced synchronized sound in the cinema: with its perfectly matched orchestral accompaniment, Alan Crosland's 1926 *Don Juan* ushered in the technology that would soon find stars wooing on-screen lovers and audiences alike with sound to accompany pictures.[4] In fact, Don Juan first emerged on screen practically at the birth of cinema.

Salvador Toscano Barragán's *Don Juan* of 1898 is credited as Mexico's first fiction film. Over time, Don Juan has attracted some of Hollywood's greatest stars to his story. Thus, John Barrymore's psychologically damaged Don Juan, in Crosland's 1926 version, witnesses his mother's adultery and his father's renunciation of women, which leads him to indulge in a string of broken affairs. Douglas Fairbanks played the part of an ageing Don Juan who stages his own death in order to reflect on the theme of fame and celebrity in Alexander Korda's *The Private Life of Don Juan* (1934). Errol Flynn was for some the encapsulation of the swashbuckling hero in *The Adventures of Don Juan* directed by Vincent Sherman (1949), while Vadim's Brigitte Bardot vehicle *If Don Juan Were a Woman* (1973) tested gender boundaries while providing the opportunity for a series of erotic vignettes for Bardot within a heightened urban landscape.

Johnny Depp is the star of *Don Juan de Marco* directed by Jeremy Leven (1995), a magical-realist fantasy with Marlon Brando in the role of Don Juan's psychoanalyst. More recently, audiences at Jim Jarmusch's *Broken Flowers* (2005) enjoyed the postmodern intertextuality as the protagonist

Tales of Seduction

Don Johnson (a play on the name Don Juan) played by Bill Murray, watches Korda's *The Private Life of Don Juan* on a US television channel showing bygone classics, symbolic of his depleted Don Juanism, before setting out on a quest to revisit his past lovers.

Theatricality and Trickality in de Baños's *Don Juan Tenorio* (1922)

The earliest Spanish Don Juan film, an adaptation of José Zorrilla's 1844 play entitled *Don Juan Tenorio*, was made by the brothers Ricardo and Ramón de Baños in 1908, swiftly followed by a second version in 1910.[5] A longer, more accomplished version lasting two and a quarter hours followed in 1922.[6] Appraisals of all these versions have threatened to attach to it the label of theatricality, of mere '*teatro filmado*' (theatre on film).[7]

In 1922, fresh from a viewing of Abel Gance's silent cinematic triumph *La Roue*, French Cubist painter Fernand Léger mused on the possible future of the cinematic medium. Rather than attempting to imitate 'the movement of nature' or taking the 'mistaken path' of similarities to theatre, cinema ought to harness its potential as a *matter of making images seen*'.[8] Theatricality became a pejorative way to describe the cinema, associated as it was with artificial sets, static longshots and a 'dramatic construction imitated from the theatre' involving exits and entrances 'stage left' and stage right'.[9]

We can see many of these elements in the earliest versions of *Don Juan Tenorio* by the de Baños brothers who had undoubtedly chosen this theme for its popularity in the theatre. A well-known popular theatre actor was chosen as the protagonist. The sets are artificial-looking and resemble a stage. The scenes are presented as a 'succession of discontinuous "tableaux"' in which the passage between scenes is indicated by an inter-title, which corresponds to Mitry's definition of the worst kind of theatricality in the cinema'.[10]

Screen Seductions: Negotiating Theatricality in Don Juan Films

2. Pamphlet from *Don Juan Tenorio*. Ricardo de Baños. Courtesy of Fototeca, Filmoteca Española

Tales of Seduction

Turning to the 1922 version, de Lasa excuses the film, explaining that *'la absurda teatralidad'* (the absurd theatricality) was a feature of many Spanish productions of the times, *'que olían a rancio por los cuatro costados'* (which smelled rancid through and through).[11] But, despite this version featuring many of the same tableaux as the earlier ones, but with a new cast, we find a film that is happy to display its theatrical roots while simultaneously revelling in the new cinematic techniques at its disposal. The film opens with a masking technique in which the sides of the frame are blocked out to look like stage curtains. These part to reveal the initial scene: the *Hostería del Laurel* (Laurel Inn) where Don Juan and Don Luis will recount their bellic and amorous adventures.

Masking, like the iris, which is also employed in the film, was common in silent cinema (Abel Gance's *La Roue* employed a variety of circular and oval masks). But de Baños self-consciously uses a filmic technique to reproduce a theatrical practice. As the title of the film flashes across the screen, we are reminded that this is an adaptation of Zorrilla's play. The inter-titles reproduce famous lines from the play, which would have been well-known to audiences of the time who may well have delighted in seeing the text paraded alongside images. Like theatrical Don Juan productions of the time, the film delights in the reproduction of elaborate costumes for the male characters (tights, sword, doublet and mask); the clean lines of a nun's habit for Doña Inés. Elaborate sets are created for interior and outdoor scenes.

In the retelling by Don Juan and Don Luis of their conquests, a succession of different sets illustrates the number and variety of the women seduced – from the *'más altiva'* (highest born), a princess on a balcony dressed in fine robes, to a fisherwoman mending nets beside a boat on the beach. Swift cuts between scenes at times make the different narrative threads difficult to follow, but as Andrew Ginger has astutely noted in his excellent study of the film, these fast cuts add to the theme of the advancing of time so important to Zorrilla's play.[12]

Furthermore, parallel editing creates urgency and suspense as we cut between Don Juan's kidnapping of Doña Inés, aided and abetted by her maid, Brígida, and her father's entrance into the monastery. Having first been held-up by the protocol of the nunnery, he finally opens the door of the convent to find an empty room, with a note from Don Juan to Doña Inés still lying on the ground where Doña Inés had dropped in a swoon.

Time is undoubtedly the main theme of Zorrilla's romantic play: Don Juan's blatant disregard for the passage of time threatens to take him to a death without repentance, but the film is able to explore time in other ways too. Time past is explored through the flashback, as Don Juan and Don Luis narrate their bellic and amorous adventures. These are preluded by an iris that signals the move into another time and space. As well as present time, the future is also rendered visible on screen, as Don Juan witnesses his own burial towards the end of the film. The *Comendador* draws his attention to a group of hooded figures slowly carrying a body out to the graveside before solemnly warning him that he is witnessing his own funeral.

The film also visualizes a scene that never took place at all. Brígida and Don Juan tell Doña Inés that they had to remove her from the convent owing to a fire (but the real reason was Don Juan's desire to kidnap her). She believes it, and for a moment, we do too as we witness flames roaring through the convent in an early example of stunt effects. Finally, in another scene located 'outside time', daydreaming becomes reality as we see Doña Inés, in her convent, praying before a religious icon. However, if we look closely we can see that rather than a Madonna and

Tales of Seduction

child, the figure in the frame is none other than Don Juan, symbolic of her adulation of him. In later scenes this vision has disappeared from the painting.

The exciting possibilities of film to move us through time and space permit the audience to experience visual landscapes differently from those of a theatrical production. In addition to this, while some scenes present a static long shot on events, others quite pointedly present a point of view, such as the scene where Don Juan duels as part of his flashback in which we seem to be below Don Juan, looking up at him as his interlocutor in the duel. Although used sparingly, the close-up works to good effect, such as the extreme close-up of the face of Doña Inés, in ecstasy, staring to the heavens as she swoons in Don Juan's arms.

The iris effect seems often to be used in place of the flashback, and it directs our gaze, such as in the framing of Ciutti's knees knocking together in fear as the stone statue knocks at the door of the palace, requesting to be let in for dinner. In different ways, *Don Juan Tenorio* explores the matter of 'making images seen', as Léger would have it. The de Baños brothers present themselves as the originators and narrators of the story, as cinematic showmen delighting the audience (underlined by the equal billing afforded the de Baños brothers and Zorrilla, whose portraits appear in the pamphlet handed out during screenings).[13] The narrative advances by the juxtaposition of a series of visual displays, held together by editing that is self-conscious in its flamboyance of the technical possibilities offered by film. The film shows no desire to hide its theatrical roots. Rather, cinematic techniques enhance the theatrical elements of the story.

Nowhere is this clearer than in the final part of the film, when Don Juan encounters the stone statue of the *Comendador* and the ghost of Doña Inés. The ghosts are produced by double exposure,[14] which enables the *Comendador*

Screen Seductions: Negotiating Theatricality in Don Juan Films

to appear to walk through walls, and Doña Inés to disappear in the blink of an eye. These are trick-shots (what Gaudreault refers to as 'trickality'[15]) and in a sense represent the apotheosis of the de Baños brothers' showy, spectacular, even theatrical approach to the cinema.

This is what Tom Gunning would call 'the cinema of attractions', and it owes its roots to vaudeville theatre, until around 1905 the primary place of exhibition for cinema, alongside magic tricks, star turns and variety turns.[16] A marvellous scene in the film in which Doña Inés summons a group of skeletons, who appear to be dressed in nuns' headscarves and advance menacingly towards the screen, recalls cinema's roots in the magic lantern ghost show of the nineteenth century.[17] The ghosts and skeletons illustrate in a spectacular manner the main theme of the Don Juan story, which is fear of the afterlife, conceived as a retribution for a life lived dissolutely. Yet I would suggest that 'nameless dread' is not what is conjured up by these images.[18] Rather, there is awe and wonder, not at the afterlife, but at cinema's ability to conjure up marvellous visual worlds for the enjoyment of an audience.[19] The 1922 *Don Juan Tenorio* therefore departs from the crude descriptions of cinema as theatrical in a pejorative sense (uninspired camera work and artificial sets), and instead delights in the showy, spectacular and theatrical possibilities of the cinematic medium.

Surveying Don Juan films from Spain over the last century, Kristeva's 'nameless dread' does not seem to feature in any of these works. Rather, through the icon of the mask, these works return us to Don Juan's roots in the theatre. These films (and arguably all Don Juan films) appear to be stalked by the reminder of Don Juan's theatrical origins.

In the first place, there seems to be something highly theatrical about the costume drama, a genre adopted by so many Don Juan films. García-Berlanga's 1997 film *Don Juan*, made for TVE (Televisión Española), opens with a series of slow tilts and pans over various costumes from the production as the credits roll. The costumes emerge out of the darkness, glistening as they reflect the light, gold brocade, cream silks, pearls, corset panels and swords: they present an iconography of accoutrements to the film, and also, metonymically, their plush regal textures represent the 'quality' drama we are about to watch. They serve to underline the fetishization of the costume in lavish period pieces, as important as any individual character. Like the museum pieces they seem to evoke, they stress the notion of spectatorship, a theatrical and visual display put on for the gratification of an audience.

Spectacular clothing, alongside lavish interiors and breathtaking landscapes are a feature of many of the Don Juan films from Spain. Al Bradley's *Los amores de Don Juan* (Don Juan's Loves) (1971) recreates orientalist scenes from Morocco; Jacques Weber's *Don Juan* (1998) moves effortlessly from rugged mountainous countryside to windswept beaches, giving a sense of the freedoms afforded by Don Juan's libertine lifestyle. In Tomás Aznar's *Viva, muera, Don Juan* (Live, Die, Don Juan) (1974) the various undressings and the *'mundo al revés'* (upside-down world) theme of the carnival contribute to the idea of eroticism as a sign of liberation during the *destape*.[20]

Víctor Barrera's *Amar y morir en Sevilla* (To Love and Die in Seville) (a fairly 'stagy' production, in a pejorative sense, in that the characters adopt a rather mannered acting style and fight to make Zorrilla's verses their own) prefers to focus on the candlelit interiors of monasteries and bedchambers. In Suárez's *Don Juan en los infiernos* (Don Juan in Hell) (1991), featuring the ageing Fernando Guillén in the place of the young rake,[21] the landscape is so heavily stylized as to transport us at once to the level of myth and

Screen Seductions: Negotiating Theatricality in Don Juan Films

to hold us gazing at a theatrically staged outdoor *mise-en-scène*. Javier Hernández Ruiz has shown how the film recreates scenes from paintings: the large conch shell that is transported across the countryside is a recreation of an etching from Athaneseus Kircher's *Misurgia universalis* of 1673, the ending is a reproduction of Patinir's *El paso de la laguna Estigia* (1510), while the female form retains echoes of Velázquez's *Venus del espejo*. These recreations form a series of *tableux vivants*, which temporarily halt the action, presenting a theatrical *mise-en-scène* in place of a naturalist backdrop to the action.[22]

In other films, meta-theatre, or the theme of the play within the play, is chosen as a trope. John Berry's *El amor de Don Juan* (*Pantaloons* was the English title) is a comedy that dwells on the theme of mistaken identity as Sgaranelle (Don Juan's servant) adopts his master's costume to gain success in his own seductions.[23] The comparisons with Bob Hope's *Casanova's Big Night* (1954) have not gone unnoticed by critics, but it also recalls Korda's *The Private Life of Don Juan* (1934) in which a young pretender impersonates the legendary seducer to achieve the latter's fame.

The theme of meta-theatre from that film, in which Don Juan (Douglas Fairbanks) walks into a production of the play of his life, is recreated by Antonio Mercero in *Don Juan, mi querido fantasma* (Don Juan, My Darling Ghost). In this film, in which the credits are flamboyantly sung by a flamenco troupe, we are asked to accept that Don Juan has returned from the dead and walked into rehearsals of the play of his life just at the moment when the actor playing Don Juan (a lowlife criminal) has absconded.[24] The comedy results from the innocence of the real Don Juan thrust into the shoes of a petty gangster. At the end of the film, the real Don Juan redeems himself and is rewarded with his life, while the impostor is banished for good.

The contrast between the theatricality of the 'real' Don

Juan of the seventeenth century and the one placed in Spain in the 1990s, does not so much provide a focus for a discussion of *theatrum mundi*, as in say Bergman's *The Devil's Eye* (1960), but rather unleashes a bedroom farce that recalls the theatrical parodies of Don Juan that have been present in Spain throughout the twentieth century. Mercero's 1974 version of *Don Juan* features a group of actors rehearsing for a production of Zorrilla's play with the aim of deconstructing the myth of Don Juan, presenting him as a homosexual in the first place, and secondly as a type of doll that deflates when pricked with a pin. Finally, whether consciously sought or not, whether theatrically drawn upon or quietly ignored, intertextuality is arguably a feature of all Don Juan films.

In what follows, I explore further the notion of theatricality with reference to Sáenz de Heredia's *Don Juan* (1950). The film was produced at the height of Franco's powers, and by a director who openly sided with the regime. I wish to explore the ways in which the film uses theatricality as a device to encourage a form of spectatorship that would be in keeping with national Catholic ideology.

Theatricality and Absorption in Sáenz de Heredia's *Don Juan* (1950)

Don Juan exists in the popular imagination as the legendary seducer of women, charismatic rogue and transgressor. As an iconoclast, liar, libertine and marriage-breaker, he may seem a curious choice of subject for José Luis Sáenz de Heredia, who, despite early collaborations with the rebellious Luis Buñuel,[25] is best known for his allegiance to the Franco regime, a loyalty that would continue long after the death of the dictator.[26]

Sáenz de Heredia, described in obituaries as the Leni Riefenstahl of Franco's Spain[27] and the '*máximo cineasta del*

Screen Seductions: Negotiating Theatricality in Don Juan Films

franquismo militante' (greatest *auteur* of militant Francoism),[28] produced the fascist epic *Raza* (Race) (1941) based on a script allegedly drafted by General Franco. The film showcases the victorious triumphalism and reactionary gender typologies of national Catholicism, while the racial characteristics of the Spanish nation of the film's title 'are defined in large part … through an obsessive insistence on sexual purity'.[29] *Don Juan* (Cifesa, Chapalo Films, 1950)[30] was made at the height of Franco's power, when state censorship snipped, erased, inscribed and rewrote all artistic productions in order to promote Francoist family values, the sanctity of marriage and the monolithic law of church and state. *Don Juan* was endorsed by the censors, declared a 'triumphant success' by the Francoist press and propaganda, and awarded the National Interest Prize, a classification that guaranteed wide publicity and distribution in prime exhibition theatres (the film opened in the Cine Avenida, Gran Vía, the heart of Madrid's public leisure space) as well as a healthy return on production-costs.[31]

The mid-1940s to early 1950s saw the birth of a national cinema in Spain as a 'deliberate project undertaken by the dictatorship',[32] and witnessed a plethora of high production value adaptations of the classics, which appropriated literary or historical figures as vehicles to endorse the principles of empire, family and church and provide the setting for Francoist ideology to appear to stretch back into a seamless past. To name but a few, *Alba de América* (Dawn of America) (Juan de Orduña, 1950) depicted Columbus's voyage to the Americas; *Locura de amor* (Mad with Love) (Juan de Orduña, 1948) told the epic story of Queen Joan the Mad; *La leona de Castilla* (Lioness of Castille) (Juan de Orduña, 1951) concerned the sixteenth-century Comuneros Revolt; and *Bambú* (Bamboo) (Sáenz de Heredia, 1945) was an ode to Spanish imperialism.

Don Juan is a lavish costume drama, a '*grandiosa super-*

Tales of Seduction

producción nacional' (magnificent national super-production), a glamorous antidote to the years of poverty that had continued since the end of the civil war in 1939. The setting of the film in Seville, 1553, emphasizes aspects of Spanish heritage connected with a golden age of empire, conquest and religious crusade.[33] Contemporary press reviews highlight the 'Spanishness' of the figure of Don Juan, a *'personaje de españolísimos rasgos temperamentales'* (character of truly Spanish temperament)[34] and stress that while the figure has been appropriated by many different nations, each trying to *'aclimatarlo a su geografía'* (adapt it to their own geography), Don Juan can be achieved in its *'dimensión exacta'* (exact dimensions)[35] only in Spain.

These articles map the contours of a national pride, elided with the figure of Don Juan, implicitly eschewing the Hollywood vehicle *The Adventures of Don Juan* (Vincent Sherman, 1949) starring Errol Flynn as a pale imitation of the Spanish incarnation, which is the *'el único auténtico de los muchos que se han intentado en otros paises'* (only authentic Don Juan, out of the many that have been attempted in other countries).[36] But it is precisely Don Juan's internationalism that makes him such an important figure for an industry that still hoped to establish a *niche* with films that would appeal in international markets as well as to compete with Hollywood in domestic spheres.[37] Like a wayward prodigal son returning after a long journey through foreign lands, Don Juan is gathered back into the Spanish fold.

Furthermore, if we trace a genealogy of Don Juan through a Spanish literary heritage, we find that Sáenz de Heredia's choice of theme is far from unorthodox. The canonical version by Tirso de Molina is a supernatural morality tale featuring Don Juan as the archetypal *'dissoluto punito'*, the rake punished for his misdemeanours by a horrible ending in the bowels of hell. José Zorrilla's romantic revision offers a pious lesson in Christian redemption.

Sáenz de Heredia's adaptation pays homage to both versions (while coquettishly declaring fidelity to neither); his chosen ending emphasizes the redemptive potential of the myth. Nevertheless, the film devotes significantly more screen time to a capricious revelling in the sexual and moral transgressions of our charismatic hero, remedied by a hasty Christian rebirth at the end of the film.[38] This rapid shift in theme is signalled by a switch in genre – from a cheerful comedy of errors, interspersed with swash-buckling scenes and episodes of *españolada*[39] – the film moves into melodrama, a tear-jerker of the first order.

In this context, I focus on the tensions offered by this film in terms of its abrupt change of genre, pace and theme and reflect on the effects of these on spectatorship. My access to the film is on video, in the *Clásico español* series, which bears testament to the importance the Franco regime attached to the storage of its filmic treasures. My viewing of the film, restricted to video, brings an awareness of attendant changes in mode of consumption and control over the pace, sequence and repetition of the visual events, which may serve as a reminder of the fixed temporality and totalizing claims of classical cinema spectatorship.

Moreover, the slippage between past and present, which the graininess of the film inevitably evokes, may make any attempt to account for viewing practices in this film seem a quixotic gesture, a mere act of 'nostalgic contemplation'. Yet, as Miriam Hansen has observed, 'now that cinematic spectatorship is becoming sufficiently contaminated with other modes of film consumption, we can trace more clearly its historically and theoretically distinct contours'.[40]

Pamphlets by Spanish Catholic commentators on cinema spectatorship from the period provide insights on the power and pleasure accorded cinema in the 1950s and the ways that it was depicted as a struggle between willpower and unconscious desires, intelligence and dupery, pious

Tales of Seduction

doctrine and Hollywood glamour. Two modes of looking and receiving cinema are brought into play: one based on distance from the visual event, the other grounded in identification, closeness and absorption in the image.

In the light of this dialectic, I address viewing praxis in *Don Juan* and suggest that an ideal spectatorship depends on a move from theatricality (which engineers a form of distance from the image) during the sequences that focus on Don Juan's sexual and moral misdemeanours, towards a closeness, identification and absorption during those that deal with Don Juan's Christian redemption. The film is contextualized by interviews, reviews, studio publicity and articles in fan magazines, 'sources that at once document, manipulate and constitute its reception'.[41]

While the film is seen to enunciate an ungendered (but structurally male) subject position for the viewer, I explore the ways in which diegesis interlocks with publicity material to acknowledge the presence of a female consumer, using the glamour of the star system to promote 'spectacular moments' of rapt contemplation towards the male as an erotic object. This modern mode of idolatry is then seen to be profitably inserted within a history of beholding reserved for devotional painting. Cinema hijacks the glamour of the star system and turns it towards more pious goals. The film's packaging as a love story eases the narrative and generic transition from a comedy of errors to a melodrama. Drawing on Michael Fried, I explore how the melodramatic mode permits the full absorption of the spectator into the field of the image: the desire of the spectator is realigned with the dominant ideological positions that cinema may facilitate.

In a final section, I examine the tensions evoked by this film, and reflect on the opportunities offered the spectator to resist an 'ideal spectatorship' and find pleasure in viewing outside the demands of Francoist ideology.

Screen Seductions: Negotiating Theatricality in Don Juan Films

Seductions in the Dark

For fascist ideologue Ernesto Giménez Caballero, writing in 1944, cinema is like *'un Don Juan delirante'* (a feverish Don Juan), producing *'descendencia incontrolada'* (uncontrollable progeny). He speaks of the kilometres of film reels that wind around ancient literary themes, like unending serpents. Mixing metaphors, he claims that films flower for a day before lying, trodden into the ground, like *'maleza de putrefacción'* (putrefied weeds).[42] Giménez Caballero is one of a series of cultural commentators, most of them Catholic counsellors, who wrote about the negative effects of cinema spectatorship during Franco's regime.

On examining writing on spectatorship from the period,[43] we find a sense that if cinema is like a delirious Don Juan, then the spectator is a vulnerable passive victim, susceptible to screen seductions in the darkness of the auditorium. Miguel Siguan writes of the *'placer solitario'* (solitary pleasure) that is cinema, where the audience is plunged into darkness, causing the spectator to forget those around him or herself.[44] For Gutiérrez del Egido writing in a pamphlet whose cover features a cross with film reels winding threateningly around its base, darkness itself has a magic power: *'qui male agit. Odit lucem'*, he warns, 'evil is a friend of darkness'.[45] Siguan writes that the largest group tolerated by cinema is the romantic couple who can find protection for their desired intimacy in the shadows of the auditorium.[46] Otherwise, the cinema public is not a mass, but a group of solitary beings, who hold up no resistance, whose defences are down, who are hypnotized, dreaming, passive and dominated by *'este ojo mágico y subjugador que es la pantalla'* (the magical and subjugating eye that is the screen).[47]

The perceived danger presented by cinema is that the spectator appears to become absorbed by the screen images. In a state of susceptibility, the spectator is open to the influence of cinema (Siguan compares it with hypnosis, opium or alcohol) which leaves a *'huella'* (mark) that can have an effect on behaviour. Of particular concern in articles by a series of writers is the enticement cinema offers to imitate behaviour. José Manuel Vivanco is interested in the portrayal of love, the kiss and the caress in the cinema, as well as the representation of marriage, home and divorce, vice, virtue and materialism on screen.[48]

Of special concern to many writers is the effect of screen-images on children and adolescents. For example, García Escudero examines the link between cinema and behaviour in terms of adolescent delinquency and eroticism,[49] while Juan García Yagüe draws on French empirical research to compile an inventory of gestures, behaviour and dress styles that have been copied from cinema, which include *'dar besos con limpieza y ansiedad'* (kissing chastely and anxiously), 'a man who was smoking' and 'being Rita Hayworth'.[50] Siguan writes that the teenager who goes to a night-time party for the first time carries with her like baggage the memory of all the parties she has seen on screen that have left a mark on her 'toilette', her mannerisms and gestures, the way she dances and above all on her behaviour with a potential partner.[51] A pamphlet tells the morality tale of a teenager in Italy who was so influenced by the cinema that she ran away from home (films with Joan Crawford are cited because they encourage young women to lead independent lives), only to be found later as a corpse.[52]

Repeatedly, these articles stress the fictitiousness of the cinema. It is *'mentira'* (lies),[53] *'engaño'* (deception),[54] it presents a false vision of the world,[55] an artificial paradise.[56] At the same time, cinema is linked with eroticism, and screen seductions cause lasciviousness. For these writers, censorship is not uniformly reliable as a filter for negative images. The cinema also has mass appeal, being naturalized by Spanish citizens into a regular fixture of the week's activities.⁵⁷ Thus, in the face of the overarching mass power of cinema, these writers urge that members of the public be educated in cinema, strengthening (*'fortaleciendo'*) their personalities and their sense of responsibility,⁵⁸ in order to learn to distinguish between positive and negative images.

The intelligent aficionado, the member of a film club, is less in danger of being seduced by the screen because he adopts a less passive position.⁵⁹ Active resistance to absorption by the filmic image can be achieved through an understanding of cinematic techniques. In this vein, Garmendía de Otaola provides a guide to the aesthetics of cinema (explaining shots, sound, dialogue, lighting, colour and photography) as well as its ethics.⁶⁰ A pamphlet entitled, *¿Sabes ir al cine?* (Do You Know How to Go to the Cinema?) appeals to the intelligence of the female spectator.⁶¹ *'Naturalmente sé ir al cine'* (Of course I know how to go to the cinema), it begins:

> *Cuando voy a la peluquería me leo todas las revistas que hay allí, además de las que compra Clara, que es la más entusiasmada por las cosas de las artistas. Como que estoy segura que si no fuera por lo feílla que es la pobre, se presentaría a esos concursos que organizan para buscar caras nuevas en el cine español. Su ilusión sería ser artista.* (When I go to the hairdresser's I read all the magazines there, besides the one my friend Clara buys – she is the one who is really enthusiastic about the lives of the stars. I am sure that if the poor thing were not so ugly she would enter one of those competitions to find new faces in Spanish cinema. Her dream is to be a star.)⁶²

After separating its target reader from her fictional friend Clara, who is duped by the cinema and above all by the bright lights of the star system, it urges: (*'una cosa es ir al cine y otra SABER ir'* (it is one thing to go to the cinema and another to KNOW how to go). It exhorts the reader to 'learn to put the filter of your intelligence between your senses. *'Busca en cada película la IDEA de su creador, el mensaje que a través de esa cinta ha querido lanzar al mundo. ... No hagas el juego de la publicidad. Ve al cine* inteligentemente *y piensa y habla de él inteligentemente'* (In each film, seek out the IDEA of its creator, the message that the film is trying to communicate. Don't enter into the advertiser's game. Go to the cinema *intelligently* and think and talk about it intelligently).[63]

Furthermore, it warns, 'Distrust. This should be your first position.' *'Desconfianza de los sentidos'* (Distrust your senses) *'y aplicación de la inteligencia sobre la película'* (and apply intelligence to the film).[64] Intelligence, then, becomes a form of distrust or distancing from the spectacular resources employed by cinema, achieved through observation of the film's ideological message. The anonymous writer of this pamphlet therefore provides a model for a form of Catholic spectatorship in which an intelligent reading of film provides the necessary distance required to neutralize the threat of being *'narcotizados por la imagen y el color'* (drugged by the image and colour).

The articles on spectatorship in 1950s Spain meditate on the possible effects of two ways of viewing film: moving between absorption in and distance from the image.

Synopsis

In Seville, in 1553, a dying man asks for a royal pardon for his son, Don Juan, who has been exiled to Italy. Don Juan returns to Spain with his faithful manservant Ciutti. During the voyage home he meets Lady Ontiveros, a married English noblewoman with whom he begins an 'open' relationship. On arrival in Seville, he is brought news of the death of his father and of the conditions of his

Screen Seductions: Negotiating Theatricality in Don Juan Films

inheritance: he must marry Doña Inés, daughter of Don Gonzalo. Don Juan lies, declaring that he is already married, and continues with his multiple seductions. Later, upon hearing that Dona Inés is to attend a popular fair, he arranges for bandits to create a stampede of bulls. In the ensuing chaos, he kidnaps Doña Inés. There she persuades him not to seduce her and, as she tells him of her religious faith, he starts to fall in love with her. When Don Gonzalo arrives, he is killed by Don Juan. Doña Inés swears that she wishes to enter a convent. When Don Juan tells Lady Ontiveros of his love for Doña Inés she betrays him to the guards. As he dies, Don Juan swears his love of God.

Theatricality

The film opens with the credits being shown over a series of scenes from the film, a trailer of dissolving tableaux vivant that crosscut sword fights with scenes of Don Juan's multiple seductions. The first of these scenes is a close-up of the face of Antonio Vilar, playing the lead, Don Juan, wearing a mask that covers most of his face. Vilar's hands can be seen on either side of the frame to pull up the mask as the film's title, *Don Juan*, appears across his newly revealed face. The mask in the image is motivated by the *mise-en-scène* of the sequence from which it is taken – a masked ball at carnival time.

    Masquerade is also present as a visual and thematic 'hook' throughout the main body of the film as we witness Don Juan's manifold conquests, involving cases of mistaken identity, lies, tricks and subterfuges. The alignment of Don Juan with masquerade at the start of the film flamboyantly posits Don Juan as an enigma.[65] The film will propose plot-driven resolutions to open-ended questions of Spanish masculinity, questions that derive from a pro-filmic 'scene' outside the diegesis. Furthermore, the film highlights theatricality as trope – an element that extends

Tales of Seduction

3. Don Juan as masquerade. *Don Juan* by José Luis Sáenz de Heredia

beyond the stagy elements of the plot and *mise-en-scène* and into cinematic resources and spectatorship.

If masquerade is about who is looking and its specific discursive formation in a given historical juncture,[66] then by looking at the publicity material surrounding the film and its interlocking with diegetics we are reminded that *Don Juan* inserts itself into a heritage of literary, medical and philosophical theories that centre on the figure of the Spanish seducer. While the stagy titles at the beginning of the film inform us that this version will borrow from both Tirso and Zorrilla, but be faithful to neither, the reverent wordiness of the script (by Carlos Blanco) likewise serves to remind us of the film's literary origins.

An article in *ABC*, meanwhile, notes the homage to Spanish physician Gregorio Marañón, when Don Juan asks his faithful sidekick Ciutti if he has grown any grey hairs.[67] Marañón, whose volume on Don Juan was published in 1942, was infamous for his 'queering' of Don Juan as we saw in Chapter 2.[68] Sáenz de Heredia invited Marañón to attend a private screening of the film, which the doctor reportedly disliked.[69] But in his invocation of Marañón, Sáenz de Heredia was opening up an old debate in Spanish public discourse, an unresolved tension over the sexuality of the archetypal Spanish lover.

Screen Seductions: Negotiating Theatricality in Don Juan Films

In publicity shots for the film, Vilar appears resplendent in (feminizing) accoutrements, tights, ruff at the neck and cuffs, lavish buckles, a cape and sword. In an interview accompanying such a picture, Vilar offers an ironic detachment to his attire: *'no me imagino a Don Juan con aquella ropa, en nuestro tiempo, ... pugnando por hacerse sitio en el estribo de un tranvía'* (I cannot imagine Don Juan with those clothes in our time, fighting for space on the running board of a tram.)[70] Press coverage, meanwhile, fetishizes Vilar's beard, associating it with manliness – we learn that Vilar cut himself while shaving, and that Carlos Nin, responsible for make-up, will have to work hard to cover up the scar.[71]

Another piece, meanwhile, records that Vilar attended a concert despite his embarrassment at displaying his 'beard and sideburns' (*barba y platillas*).[72] Vilar is portrayed as all-round Renaissance man: aside from attending concerts, he reads long psychological tracts to help him sleep, speaks several languages, is a 'gentleman' (*caballero*), holds, cocktail parties for the press and is a *'gran amigo, excelente padre y maravilloso marido'* (great friend, excellent father and marvellous husband).[73]

This is far removed from the star publicity surrounding Errol Flynn for his Don Juan vehicle, which repeatedly describes Flynn as a womanizer in real life[74] and, though not reported here, he had been tried on statutory rape charges. Referents external to the film therefore inscribe a distance between Vilar and his role while the suggestion of Don Juan's effeminacy alluded to by his sumptuous costume is steadfastly ascribed to theatricality. Within the film, Don Juan's costume is authorized and naturalized in contrast to the comedy cow costume worn by a rival at the masked ball. Moreover, at the level of plot, Don Juan's heterosexuality is reinforced: he is saved by the love of a good woman.

The threat implicit in all this dressing up and posturing

on the part of Don Juan is the implication that masculinity, like Don Juan, is no more than a masquerade, a series of empty accoutrements to gender. But this tension will also be 'resolved' (however heavy-handedly) at the level of plot. The association of Don Juan with emptiness, through the masquerade (the mask that disguises a lack), leaves the way clear for the suggestion of wholeness and plenitude (beneath the mask is a soul) associated with the redemptive, religious Don Juan at the end of the film.

Elaborate dress and fabulous landscapes were a feature of Spanish historical melodramas of the 1950s. But this *Don Juan* goes further in the elaborate staginess of its costume and sets than, for example, Juan de Orduña's *La leona de Castilla* (The Lioness of Castille) (1951), *Locura de amor* (Mad with Love) (1945) or even his *Alba de América* (Dawn of America) (1951), the latter complete with desert island sequences.

Against the theatrical setting of the lavish interior of an Andalusian palace, luxury ship's quarters or masked ball, or exterior scenes of an impromptu street carnival or popular fair, in *Don Juan* we find an emphasis on sumptuous costumes and disguises. These can be seen implicitly to acknowledge the spectator as part of 'the theatrical display'.[75] The spectator is also implicitly acknowledged in a series of conceits that constitute Don Juan's cavalier seductions of a trail of contentedly ravished women.

In a scene close to the beginning of the film, Don Juan, still in Italy, is sprawled on a satin chaise longue, his head resting in the lap of an Italian female, his face obscured by shadows. Two whistles are heard, signalling to the lady that the lover whose hair she is stroking so tenderly is not, in fact, her suitor Don Octavio, but an imposter. A close-up of Don Juan's face reveals his eyes, gently mocking, the rest of his face obscured in darkness. In this conceit we know more than the lady, a dramatic irony at the expense of the

Screen Seductions: Negotiating Theatricality in Don Juan Films

female character. In this and numerous later scenarios featuring the hoodwinking of women for the purposes of seduction, the spectator is implicitly acknowledged in a metaphorical and theatrical knowing wink to the audience. It is as if the spectator were waiting in the wings, or before the frame, playing out the role of Don Juan's sidekick and accomplice in his multiple seductions.

The duelling scenes too, involve a 'tongue-in-cheek knowingness' on the part of the audience, which Gina Marchetti has found in cinematic swashbucklers.[76] The sword-fighting scenes are theatrically presented as a playful cinematic romp: the shot/reverse shot of the sword fight recalls the cinematic model for the conversation, in

4. The sword-fight shot/reverse shot recalls the cinematic model for the conversation.

which the camera presents the point of view of first one interlocutor and then the other.

Film theorists of the 1970s focused on the conversation model to account for the *suture*, the process by which the spectator is first enunciated and then erased from the visual economy.[77] In the first shot of the conversation, where a cinematic interlocutor appears to address the spectator directly, the spectator was seen to come close to sensing the edges of the filmic frame, aware of off-screen space, thereby destroying cinema's illusion. However, a second shot, from the reverse angle, reassuringly sutured the spectator back into invisibility, effectively erasing the spectator from the frame.

Tales of Seduction

The sword fight is like a dramatization of the conversational paradigm, a mobilized version that goes some way towards denaturalizing the shot/reverse shot technique. It is a jaunty revelling in the cinematic possibilities of film. The edges of the film frame are not revealed to the spectator in a troubling way, but the 'diegetic spell'[78] is weakened a little, mobilized by the movement of the camera. The members of the audience become aware of the possibilities offered by film to take them on a journey (a mobilized, virtual gaze) purely for entertainment through scenes of representation.

Another scenario provides the spectator with a chance to reflect on the deceptiveness offered by the film's scopic regime. Lady Ontiveros, an English noblewoman with whom Don Juan will maintain an 'open' relationship throughout the film, is bathing in her luxury ship's quarters as an arrogant Don Juan enters and, under the pretence that he is a Spanish royal, attempts to take over the compartment for himself. On his promises that he will keep his back turned, he coaxes Lady Ontiveros to come out of her bathroom in her robe and approach him. The camera, purportedly aligned with her gaze, advances towards him (taking in the full spectacle of his rear view in tights). But as he turns to face her (reneging on their deal) he finds to his (and our) surprise, that he is facing the black maid, whose wide-eyed comic reaction recalls the stereotypical depiction of domestic servitude in classical prewar Hollywood films (such as *Gone with the Wind*, 1939).

With its incongruous hand-held camera technique, the sequence also recalls the early horror genre and similarly works to 'other' blackness.[79] The spectator is drawn up short (our shock is cued by the look of terror in the eyes of the maid) in looking at the male as an object of desire. The scene also dramatizes the oscillation between subject viewing positions as Don Juan is both object and subject of

Screen Seductions: Negotiating Theatricality in Don Juan Films

5. Lady Ontiveros confronted by Don Juan.

6. The maid's reaction recalls stereotypical depictions from postwar Hollywood.

the gaze. His point of view drives the narrative forward, but he is simultaneously the prime erotic spectacle. Principally, it self-consciously flaunts cinema's power to deceive. The cinema, like Don Juan, has the power to dupe: Don Juan as masquerade points to the deceptiveness hidden within cinema's resources.[80]

In different ways, *Don Juan* reminds us that there is another 'scene' beyond the diegesis, whether by interlocking with a popular imaginary to provide a meta-discourse on masculinity or by reminding us of cinema's power to entertain and to deceive, it creates the distance necessary to enunciate a spectator before the filmic frame.

Stardom and the Female Spectator

'*Una película tan universal, como la figura que la inspiró*' (A film that is as universal as the figure that inspired it) is the tagline on the back cover of a pamphlet handed out during screenings. The accompanying images highlight male rivalry and foreground the importance of the sword fight. But the front cover showcases the presence of the female consumer as a costumed Vilar appears, hand on hip, among a constellation of female heads, the heads of actresses from publicity stills, which appear to have been cut out and stuck

Tales of Seduction

on, surrounding Vilar in a montage of female spectatorship in which we close the circle. The paste-and-stick nature of the composition, the touched-up colour, makes the image appear like a pastiche of Botticelli's *Birth of Venus*, but here with Vilar rising on the horizon as an image of male perfection for female erotic contemplation.

At the same time, however, the decoupage effect recalls the female and intensely private and domestic pastime of cutting out and collecting pictures of famous stars (in fact, the copies of *Primer Plano*, a glossy fan magazine I consulted (that ran from 1940 to 1962), included sections that had been cut out as well as pencil notes alongside photographs containing information about the ages of particular male film stars). The pamphlet continues the association of cinema with pleasure palaces (the film opened in the Cine Avenida, whose luxurious vestibule boasted ornamental paintings and stained glass windows by Mauméjean). But principally, the composition dramatizes the glamour of the star system and its appeal for a mainly female audience.

Walter Benjamin, musing on the loss of the uniqueness of a work of art in the age of mechanical reproduction, reflects that 'film responds to the shrivelling of the aura with an artificial build-up of the "personality" outside the studio'.[81] In this case, the aura of the movie star is specularized in an arrangement that stresses that Vilar/Don Juan is so charismatic that he 'has all the women'. Moreover, the composition dramatizes a specular regime that the star brings into the frame. Looking at stars becomes a discreet action, which 'eludes the formalist focus on narrative (principles of thorough motivation, clarity, unity and closure)',[82] by enacting a discourse that derives from beyond the diegesis but that interacts with it to produce a 'string of spectacular moments' within the film,[83] a series of opportunities for looking and gazing in rapt attention at stars. Furthermore, a second look at the image reveals further depth.

7. Cover of publicity pamphlet distributed during screenings.

The image is sprinkled with tiny stars from the night sky, which act as a dialectic between two discourses: Don Juan is poised between stardom and the sky. He is standing jauntily at the opening of a path of light that leads upwards towards the heavens. Now, the composition appears like a religious icon, surrounded in an aureole of brightly shining stars. This visual pun stages a matrix of looking relations, inserting a modern system of looking (cinematic stargazing) within a history of gazing at religious icons. Or rather, it encodes the religious gaze syncretically, harnessing the glamour of the star system for devotional goals. Religion is glamorized within the metonymic chain of associations generated by the star.

Absorption
A shift in film style, aesthetics and narrativity at the end of *Don Juan* is eased by the development of the theme of a love triangle, which develops into a full-blown tragic love story at the end of the film. The love story theme, like the metonymic signifier the star, works syncretically to present a lesson in Christian redemption masquerading as a tale of romantic love. Carmen Martín Gaite has recorded how postwar audiences in Spain knew that a Spanish film would present either historical heroics or the delights of a sacrificed and decent love, a foreclosure of the narrative that removed suspense and significantly reduced the appeal of Spanish films compared with their Hollywood counterparts.[84]

Publicity material from *Don Juan* cleverly helps to build up suspense within the film by presenting two alternate endings, revealing Don Juan torn between two women, the English noblewoman Lady Ontiveros and the Spanish maiden Doña Inés.[85] A repertoire of iconography plays out their differences. Lady Ontiveros is a *femme fatale*, a female form of Don Juan, marked by adultery and treachery.[86] She mocks her husband by making love to Don Juan in full view of the parrot she keeps in a birdcage, and which, with its mimicking of her husband's stock phrases, comes to represent the absent spouse. Her relationship with Don Juan is based on their mutual promiscuity. She has an affair with an exotic gypsy, symbolized by the red carnation Don Juan will tread into the ground.

But as Lady Ontiveros falls for Don Juan, she is forced to lie to cover her feelings. Thus, as she is bathing in a scene at the Hostería del Laurel, Don Juan calls her *'hermosa, comprensiva y ausente de lágrimas'* (beautiful, understanding and lacking in tears), which he reinforces with, *'dime de nuevo que no me amas'* (tell me again that you don't love me). *'No te amo, ni te amaré jamás'* (I don't love you and I never will) is her reply. At the end of the film her whispered *'amor mío'* (my love) reveals her true feelings: realizing that Don Juan is in love with her rival, Doña Inés, she betrays him to the guards, who literally stab him in the back.

Repeatedly, Lady Ontiveros is associated with an array of empty or mendacious signifiers. She is also doubly marked by her foreignness: a French actress playing an English noblewoman (the foreignness of the French actress Annabella is emphasized in publicity for the film, for example at the Venice Biennale where the film was showcased, her French pronunciation (*'erre'*) is mocked).[87] Double-dealing, adultery, immorality and the active pursuit of sexual pleasure are thus clearly marked as 'foreign', other to the ideals of Spanish femininity.

Doña Inés, meanwhile, is consistently associated with purity, Christianity and Spanishness. She is symbolized by the pearl necklace she loses (suggesting the threat to her maidenhood and honour) and appeals to Don Juan to return to her and by the handful of earth Don Juan (with casual callousness) tenderly asks her to save for him in a velvet purse and throws away by the roadside.

At the end of the film the slippery signifiers appear to gain depth. The head guard proudly wears a plumed helmet, reminiscent of the parrot's feathers of the earlier scene, suggesting that the helmet wearer is a stand-in for the husband and will enact his revenge. The soil from Doña Inés's feet, once discarded, is now found by Don Juan and treasured. It has become the 'dark, ardent Spanish earth',[88] has a religious depth, and has taken on a sacred status. Where Don Juan's lies formerly drove the narrative forward, now it is Doña Inés's words about divine love that make Don Juan love not just her, but also God. Lady Ontiveros now acts as a marker for Don Juan's sincerity at the end of the film. In a scene where she swears to Don Juan that she does not love him, her final 'my love' (*amor mío*) betrays her, she is still lying, but we remember that it is with her alone that Don Juan has been truthful. Therefore, when he confesses to her his love for Doña Inés, he appears sincere for the first time. Don Juan drops his masquerade to reveal a warm heart and shining soul. The story of love as narrative thread eases the generic shift, smoothing over the filmic creases as mendacity turns to sincerity, and comedy switches to poignancy and melodrama.

A change of mood, pace and genre towards the end of *Don Juan* marks a shift from the whirling cavalcade of masks, disguises and mistaken identities of the main body of the film towards the expressive *mise-en-scène*, sombre music and tableaux of grandiose gestures of its finale. This move from theatricality to melodrama, involves a similar variation in viewing praxis, from ironic detachment to absorption in the image.

Michael Fried, an art historian who takes as his example French painting of the mid-1700s, in his book, *Absorption and Theatricality,* has analysed what he terms a shift in the ontological status of painting, in representation itself, in which the problematic relationship between painting and beholding lost its earlier 'theatricality' and began to embrace a new strategy of 'absorption'.[89] Using Diderot's writings on painting and drama as a point of departure, Fried conceives of this historical shift as ushering in a new form of spectatorship: he contrasts two ways of looking.

Thus, for Diderot, the very condition of spectatordom 'stands indicted as theatrical', in other words it is a medium of 'dislocation and estrangement', where the audience's empirical presence is acknowledged in front of the frame.[90] Such a beholding, with its cold awareness of the representational effects of painting, prevented the *exemplum virtutis*, or lesson in virtue, an intensity of dramatic effect felt as a major expression of the human spirit that would only be possible with the advent of a form of spectatorship that encouraged 'absorption, sympathy, self-transcendence'.[91] 'Detheatricalize beholding', is Diderot's exhortation, 'make it once again a mode of access to truth and conviction'. 'Act as if the curtain never rose!'

For Diderot, the detheatricalization of spectatorship was possible if the artist could find a way to 'neutralize or negate the beholder's presence, establishing the fiction that no one is standing before the canvas'.[92] However, paradoxically, this could only be achieved if the beholder could be stopped and held there: for the painting to obliterate the spectator's presence, it must occupy itself with its own, autonomous, represented space. At the same time, it must arrest the viewer's attention, capturing it in its thrall.

Fried identifies the actualization of Diderot's call to arms, in a series of paintings from mid-eighteenth-century France, which depict figures 'wholly absorbed in their actions, passions, activities, feelings, states of mind'. He chooses examples from artists such as Greuze, Chardin and Fragonard to trace a history of absorption: of figures engaged in reading, gazing, praying or otherwise completely absorbed in their own autonomous space. Futhermore, Fried shows how these figures are often arranged in a unified compositional structure, thereby giving the painting as a

Tales of Seduction

8. An attempt at the de-eroticization of the gaze.

whole the character of a closed and self-sufficient system.

I submit that at the end of *Don Juan*, we find similar tableaux of states of absorption. In a scene close to the end of the film, Doña Inés is in conference with her priest as she tells him of her decision to enter a convent. We begin with a long single-take close-up of Salgado, who appears absorbed in her own words, her eyes looking out to the top of the frame as if at some distant horizon. A medium shot of the priest, shows that he is gripped, enthralled and excited by her speech. A close-up of Vilar reveals that he has been spying on the conversation; his face is framed and partially obscured by heavy vestry curtains as he peers on the scene. He too appears absorbed as he observes. The repeated cuts between the three characters encircle them within a closed system, but we are not completely excluded from the scene as the reverse shot of Don Juan creates a space for our gaze even if it is neither reciprocated nor acknowledged.

Moreover, Don Juan's mode of looking, while recalling the conventions of voyeurism (a medium shot of Doña Inés and the priest is framed by the curtains, signalling Don Juan's point of view) is, nevertheless, not a reduplication of a voyeuristic male look, but rather an attempt at a de-eroticization of the gaze. The sexual erotics implicit in the voyeuristic gaze are overlaid with a mode of looking reserved for the contemplation of devotional art. In the

Screen Seductions: Negotiating Theatricality in Don Juan Films

iconography of devotional painting, curtains are symbolic of Christian revelation. The masking of Don Juan's face is here connotative of his conversion. Don Juan's partially obscured view signals his desire, not for sexual union but rather to enter into a system to which up until now he has remained an outsider: religious faith.

In the final scenes of the film, Don Juan lies dying (stabbed, quite literally in the back, by an adversary) as he is led away on a wooden cart. Using the resources of melodrama, emotions (mourning Don Juan's death) are expressed in the musical dirge, excessive and mannered acting style, as well as the heightened *mise-en-scène*: flushed sky, rustling trees, swaying cart and rhythmic plodding of the horses contribute to a rhapsodic montage of chiaroscuro effects. A shot of the cart, travelling towards the distance, uses a slightly canted low angle to appear to point the way to the heavens. A reaction shot from the face of María Rosa Salgado, signals the distress of Doña Inés. But it is from the face of Ciutti (Ramón Giner), in an extreme close-up as he joins Don Juan on the cart, tears glistening on his face, which appears contorted into an absorbing anguish, that we take our emotional cue.[93] Ciutti's tears signify his sincerity, authenticate his grief and also testify to Don Juan's redemption. The extreme close-up of Ciutti's face encourages an easy empathy that absorbs us in the image.

Following Fried, we could say that the spectator is paradoxically at once struck by Ciutti's rapt contemplation and at the same time removed from the scene: there is no place for the empirical subject in the formal logic of this viewing event. This dismissal of the empirical subject could be equated with the logic of cinematic suture, in which the dismissal of the empirical subject necessitates 'the emergence of a different beholder, this time in the order of the real', paradoxically present, and yet erased from the scene, saturated and absorbed by the image.[94] Thus, the spectator

Tales of Seduction

9. Ciutti's tears provide an emotional cue.

of this film moves from a position of detached, tongue-in-cheek enjoyment, addressed in an ironic aside, to a passive position before the image. In that last sequence, then, we are sutured between Don Juan and Ciutti, in a final, absorbing grief.

Plot and cinematic resources thus unite to respond to Don Juan's earlier duplicity and emptiness with a final 'imaginary plenitude'.[95] Absorption and suture (with its structure of enunciation and cancelling of the subject) therefore form part of the fascist aesthetic created by Sáenz de Heredia's film. In its invocation of a passive, absorbed spectatorship, at once present and erased from the scene, *Don Juan* finally clears the way for the interpellation of a subject firmly entrenched within a national Catholic ideology.

Subversive Pleasures: Glamour and Eroticism
While there is insufficient space to do justice to the topic here, a quick review of historical melodramas of the 1940s and 1950s in Spain reveals that the use of absorptive poses is widespread. For example, in *Alba de América* (Juan de Orduña, 1951), the figure of Columbus, again played by Antonio Vilar, at the end of the film stares out melancholically to the night sky, his figure silhouetted, petrified to mimic the familiar Columbus monument in Barcelona.[96]

Screen Seductions: Negotiating Theatricality in Don Juan Films

Repeatedly, whatever their theme, these historical extravaganzas overlay images and motifs with Catholic iconography (a bank of tears, heavens and crosses), with the effect that these absorptive poses are most often associated with Catholic iconography.

Thus, we witness the repeated framing of heroines as Spanish Madonnas – for example, Juanita Reina as the mantilla-wearing singer Lola in *La Lola se va a los puertos* (Lola Goes Back to the Sea) (Juan de Orduña, 1947); Amparo Rivelles as the Catholic Queen Isabella in *Alba de América*; and Aurora Batista as the heroine in *Agustina de Aragón*, whose gaze is once again raised to the heavens at the end of that film.[97] The effect is a gallery of absorptive poses, a reification of Catholic imagery crystallized or petrified into position, creating a Catholic spectatorship and a fascist aesthetic that repeatedly sutures the spectator into a passive absorption before the image.[98]

Yet *Don Juan*'s shift in genre and its theme of multiple seductions arguably present tensions that offer certain opportunities for spectators to resist an 'ideal spectatorship'. Returning to Kristeva's conceptions of the specular seductions at work in film as cited in the opening of this chapter, a process by which the spectator is sutured between a reassuring identification on one hand and a terror of nameless dread on the other, her notion of the fascinating specular nevertheless involves a complicitous distillation of the image, a distanciation that may allow for a resistance of the hegemonic visual order.[99] Above all, in *Don Juan*, perhaps, it is the film's metonymy, the way it attempts to overwrite the secular with the religious, that allows for multiple interpretations.

Examples of the film's metonymy continue right to the end of the film as Don Juan says he has a 'date in heaven', referring at once to Doña Inés and to God. Repeatedly, the film harnesses eroticism or glamour for Catholic aims, but one senses that a spectator could just as easily yield to its secular charms – with its play of signifiers, the film can be seen to 'secularise the absorptive tradition' in certain instances rather than the reverse.[100] In the first place, for example, the film's attempts towards the end of the diegesis to de-eroticise the gaze (a structurally difficult enterprise according to the classical paradigm of pleasure in looking) do nothing to disavow the erotic pleasure of a series of scenes from the film that offer up the male body (that of Don Juan) for the voyeuristic contemplation of the audience composed of both male and female spectators.

At the same time, the opportunities offered by cinema for multiple scenarios of identification mean that star performance can undermine the deliberations of the plot. Thus, while the narrative of love and betrayal encourages an identification with Doña Inés, the symbol of homegrown sexual purity against the infidelities and betrayals of foreigner Lady Ontiveros, one critic of the film nevertheless described María Rosa Salgado's acting style as '*insípida*' (insipid), while French actress Annabella is more fashionably dressed in 1950s hair scarf and revealing *décolleté*: the triumph of style over substance.

Carmen Martín Gaite has described the subversive images offered by a handful of film actresses as '*brechas aisladas*' (isolated breaches), which worked in opposition to the stifling recommendations for hairstyles that the female section of the Falange issued.[101] Lady Ontiveros is not only more stylish and lively than the rather stiff Doña Inés, but she also picks up men and discards them at will: to the gypsy lover who serenades her at dusk she remarks, '*de modo que eres espabilado. Creí que no eras más que guapo*' (so you are clever too; I thought you were just a pretty face). Lady Ontiveros offers far more interesting possibilities for a female fantasy than her insipid female counterpart Doña Inés.

Finally, at the end of the film we are left with the feeling that Don Juan's Christian rebirth has been tacked on, a hasty Catholic redemption after almost two hours of sexual shenanigans. The final scenes are dependent on the figure of Ciutti for the whole weight of their emotional appeal, while Don Juan's rather wordy speech and climactic punchline '*Don Juan, español*' (Don Juan, Spaniard) retains touches of a theatrical inauthenticity that borders on camp. Possibly, the film's function is that of a carnivalesque revelling in disguise and sexual misdemeanours in the realm of fantasy, a liminal trying on of illicit subject positions, before the audience returns to a life of piety outside the pleasure palace.

If the expressive *mise-en-scène* of the final scene stands for what cannot be expressed, then clearly what is missing from this scene is an articulation of Don Juan's *jouissance* – a sexual energy repressed.[102] Throughout the film Don Juan's sexual exploits have been referred to or insinuated, but they always take place outside the filmic frame. Expelled from the order of the symbolic, *jouissance* occupies the order of the real. Thus, Don Juan's words to Ciutti, '*cuando sientas en el cielo el ruido de espuelas*' (when you hear my spurs galloping against the sky) recalls hallucinatory *jouissance* that lingers, unspoken, in the desires and fantasies of the audience long after the lights have gone up.

4. REPETITION COMPULSION: REDOING THE TENORIO

On the eve of All Souls' Day in 2004, Mario Gas, director of the Teatro Español in Madrid, organized what he termed a theatrical 'jam session' entitled *Tres noches con don Juan* (Three Nights with Don Juan). Alongside the screening of Don Juan films (*Cuatro películas sobre el mito*/Four Films on the Myth) and street productions by the Morboria Teatro, the highlight of the piece was the *Cincuenta voces para don Juan* (Fifty Voices for Don Juan), performed by 50 stars of Spanish stage and screen, in a dramatized reading of José Zorrilla's *Don Juan Tenorio*.

Among the actors were *grande dame* of Spanish theatre Nuria Espert, Imanol Arias (Pedro Almodóvar's *La flor de mi secreto*/The Flower of My Secret) and stalwart of Spanish stage and screen José Luis Gómez, all alternating in the role of Don Juan. Veteran actress Concha Velasco read Brígida, while Aitana Sánchez Gijón (*A Walk in the Clouds*), Emma Suárez (star of the TV series *Cuéntame cómo pasó*/Tell Me How It Happened) and Leonor Watling (Almodóvar's *Hable con ella*/Talk to Her) alternated as Doña Inés. The 50 Spanish voices, on three nights and alongside four films, may remind us of the passions of the collector.[1]

The 50 actors and actresses represented the different generations of actors who over the years have taken on the main roles in Zorrilla's most famous work.[2] Moreover, the sense that this dramatized reading was adding another to the long list of performances of the play since its inception was emphasized in the theatre's press release, which noted that the aim was to 'continue the tradition of performing this Spanish classic on the eve of All Souls'. Year upon year, Zorrilla's *Don Juan Tenorio* is staged on the *Día de difuntos* (literally *Day of the Dead*) in Spanish cities and provinces.[3]

The feast of All Saints and All Souls forms part of the Catholic calendar and commemorates the faithful departed with prayers to cleanse them of their sins. 'To attend a representation of *Don Juan Tenorio* on or near All Saints' Day', writes Timothy Mitchell, 'has been as traditional in Spain as jack-o' lanterns and Halloween costumes in America'.[4] The celebration of a feast at the beginning of November has religious and pagan associations. While the prayers for the departed have been traced to St Odilo of Cluny in the eleventh century, the pagan sources stretch back into immemorial antiquity. Otto Rank sees it as part of the ancient folklore of the figure of avenging death and a 'series of customs which can be understood as measures of protection against the return of the dead'.[5] Víctor Saíd Armesto cites a sixteenth-century custom in Galicia for eating and drinking at gravestones as part of its prehistory, although he takes this custom back to ancient Rome.[6] The tradition of performing 'el *Tenorio*' at the beginning of November therefore affords the play religious as well as pagan associations. The play's constituent parts, which include a revenant and a denouement of redemption, make these associations seem natural and timeless. The association of the play with All Saints and All Souls therefore confers on the play the status of sacred rite, of ancient ritual.

Confusion reigned for some time over the origins of this

twinning: perhaps it began with Antonio de Zamora's *No hay plazo que no se cumpla ni deuda que no se pague o El convidado de piedra* (1713), or perhaps with Tirso de Molina's *El burlador de Sevilla y convidado de piedra* (*c*.1630), the Mercedarian friar believed to be the author of the 'original' work. But in '*La implantación del rito del Tenorio en Madrid (1844–1877)*', Hans Mattauch has revealed how the association can be traced to a specific time and place: Barcelona in 1814.

On 2 November 1847, Zorrilla's play, *Don Juan Tenorio*, which had enjoyed limited success in Madrid, opened in Barcelona with the title, *Don Juan Tenorio o sea el nuevo convidado de piedra* (Don Juan Tenorio or the New Stone Guest). The title was a reference to Zamora's earlier variation on the Don Juan theme, *No hay plazo que no se cumpla ni deuda que no se pague o El convidado de piedra*, which had been relatively successful in Barcelona. As Mattauch explains, Zamora's play had been performed on the Catholic feast in Barcelona since 1814, when it was presented '*en tributo de homenaje ... a la memoria de los que dejaron de ser*' (as a homage to the memory of the dearly departed).[7] Rather than timelessness, this detail reveals the superb marketing skills of a Barcelona theatre.

Zamora's work and that of Zorrilla were rivals for a period of 12 years, until 1859 when Zorrilla's *Don Juan Tenorio* eclipsed its predecessor on the Barcelona stage. It was not long before the fashion for staging Zorrilla on the feast day took off in Madrid, '*suscitando una verdadera tenoriomanía*' (provoking a real Tenorio mania),[8] with stagings in large theatres as well as private performance spaces. J. L. Abellán states that, '*la representación de* Don Juan Tenorio *tiene ... un carácter ejemplar para la España católica de todos los tiempos, realiza la función de una* meditatio mortis *popular*' (the performance of *Don Juan Tenorio* is exemplary for the Catholic Spain of all times, it carries out the function of a popular *meditatio mortis*).[9]

Abellán emphasizes the sense of a sacred rite being conferred on the play. If it is true that any literary canon is formed out of nostalgia, out of reaping the treasures of the past, then this work, with its apparent past in time immemorial, is lifted beyond the realm of the 'Spanish classic' and into the arena of sacred rite, ritual and immovable tradition. Francisco Nieva has written of the unique *'sacralización ritual de un mito a través de una obra dramática'* (ritual that renders a myth sacred through a dramatic work) that operates in connection with Zorrilla's incarnation.[10] This bedrock of the Spanish literary canon has become a national treasure, as much a part of Spanish heritage as Cervantes and the Inquisition, but with obscure roots that make it seem as natural a part of Spanish culture as flamenco and the bullfight.[11]

Reflecting on the overwhelming popularity of the play in the nineteenth century, critics have debated the academic merits of the work. Even Zorrilla disparaged his own play, although this had more to do with his anger at the restrictive copyright laws that prevented him from profiting from his own work. Most have situated it in the context of the nineteenth century.

For example, David Thatcher Gies sees the duality in Don Juan's behaviour and character (at once rebellious of the social order and submissive and cooperative) as corresponding to twin tendencies in Spanish Romanticism.[12] For Donald Shaw, the play centres on popular concepts of romantic love combined with traditional values.[13] José Alberich sees the play responding to an *'acto patriótico'* (patriotic act), containing elements that are more Spanish than those of Tirso's drama.[14] Eamonn Rodgers sees the 'appeal of such stylized images of Spanish valour and chivalry, and of a world which seemed in every respect more colourful and exciting than that of the second half of the nineteenth century, the age of prose, of moral compromise, and consensus politics'.[15] Timothy Mitchell has explored how the play was an aesthetically pleasing synthesis of the social and religious values (divine justice, Marianism, martial valour, indulgent mothering and blasphemy) important to the popular classes of Spain in the nineteenth-century.[16]

Interestingly, the play was not immediately popular. Zorrilla's reworking of Tirso's (and Zamora's) text into a denouement of redemption for a transgressive sinner attracted fierce criticism from the Catholic Church, which influenced the play's critics in their assessment of the piece.[17]

Its opening in 1844 at Madrid's Teatro de la Cruz enjoyed limited success, attributed by scholars to the inappropriateness of Bárbara LaMadrid, who was corpulent and advancing in years, to fill the role of the blushing Doña Inés. The play's popularity is seen to originate with Pedro Delgado's 1866 version at the Teatro Español, Madrid, with the younger and prettier Teodora LaMadrid in the main female role.[18] Zorrilla's *Don Juan Tenorio* is interesting in that its fortunes have been inexorably tied up in the history of its performances on stage.[19] This is perhaps not surprising given that Jesús Rubio Jiménez reminds us of the importance of performance by showing us how the work is extravagantly theatrical: '*las escenas de gran brillantez colorista, las apariciones fantásticas, la musicalidad de los versos, ripios pero sonoros*' (the scenes of brilliant colours, the fantastical apparitions, the musicality of the verses, verbose but resonant).[20] Unlike other works of the Spanish canon, it gained its literary status through direct interaction with a Spanish public. Parodic versions sprang up almost from its inception (the first of these dates from 1848), offering myriad variations on a theme in theatres alongside the 'mainstream' productions. These parodic versions reinforced the status of the source text, allowing it to take root in the psyche of the Spanish public.[21]

Repetition Compulsion: Redoing the Tenorio

Performing a play year upon year creates a peculiar set of circumstances. Audiences quickly begin to know the verses off by heart. The designation of *Tenorio* to Zorrilla's text stresses our familiarity with it. Ortega y Gasset noted in 1935 that *'todos los años, los españoles, que no solemos ir a ninguna parte, vamos a ver y oír el "Don Juan" de Zorrilla ... vamos a escuchar una vez más los consonantes que nos sabemos todos de memoria'* (every year we Spaniards, who do not usually go anywhere, go to see and hear Zorrilla's 'Don Juan' ... we go to hear once again the consonants that we know off by heart).[22] Andrés Peláez Martín notes that *'sus versos y sus ripios se repiten incesantemente hasta el caso que algunas de sus situaciones son tópicos ya en muchos usos amorosos'* (the verses and jingles are repeated incessantly to the extent that some of the situations have now become clichés in courtship customs).[23]

Javier Villán writes of the infamous case of a spectator who acted as impromptu prompter for an actor who had forgotten his lines during a performance.[24] The play became so central a part of Spanish theatre that it became a sort of proving ground for actors and actresses: *'todos los primeros actores debían librar el reto del personaje para probar su condición de tales'* (all the major actors had to take on the character to prove their worth).[25] César Oliva writes that spectators *'iban a ver el Tenorio por los actores, más que por otras causas'* (went to see the *Tenorio* for the actors more than for other reasons). Audiences knew the work so well, that it became a question of exciting them with something different year upon year: *'ni el público tenía otra intriga que la de ver cómo realizarían la obra'* (the public had no other thrill than to see how they would perform the work).[26] On the one hand, then, audiences wanted the familiar verses, on the other, they wished to be excited by the starry cast or showy theatrics.

Finally, while the play itself owes a debt to other works

(Tirso's and Zamora's as well as other references) each performance could be seen to operate in an intertextual arrangement to previous stagings. Directors have tended to manage this phenomenon in one of two ways: either to stress the intertextual genealogy of the play in a knowing wink, or else to promise to present the play afresh, as if seeing it for the first time.

'Tenoriomania' was in evidence again in the 1920s in Spain, and saw intellectuals such as Ortega y Gasset, Unamuno and Marañón all contributing to a debate on the sins and virtues of the Don Juan figure. Such a frenzy of activity surrounding Don Juan ensured a lively interest in both stagings of the original and parodic versions. It also gave rise to serious reflections on the theme from some literary heavyweights. Miguel de Unamuno, for example, in his *El hermano Juan o el mundo es teatro* of 1929 reflected on theatre as a metaphor for life, on the existence of God and on the binary systems that make up the world through his reworking of Don Juan as Brother Juan. Juan Ignacio Luca de Tena wrote *Las canas de Don Juan* (1925), Federico Oliver, *Han matado a Don Juan* (They Have Killed Don Juan) (1929), María Lejárraga (writing under the pseudonym of her husband, Gregorio Martínez Sierra) wrote *Don Juan de España* in 1921.[27] And what about the Condesa de San Luis's *Don Juan no existe* (Don Juan Does Not Exist) (1924); Manuel y Antonio Machado's *Juan de Mañara* (1927); and the Quintero brothers' *Don Juan, buena persona* (Don Juan, Good Person) (1918)? The list is seemingly endless.[28]

Even the Spanish Civil War, which disrupted so much cultural activity, failed to call a halt to the stagings of the play. On 28 October 1939, Guillermo Marín and Niní Montián staged the play at the Teatro Español, beginning a trajectory that was to continue almost unbroken throughout the 1940s and 1950s. In fact, the Franco regime actively encouraged the play and lauded its message of Catholic redemption. It incorporated it into the *Teatros Nacionales* project and encouraged the creation of a traditionalist repertory theatre.[29] The centenary of the play was celebrated in 1944 with Narciso Alonso Cortés's *Zorrilla: su vida y su obra* (1943) and his edition of Zorrilla's *Obras completas*. Fernando Jiménez Placer et al. *Centenario del estreno de Don Juan Tenorio (1844–1944)* featured illustrations of scenes from the play by Sáenz de Tejada, a study of the *'valores plásticos'* (aesthetic values) of the play as well as an in-depth commentary on the copyright issues facing Zorrilla in his day.[30]

Throughout the 1940s and 1950s, the Teatro Español and the Teatro María Guerrero staged performances by directors such as José Franco, Luis Escobar, Huberto Pérez de la Ossa, Cayetano Luca de Tena, Luis Fernando de Igoa, Modesto Higueras and José Tamayo, with actors such as Enrique Guitart, Guillermo Marín and Mercedes Guerrero, and scenographers such as Siegfried Burmann. In 1949 there was no production at the Teatro Español owing to the runaway success of Antonio Buero Vallejo's *Historia de una escalera*. But María Guerrero produced a landmark version of the play, directed by Luis Escobar and with scenography and costumes by Salvador Dalí.

That production changed the landscape so much that from then on directors concentrated on trying to find the latest innovation. The production was repeated in 1950, and then again in 1964, but with a young Concha Velasco in the role of Doña Inés. Here the trajectory comes to an end in the Teatro Español and productions on the Spanish stage are seen practically to die out also.[31] Miguel Narros, for example, preferred to stage Tirso's *El burlador de Sevilla*. He did stage Zorrilla's *Don Juan Tenorio*, however, in 1968 with José Luis Pellicena and a young Ana Belén. '*Es el último* Don Juan *de Zorrilla innovador en el Teatro Español*' (this is the last innovative Don Juan by Zorrilla at the Teatro Español), César Oliva has remarked.[32]

Tales of Seduction

The 1970s and 1980s did see some interesting productions, such as the Asamblea de Trabajadores del Espectáculo de Cataluña, which in 1976 performed the play on seven stages, with seven directors and seven different casts.[33] Carmen Martín Gaite, meanwhile, was more tempted by Tirso's *El burlador de Sevilla* for the production in 1988 in a coproduction of the Compañía Nacional de Teatro Clásico and the Argentinian Teatro San Martín, in which she sought to provide depth to the female characters,[34] '*de justificar ciertos comportamientos y de que no queden excesivamente empequeñecidas con respecto a Don Juan*' (to justify certain behaviour and to make sure that Don Juan does not belittle them).[35] The work was criticized for Martín Gaite's stripping of the text of certain passages, the attempt to '*retocar una obra de arte*' (touch-up a work of art).[36]

In general, the 1970s and 1980s saw a decline in productions of the *Tenorio*. This is perhaps unsurprising, given the play's associations with Francoism. Eduardo Vasco notes the reluctance of directors to produce performances of a play that had become bound up in notions of the numbing propaganda of the regime.[37] Lluís Pasqual's rendition of the Mozart/Da Ponte opera *Don Giovanni* of 2005 portrayed Don Juan as a fascist icon.[38] On the occasion of Gas's *Cincuenta voces para Don Juan* in 2004, Imanol Arias noted that Zorrilla's was not a play that his generation knew well: *Don Juan Tenorio* by Zorrilla had become staid, the staple of a rather tired theatrical style.

Since 1990, however, the Teatro Español has once again become committed to Zorrilla, for the first 14 years under the directorship of Gustavo Pérez Puig, and currently under Mario Gas. The 1990s saw a mini revival of interest in the theme, with, for example, Vicente Molina Foix's *Don Juan último* (The Latest/Last Don Juan) directed by Robert Wilson at the Teatro María Guerrero in 1992, which featured a 'luminous, geometrically divided space, ... Magritte colours, the speak-dance of the play figures who move along their angular tracks as abstractly as in a chess game; the ambivalence of gender in the male characters (they wear high heels and the lower halves of their bodies appear to be female)' in a serious and complex game of doubling.[39]

The year 1994, meanwhile, saw ¡Hombres! (Men!) by the Companyia T de Teatre open at the Mercat de les Flores in Barcelona. This all-female theatre group (Miriam Íscla, Mamen Duch, Àgata Roca, Carmen Plá and Rosa Gàmiz) opened with a series of famous quotations on the subject of men (all by men, from Nietzsche to Shakespeare), followed by excerpts from the writings of famous libertines (from Casanova to Sade), before proceeding to a series of vignettes commenting on masculinity. In the background, a mock conference on masculinity is taking place featuring pressing questions on such matters as the effect of alopecia on masculinity. Texts and vignettes were by male authors (Sergi Belbel, Francesc Pereira, Ferran Verdés and Josep M. Benet i Jornet) while the (male) protagonists were all played by actresses in this ironic and by turns bitter and tender homage to masculinity.

In 2000, the INAEM (Instituto Nacional de las Artes Escénicas y la Música) announced its initiative to stage *Don Juan Tenorio* with collaboration from public and private theatre companies (a state-funded initiative launched during Aznar's Popular Party government), although the project only lasted for four years (it included Alfonso Zurro's 2001 setting of the play in an old people's home in modern-day Madrid in which the average age of the actors was 65).[40] The play continues to be performed into the twenty-first century. Salvador Távora's *Don Juan en los ruedos* (Don Juan in the Bullring), was a flamenco version complete with Arab stallions on stage. The play *Don Juan en*

Alcalá (directed by Jaime Azpilieveta), an *'adaptación local del histórico* Don Juan Tenorio' (a local adaptation of the historical *Don Juan Tenorio*), collaborated with the council of the town of Alcalá as well as the ministry of tourism, in a project designed to lure spectators to the town to show off its status as a *'patrimonio nacional'* (national heritage) site. This is not to speak of the myriad parodies that propagated from 1948 onwards. Don Juan remains a 'national treasure', as an exhibition from 2004, testifies.[41]

Repetition is therefore a key element in the history of *Don Juan Tenorio*. Stagings and critiques of Zorrilla's play return obsessively to the question of 'firstness'. Ramón Pérez de Ayala has noted the impossibility of seeing Don Juan for the first time.[42] Pérez de Ayala's discussion is filled with longing and nostalgia for an irrecuperable sense of 'firstness':

> *Recuerdo que, en una ocasión, viendo* Don Juan Tenorio *en una provincia, muy mal interpretado por cierto, me produjo una viva emoción. Y yo pensaba: 'Lo que yo daría por ver el* Tenorio *por primera vez'. Éste es el canon estético fundamental: procurar ver las cosas por primera vez. Lo torpe y risible de ese público especial de Madrid que asiste a los estrenos, y nada más que los estrenos, es que, en general, se compone de personas incapaces de ver una obra por primera vez, permítaseme la paradoja; un público que no busca en las obras sino el parecido con obras anteriores'.* (I remember that, on one occasion, watching *Don Juan Tenorio* in one of the provinces, very badly done by the way, I felt pure emotion. I thought, what I would give to see the *Tenorio* for the first time. This is the fundamental aesthetic canon: to try to see things for the first time. The awkwardness and risibility of that special Madrid public who attends opening nights, nothing other than opening

nights, is that in general these are people incapable of seeing a work for the first time. Permit me to describe the paradox: a public who looks for nothing in plays but their similarity to previous works.)[43]

Zorrilla's drama is a *refundición* of Tirso de Molina's work, while critics have also debated Zorrilla's debt to Zamora as well as to other sources.[44] James Mandrell goes so far as to describe the mythology of Don Juan as a 'mythography', a discourse about discourse. The search for the play's origins has given rise to page upon page of criticism. Zorrilla's text also returns us to Romanticism or to a nineteenth-century Catholic revival, but it equally returns us to sixteenth-century imperial Spain.

Criticism appears therefore to be always looking backwards towards a previous time, or earlier reference, *ad infinitum*. At the same time, the association of the play with the Catholic feast of All Souls and its syncretic fusion with pagan ritual allows it to appear ahistorical, created out of an originary past that by definition is elusive, which Susan Stewart describes as a definition of nostalgia: 'Nostalgia, like any form of narrative, is always ideological: the past it seeks has never existed except as narrative, and hence, always absent, that past continually threatens to reproduce itself as a felt lack.'[45]

This 'desire for desire' means that many mainstream productions of *Don Juan Tenorio* appear to be shot through with nostalgia.[46] The costumes (usually from sixteenth-century Spain) are markers of 'history', while Don Juan is evoked as an avatar of Spanish heritage, a reminder of a time when Spain was an imperial power and produced literary greats as well as figures worshipped the world over. A sense of longing is provoked by the scene of the Stone Guest, evoking a time when it was possible to feel awe and wonder at contemplation of the supernatural, or of an afterlife, such

Tales of Seduction

10. *Última escena de Don Juan Tenorio* by Antonio Muñoz Degrain
(1840–1924)

as that depicted in Antonio Muñoz Degrain's *Última escena de Don Juan* (Last Scene of Don Juan) of 1922.

Critics of mainstream productions often centre on this key scene as an indicator of the success of the production. A production should achieve a sense of 'firstness', allowing the spectator to imagine what it must be like to experience awe, linked to a time gone by.

In mainstream productions of the *Tenorio*, the attempt to regain 'firstness' can manifest itself as a desire endlessly to compare aesthetic or directorial decisions with an original source text. In the case of Zorrilla's *Don Juan*, such a project is thwarted from the start in that the source text, rather than being a stable referent, enjoys an uncertain status, and uncertain paternity. The metonymic nature of Zorrilla's *Don Juan Tenorio*, the way it constantly refers back to a predecessor, means that most productions of Zorrilla's work are always already shot through with nostalgia.

This sense of firstness also extends to the many reworkings of the Don Juan theme, whether parodic or the more serious offerings of Spanish literati. In this case, firstness takes on the connotations of newness. Works that employ this method rely for their power on their variation from a main theme, constantly referring the spectator back to an earlier text. In this sense, and in the sense that they constantly strive to offer something new, they too can be described in terms of firstness.

Jesús Rubio Jiménez has noted two tendencies in connection with Zorrilla's play: '*una sacralizadora que lo convirtió en paso obligado dentro del ritual que acompaña el día de difuntos el primero de noviembre y otra desenfadada y paródica*' (a sacralizing one that made it into an essential part of the ritual accompanying All Souls on 1 November, and another casual and parodic one).[47] It is these two tendencies, and their associations with firstness that I will explore in the rest of this chapter. I begin with a brief examination of some of the parodies from the early part of the century. I then move to examine a performance from 1949, which still stands as a landmark production: Zorrilla's *Don Juan Tenorio*, directed by Luis Escobar and with scenography by the painter Salvador Dalí.

Between Profanation and Sacralization: Parodies of the *Tenorio*

Parodies of the play sprang up almost immediately after the first stagings of Zorrilla's work. Neither Tirso's *El burlador de Sevilla*, nor Zamora's *No hay deuda que no se pague ni plazo que no se cumpla* gave rise to parodies. Nevertheless, Zorrilla's *Don Juan Tenorio* quickly gave rise to a myriad of variations on its theme. Perhaps they had to do partly with the new nineteenth-century theatre-going public '*más numerosos, pero acaso menos preparados*' (more numerous but less well-informed) who welcomed a *teatro por horas* (theatre by the hour) with entertainment in easily digestible chunks.[48]

But perhaps also, Zorrilla's '*refundición*', his changing of the ending from one of eternal damnation to one of salvation, sanctioned a host of variations on a theme. These parodies strive for firstness in the sense that their transience and rapid change seems born out of a desire to remodel the paradigm of Don Juan in a way that had never been seen before. In Carlos Serrano's *Carnaval en noviembre: parodies teatrales españolas de Don Juan Tenorio*, he lists 196 parodies on the Spanish stage between 1848 and 1944.[49] Jeffrey T. Bersett, meanwhile, in *El Burlado de Sevilla: Nineteenth-Century Appropriations of Don Juan Tenorio*, notes that this 'veritable legion of plays represents only a fraction of those that were, or were probably, written'.[50]

There is evidence of plays being performed of which the printed editions have been lost, or have yet to be found. For instance, David Thatcher Gies observes the existence of a work not documented by Serrano, the pornographic, *Don Juan Notorio, burdel en cinco actos y 2000 escándalos*

(Notorious Juan, Brothel in Five Acts and Two Thousand Scandals) of 1874, which was *'profundamente obscena y cómica'* (profoundly obscene and comic),[51] as well as female playwright Adelaida Muñiz's *La herencia del Tenorio* (Don Juan's Inheritance) of 1892. Dealing with Don Juan's inheritance rather than his immortal soul, Gies terms it the 'ultimate "middle-classization" of Zorrilla's Romantic hero'.[52] Bersett notes the 'simultaneous celebration and mocking of the *Tenorio*' inherent in the Don Juan parody, 'the mixed criticism and praise of things both contained within and exterior to the play', indicative of the fact that 'Zorrilla's text was both revered and scorned'.[53]

Many of these parodies provide fascinating insights into the preoccupations of the times. Thus, the musical comedy *Un Tenorio moderno* (A Modern Don Juan Tenorio) by José María Nogués of 1864 revealed a preoccupation with money and morals, and *Doña Juana Tenorio* by Rafael María Liern of 1875 was a riff on contemporary gender politics.[54] In the twentieth century, parodies continued to proliferate. For 1900 alone, Serrano lists the following works: *Tenorio cosmopolita* (Cosmopolitan Don Juan) (Josep Santpere), *Tenorio político* (Political Don Juan) (Segundo Cernuda), *Tenorio 'inocentada'* (Don Juan, Practical Joker) (José Molgosa Valls), *Don Joan* (Don Juan) (Adrià Gual), *Don Gonzalo de Ulloa* (Guillermo Perín), *¡Dixtos Tenorio!* (Blessed Don Juan) (Ramón Muntané), *La nit del Tenorio* (Don Juan Night) (Lluís Millà Gació), *Las noblezas de Don Juan* (Don Juan's Noble Acts) (Enrique Pelayo y Menéndez), *Tenorio en Nápoles* (Don Juan in Naples) (Joaquín Arqués y Escriña) and *Tenorios y castañillas* (Don Juan and Castanets) (Joan Manuel Casademunt).[55]

A glance at the theatre showings for 1908 reveals that spectators had a choice of Don Juan versions from which to choose: thus, while Zorrilla's *Don Juan Tenorio* was staged

Tales of Seduction

at the Teatro Español in Madrid, Pablo Parellada's parodic *Tenorio modernista* (Modernist Don Juan) (1906) was on at the Teatro Lara and *Tenorio feminista* (Feminist Don Juan) (Antonio Paso Cano, Carlos Servet y Fortuny) was showing at both the Teatro Eslava and the Regio, the latter accompanied by the '*concertistas hermanos LaFuente*' (LaFuente Brothers musicians).[56]

Tenorio modernista offers a savage parody of modernist poetry, with its parading of words borrowed from French, English and Italian and its brilliantly ingenious clock with different colours instead of numbers to tell the time (perfect for synaesthetes), in which '*el Don Juan y el Don Luis son dos* sportsmen *de los de reloj en la muñeca y monóculo en un ojo, que cuentan los estropicios que han hecho con sus automóviles en Italia y Francia*' (Don Juan and Don Luis are two sportsmen of the sort who wear a wristwatch and a monocle and tell of the havoc they have caused with their automobiles in Italy and France).[57] Ostentatious modernity is lampooned throughout. Doña Inés wears a magnificent rosary made of electric light bulbs that turns incandescent to help her read the missive from Don Juan. She and Don Juan flee her father in Don Juan's magnificent '*globo*' (balloon). In the scene in the cemetery, Don Juan frightens the sculptor away by threatening to recite verse to him and later admits to crimes against the Spanish language. The audience on the first night at the Teatro Lara, 30 October 1906, '*no cesó de reír a carcajadas*' (did not stop laughing out loud), according to one critic.[58]

Tenorio feminista (Feminist Don Juan) of 1907, like Liern's *Doña Juana Tenorio* of 1874, subtitled, '*parodia lírica mujeriega*' (lyrical womanizing parody) engineers a gender swap, substituting Doña Juana and Luis Mejía for their male counterparts. Luisa boasts that she is '*temida por las francesas y amada por los franceses*' (feared by French women and loved by French men).[59] Doña Juana sets herself a challenge to seduce the *novicio* (male novice) Ginés. She does this by presenting him with a cigarette case engraved with his initials. Ginés, who is as insipid as his female counterpart Doña Inés, swoons into the arms of Brígido. He eventually has to be rescued by his mother, Doña Gala, who rails against Juana for singling her son out '*¿pero es que tú te has creído/ que porque estoy sin marido/ me vas a tomar la trenza?*' (did you think you could pull one over on me because I have no husband?) and then threatens to sue Juana for corruption of a minor. According to one critic, the play '*pone las cosas al revés, y tales van siendo ellas en España que la invención de los autores no parece inverosímil*' (puts things in reverse, and the way the female sex in Spain is going the invention of the authors is not unrealistic).[60]

According to the list documented by Serrano, the dizzying number of parodies was to continue throughout the early twentieth century and into the 1940s.[61] Gender wars were also returned to in *La Señorita Tenorio* (Miss Tenorio) (Antonio Paso Díaz, José Aramburu, José Fuentes, 1919), and in *Las Tenorias* (The Tenorio Girls) (Onofre Carrasquer Llopis, 1920).

In the *Tenorio Sarasa* by Francisco Serrano of 1927, Apio, 'the homosexual Don Juan', whose '*especialidad es el hombre, niños, pollitos y viejos*' (speciality is men, boys, youngsters and old men),[62] seduces Ginés, a novice. If the ending appears daring, with Ulogio declaring that he gives his consent to a marriage between Apio and Ginés (before they all dance a Charleston), the humour of the play nevertheless derives from the comical nature of the lines delivered by Ginés. These, for example, include, '*¡Yo voy a ti como va/la Rambla al Paseo de Gracia!*' (I go to you like the Rambla goes to the Paseo de Gracia), which is a play on the lives of Zorrilla's text '*yo voy a ti como va/sorbido al mar ese río*' (I go to you as the river is engulfed by the sea).[63]

Apio's final speech: '*Acabó la bufonada/atrevida y sin*

Tales of Seduction

recato/Aplaudir la tenoriada/si os hizo pasar el rato' (The clowning's at an end, daring and without reserve/Applaud our Don Juan spoof/if it helped to pass the time) suggests that comedy undermines the subversiveness of the plot. As with the *Tenorio feminista*, the mere swapping of extremes means that signs threaten to dissolve into their opposite number, presenting a rather less ground-breaking paradigm than at first appears. Thus, *Tenorio feminista* ultimately reproduces heterosexist paradigms of sexual predator and victim, while *Tenorio Sarasa* descends conservatively into comedy.

Linda Hutcheon notes in her seminal text, *A Theory of Parody*, that parody is repetition with critical distance, but 'not always at the expense of the source-text'.[64] We could go further and suggest that the myriad versions that continually refer the reader or spectator back to the source text bolster Zorrilla's *Don Juan Tenorio*. Even Zorrilla's attempts to disparage his own work did nothing to dent the seductive power of his masterpiece.[65] Parodies may constitute a rebellion against a parental figure, in typically Don Juanian fashion, but ultimately they do nothing to destroy the law of the father. Increasingly, in fact, parodies began to be commissioned to accompany the stagings of Zorrilla's classic around the feast of the '*difuntos*', which, as Serrano points, out, were extended to encompass the period from around 20 October to 15 November each year.[66] Due to their 'lowbrow' status, they helped to inscribe Zorrilla's text in opposition as the 'classical', 'highbrow' 'original' and 'canonical' text. 'Firstness' therefore contributes to Zorrilla's canonical status.

In the 1920s intellectuals waded into the debate on Don Juan, despite being rather suspicious of his popularity.[67] Plays on the Don Juan theme flourished in printed form while *tertulias* and mini acting groups took on Zorrilla's classic for an evening's entertainment. Ramón María del

Valle-Inclán was not above joining in an improvization of Zorrilla's *Don Juan Tenorio*, as recorded in the memoirs of Julio Caro Baroja. Someone had to play the part of Brígida, but they did so very badly and Valle-Inclán, who *'no pudo aguantar la actuación torpe'* (could not stand clumsy acting), *'pidió una capa negra, larga, que se colocó a modo de manto rebozado'* (asked for a long black cape, which he tied around himself), tied back his beard and took off his spectacles. *'Y empezó el papel, con todos los dengues, requilorios, inflexiones de voz y convenciones'* (and began the role, with all the tantrums, embellishments, inflections of the voice and conventions) that the role required.[68]

This was not the only occasion on which Valle had cause to express his dislike of a performance of Don Juan. Joaquín Montaner's *El hijo del Diablo* (The Son of the Devil) (1927), created as a vehicle for the great actress Margarita Xirgu, shifts the focus of the tale to a woman, Doña María de Esquivel, mother of a Don Juan (born from her relationship with a Don Juan). The end of the play sees Don Juan (the son) dying in his mother's arms.[69] This production famously led to the arrest of Ramón María del Valle-Inclán who was moved to shout '¡muy mal!' during the applause.

Federico García Lorca, Salvador Dalí and Luis Buñuel also experimented with the performance of a Don Juan version, during their time at the Residencia de Estudiantes. García Lorca took the part of the sculptor, while Buñuel was the protagonist. Buñuel scribbled in his 'profanation' of a cheap edition of Zorrilla's text.[70] It includes modifications such as the following: from the original, *'Quimerista, seductor/y jugador con ventura'*, (Quarrelsome seducer/and player of fortune) Buñuel changes the lines to *'Quimerista seductor/y jugador futbolista'* (Quarrelsome seducer and player of football).[71] Photographs of the production can be seen in Sánchez Vidal's *Buñuel, Lorca, Dalí*.[72] Such

141

experiments with Zorrilla's text were to result in writers' reinterpretations of the classic.

Valle-Inclán's distortion of the Don Juan figure in his play, *Las galas del difunto* (The dead man's finery) (1926) (as well as his prose piece *Sonatas*) has been well-documented.[73] García Lorca arguably presented a variation on the Don Juan figure in his play of 1929, *Así que pasen cinco años* (As Soon as Five Years Pass). The character of the young man is a sort of reluctant Don Juan, but he shares with the legendary seducer a series of relationships with women to whom he never gets properly close, and a desire to flee from death. García Lorca's character reveals the extremes inherent in Don Juan, a figure who hovers at borders. Parody can be seen therefore, as a fruitful medium through which writers could explore the trying out of ideas for their literary reworkings of the myth.

The *mélange* of theatrical styles associated with Don Juan, from high and low culture, from parody to the mainstream, was explored in a 1992 production. José Luis Alonso de Santos's *La sombra del Tenorio* (Don Juan's Shadow) (1994) is a monologue by the protagonist, an ageing actor named Saturnino Morales, played by Rafael Álvarez. It takes place in a hospital in the 1950s (aggressively new in its setting) and yet features the same well-worn characters of old. The mirror in a corner of the room becomes a circular dressing-room mirror, complete with studded lights. The nun sitting in a corner of the room becomes Doña Inés, while Saturnino paces around the stage, puts on and takes off clothes, gets in and out of the bed and interacts with the audience.

The style is clearly metatheatrical – Álvarez the actor plays Morales the actor who reflects on the condition of theatre and life. The play is also a mixture of theatrical styles, composed from the *mélange* of styles that Don Juan has appropriated over the years, presented as the mixture of modes adopted by Saturnino as he tells his story. At once philosophical and literary, the play also incorporates popular genres – such as when Saturnino breaks off the action to address the audience in order to raffle a joint of ham. Through the character of Saturnino, Alonso de Santos is able to take the audience on a journey, an alternative history of the theatre, through anecdotes of past actors who played Don Juan.

Morales is a third-rate actor, forced his whole life to play the part of Ciutti in Zorrilla's *Don Juan*. But his lifelong desire has been to play the role of Don Juan *'en esta obra hacía el papel de Ciutti, el criado, lo que en realidad siempre deseé fue hacer el papel de Don Juan Tenorio, que es mucho más vistoso que el de Ciutti. No sé si me comprende. Más largo, mejores prendas ... más resultón ... Más papel, vamos'* (in this play I took the role of Ciutti, the servant, what I really always wanted was to play the part of Don Juan Tenorio, who is much more colourful than Ciutti. I don't know if you know what I mean. Longer, better clothes ... more impact ... more of a role, if you like).[74] This production would be impossible without the association of 'firstness' attached to Don Juan, the sense in which Don Juan constantly seeks out new genres, new theatrical styles, while the component parts of the drama remain eternally repeated. Even the myriad of parodies merely contributes to the 'sacralization' of Zorrilla's Don Juan.

Between Profanation and Sacralization: Dalí's *Tenorio*

A reconstructive staging of a 1949 production of Zorrilla's *Don Juan Tenorio*, directed by Luis Escobar, with costumes and scenery by Salvador Dalí, was produced in 2003. Under the directorship of Ángel Fernández Montesinos, the 2003 production was marketed as 'El Tenorio de Dalí' (Dalí's Tenorio).[75] In interview, Fernández Montesinos spoke of the difficulties of the *'exhaustivo proceso de investi-*

Tales of Seduction

gación y documentación' (exhaustive process of research and documentation) in bringing the work to the stage, in order to revive a play that was so important in historical memory.[76] María Delgado, in her excellent discussion of alternative theatre histories, notes that:

> the ephemeral nature of the theatrical and its gilded artifice makes it harder to fix and read. It is not surprising that directors, designers, performers and producers who have left no written traces of their work should have slipped through the 'official' documentation of Spanish theatre in the first seven decades of the last century.[77]

Critic Eduardo Haro Tecglen noted that Dalí's sketches for the 1949 production were the property of the Francoist state and have disappeared: *'España era pacata, tristona y relamida; había vuelto atrás para borrar todo el descubrimiento artístico de la primera mitad del siglo'* (Spain was prudish, melancholic and pompous; it turned backward to eliminate all artistic discovery of the first half of the century).[78] Haro Tecglen maintains that not even the pro-Francoism of Salvador Dalí and Luis Escobar could save the production from being looked upon unfavourably by some.[79] Haro Tecglen's words turn the 2003 production into a symbolic resistance to *'olvido'* (forgetting), using research and investigation to interrogate the silences and injustices of the past.

This sense of reconstructive cultural production as a counter-culture to 'official history' is deeply seductive. It purports to gather collective memory, viewing whatever, to quote Michel de Certeau, the official view of the past

> holds to be irrelevant – shards created by the selection of materials, remainders left aside by an explication – comes back, despite everything, on the edges of

discourse or in its rifts and crannies: 'resistances', 'survivals', or delays [which] discreetly perturb the pretty order of a line of 'progress' or a system of interpretation.[80]

The importance of reconstructions that seek to remember and commemorate cultural production that has now slipped into the abyss of a forgotten past should not be denied. Francoism eliminated so much creativity during its long regime. Nevertheless, Dalí's 'Tenorio' seems an unusual example of a standard-bearer for resistance to Francoist cultural vandalism.

Rather than being consigned to oblivion, in this case several attempts were made through different media to fix and shape that most ephemeral of genres, the performance, for later generations. Theatre backdrops designed by Salvador Dalí are housed in Madrid's Reina Sofía Museum; photographs of the production by Gyenes are kept at the Centro de Documentación Teatral in Madrid;[81] grainy images of the production, directors, actors and Dalí himself exist on he NoDo (state newsreel) films, while, unusually, in 1952 Alejandro Perla directed a state-endorsed version of the 1949 production. Filmed in black and white, and disappointingly unimaginative in its camera work (recreating a static, frontal view of the stage) it nevertheless gives some idea of what it must have been like to see Dalí's scenery and costumes in performance.[82]

In 2004, Eduardo Haro Tecglen reminisced that the Escobar–Dalí collaborative production of *Don Juan Tenorio*, '*tuvo mucho de escándalo*' (was quite scandalous).[83] Spectators reportedly applauded or shouted out in disgust, as Jesús Rubio Jiménez notes in his meticulous documentation of the reception of the 1949 and 1950 productions in Madrid and Barcelona.[84]

Press trailers for the production whetted the appetites of

theatre critics and public alike. Luis Escobar remarked that, *'nuestro Tenorio es de Zorrilla, pero por las genialidades de Salvador dará la impresión de que se ve por primera vez. Repito que le hemos quitado el polvo de la costumbre'* (Our Tenorio is Zorrilla's, but with Salvador's genius it will give the impression of being seen for the first time. I repeat that we have blown the dust off tradition).[85] The vexed question of 'firstness' can be seen to run throughout the play's reception. Critics were at pains meticulously to document the different ways in which Dalí's plastic renditions were seen to deviate or to comply with Zorrilla's source text. The butterflies that adorned the walls, for example, had no clear relation to the text, leaving critics and spectators alike to interpret them freely. Haro Tecglen declared that they must be symbols of inconstancy.[86]

On 13 November 1949, Sergio Nerva wrote in *España* that the play *'se ha quedado corto. Tan corto que incluso se han eludido pasajes, dígase lo que quiera'* (has been shortened. So much so that passages have been eliminated, whatever they say). A key scene *'queda reducida a una sugerencia elemental: un cabrilleo de reflejos, a través de un telón de gasa negra'* (is reduced to a mere suggestion: a ripple of reflections through a black chiffon curtain).[87] Dalí turned the *tornera* (gatekeeper) into a faceless nun. Critic Alfredo Marqueríe explained it thus: *'la tornera de un convento es siempre una voz sin rostro'* (the gatekeeper of a convent is always a voice without a face),[88] while for Jorge de la Cueva, writing in *Ya*, Dalí had turned her into a figure of fun that was nowhere to be found in Zorrilla's text: *'no se ha visto ni se verá jamás una tornera vestida de amarillo'* (a gatekeeper dressed in yellow has never been seen nor will such a thing ever be seen).[89] Critics were particularly troubled by the inclusion of the *'Parcas'* (fates), which do not feature in Zorrilla's text. Textual fidelity (faithfulness is bound up in notions of nostalgia) was a matter of most concern to most critics.

Critics bemoaned the lack of imagination used to bring the statue of the comendador to life. They expected fantasy from Dalí. Jorge de la Cueva, writing in *Ya*, writes:

> *Esperábamos ávidos de fantasía los momentos de las apariciones, cómo se habría conseguido el efecto espectral, fantasmal y etéreo, y vemos que el Comendador aparece haciendo sonar el decorado y apartando el papel del telón. Doña Inés aparece nada ingrávida ni espiritual, como pudiera entrar en cualquier comedia, menos una vez que cruza la escena en silla de mano, que nos pareció un vehículo poco sobre natural.* (We waited expectantly for the fantasy of the scenes of the apparitions, how were they going to achieve the spectral, ghost-like and ethereal effects, and we saw that the Comendador appears making the set stand out and pulling aside the paper curtain. Doña Inés is neither weightless nor spiritual, as if she were appearing in any play, apart from once when she crosses the stage on a sedan chair, which seemed to us a vehicle ill-suited to the supernatural.)[90]

What they were really criticizing, arguably, was the inability of the production to achieve a sense of the awe and wonder attached to 'firstness' (a thwarted notion from the start).

Where some critics saw the production as departing too far from the original script, or failing to return spectators to a mythical past, others criticized it for failing to deliver the expected transgression from Dalí, the master of surrealism. The reference to '*quitar el polvo de la costumbre*' (dust off tradition) surely meant radically reworking the safe, traditional productions in favour of something more ground breaking.

Dalí had for some time now been turning his attention to new ways of giving his surrealist vision plastic form. His

Tales of Seduction

famous design of the shop window for Bonwit Teller in Manhattan had been undertaken ten years earlier in 1939. After disagreeing with changes instigated by window-dressers over his display of 'Day and Night', he attempted to overturn a 'hairy bath-tub', thereby smashing the plate glass shop window, an action that led to his arrest.[91]

In 1949, Dalí had turned to set design, accepting commissions for Peter Brook's rendition of Strauss's *Salome* in London's Covent Garden as well as Visconti's version of Shakespeare's *As You Like It* in Rome, alongside Escobar's *Don Juan Tenorio* at the María Guerrero in Madrid. *Salome* was to attract expressions of indignant outrage and scornful mockery, forcing Brook to resign from his post.[92] Visconti's production fared much better, with audiences pleased with the staging, though some leftist critics accused Visconti of betraying neorealism.[93] Escobar's *Don Juan Tenorio* appeared rather tame in the light of Dalí's scandalous reputation. Eduardo Haro Tecglen saw the production as a 'timid' application of his fantasy to symbolize his ideas.[94] Alfredo Marqueríe, writing in *ABC* on 2 November 1949 agrees:

> *Parece como si por amor – ni soñar en temores – el artista hubiese querido contener su tremenda imaginación ante el gusto 'lento' del público español. Ni alegres profanaciones ni posturas docentes. ... trató esa 'mis en scene' [sic] con un surrealismo 'mínimo'. ... En general, los personajes se ataviaron como de costumbre, superados casi exclusivamente por la belleza del figurín. Hubo – sigue pareciéndonos – poquísimas arbitrariedades: ... la sugerencia de flor de Doña Inés, por ejemplo. Los bichos y todo lo demás era lo menos que se podía esperar.* (It seems as if out of love – not to mention fear – the artist had wanted to contain his tremendous imagination in the face of the 'slow' taste of the Spanish public. No

cheerful profanations or instructive positions. He created a *mise-en-scène* with a minimum of surrealism. In general, the characters were rendered as they usually are, almost exclusively taken over by the beauty of the costumes. There were – we still think – very few arbitrary elements: Doña Inés as a flower, for example. The insects and all the rest were just as one would have expected.[95]

As we have seen, Dalí's earlier associations with Don Juan had included an irreverent parody of Zorrilla's text. Later (in the 1960s), his sketches on the theme of Casanova were marked by a singularly pornographic vivacity. This production seems like a muted Dalí, unusual given the associations of Don Juan with overt sexual drive and the potential for psychoanalytic explanations of his motivations. Was Dalí afraid of offending the conservative Spanish public?

In the late 1940s Dalí had responded with enthusiasm to Luis Escobar's invitation to design the costumes and scenery for a major production of the Tenorio. This was despite a greatly reduced fee, which Dalí accepted.[96] In spite of his potential for scandal, in Spain Dalí had gone 'to considerable lengths to convince the Spanish authorities of his enthusiasm for General Franco and of his allegiance to the Catholic Church'.[97] He doubtless saw *Don Juan Tenorio* as a chance to ingratiate himself further with the regime, given that Don Juan had been enjoying a third 'tenoriomania' as a result of the Francoists endorsement of Zorrilla's *Don Juan* for the centenary of the début of the play in 1944.

Luis Escobar, then director of the Teatro María Guerrero, was part of the Francoist establishment, having been given the position of *jefe* del Departamento de Teatro y Música del Servicio Nacional de Propaganda at the end of the civil war in 1939. John London has noted how Escobar had contributed to the victory celebrations of the Falange in July 1939 with a production of Calderón de la Barça's *La cena del Rey Balthasar* (Belshazzar's Feast) surrounded by statues in Madrid's Retiro Park. 'These open-air, triumphalist productions continued well into the 1950s and played on a nostalgia for the culture of Spain's Golden Age firmly rooted in Catholic orthodoxy'.[98]

Furthermore, correspondence between Escobar and Dalí reveals that the director cautioned the painter about the possible misinterpretation of some of his ideas. In a letter of 4 September 1949, Escobar writes, '*estoy seguro de que has puesto las mariposas por su pompa fúnebre y fatídica*' (I am sure that you have put the butterflies in because of their funereal and portentous pomp).[99] Yet he is concerned that they may be interpreted differently as '*aquello que las señoras llaman mariposas a los novios que plantan a sus hijas "mariposones" y la explicación es todavía peor porque es por ir "de flor en flor" como toda esta horrible historia tiene una cierta relación con el donjuanismo, tengo miedo de que lo tomen por ahí*' (the way women give the name of butterflies to boyfriends who leave their daughters and the explanation is even worse because it is because they go 'from flower to flower' and as all of that horrible story has a certain relationship to donjuanismo, I'm afraid they might interpret it like that).

Perhaps Escobar was also afraid of the connotations linking butterflies to homosexuality, given that since Marañón the figure of Don Juan had been linked to the 'effeminate' male. As it is, Rubio Jiménez notes a tension in Dalí's designs that are causing the production to descend into parody: elements such as the *tornera* dressed in yellow, for example, produced hilarity in the audience.

Dalí's production was, however, innovative in that it pushed scenography to the fore in a way that had been unusual for the mainstream Spanish stage.[100] As the

Repetition Compulsion: Redoing the Tenorio

curtains part at the beginning of the production, a china plate falls from one of the stage walls, a symbol of evil portents. It is a self-conscious piece of staging that at first sight appears almost amateurish (did it fall accidentally?) before the realization that it is part of the grand design. This is the first of many ways in which the scenography takes centre stage in the production. It is almost as if Dalí were pushing the plate himself, like a tricksterish sprite, reminding the audience that he is behind the set designs for this elaborate production in which huge backdrops threaten almost to engulf the action.

Giant butterflies adorn the walls of Don Juan's dining room. In Dalí's Donjuanesque aesthetic for the production, the carnival atmosphere is achieved through a variety of gigantic and large-headed masks, *'gigantes y cabezudos'*. The play opens with a gnome-like figure seated on an enormous tortoise, while giant papier-mâché faces loom down on the proceedings at the Hostería del Laurel. Dalí's other thematic is the natural world (always linked to death): thus, leaves, lizards and giant butterflies climb the walls, while in the cemetery female statues hold hands and enormous sunflowers are arranged to appear from a distance like colossal skulls.

Enormous figures shuffle their way along a vast painted canvas. In scene action, the effect is of a series of characters having wandered into a Dalí painting. There is an interesting relationship on stage between movement and stasis that is rather like the inverse of a tableau vivant, the custom of arranging the static composition of actors' bodies into the form of famous paintings. Here, rather, the components of a painting are seen to move and come to life. Thus, while critics bemoaned the lack of imagination used in the production to bring the statue of the *Comendador* to life, they might have commented on the way the stage setting as a whole appears like a painting come to

151

Tales of Seduction

11. Scene from the Luis Escobar production of *Don Juan Tenorio*, with scenography by Salvador Dalí.

life. Nevertheless, the audience is never allowed to forget the subtext, which is that Dalí's designs are the core component of the performance.[101]

A critic of the 1950 production (a reworking of the 1949 one) José Camón Aznar, mused on the scant critical attention conferred on the work of the scenographer in the Spanish stage. Scenography is '*otro arte que debía de provocar una mayor actividad crítica*' (another art that should provoke more criticism). Dalí's designs, he maintains, '*abre[n] una nueva interpretación a la tarea del escenógrafo, Ya no son los telones que delimitan el espacio los que localizan y ambientan el juego escénico. Ya son inútiles esas precisiones descriptivas con que el autor encabeza los actos*' (open a new interpretation on the work of the scenographer. It is no longer the curtains dividing the space that situate and orient the scenographic action. Those precise descriptions with which the author heads his acts are now redundant).[102]

Repetition Compulsion: Redoing the Tenorio

12. Backdrop designed by Salvador Dalí for Luis Escobar's production of *Don Juan Tenorio*, 1949.

In the eyes of one critic, at least, Dalí was opening the way for a new way of interpreting theatre: one that moved away from text-based criticism and into the performative. It is certainly true that after Dalí, scenographers gained more critical recognition for their work. The likes of Gerardo Vera, Francisco Nieva, Siegfried Burmann, Wolfgang Burmann, Manuel Mampasso and Miguel Narros are respected names in the sphere of theatrical artistic design and scenography in the way that Giorgio Busato, Amalio Fernández and José María Avrial y Flores were not.[103]

Successive renditions of the 1949 Escobar production (it was repeated in 1950 and 1964) played on the 'scandal' and 'polemic' it was said to have attracted. An argument broke out when a critic, Accorde, attacked the 1950 production, leading Escobar and Dalí to respond with a letter published in *ABC* musing over why that same critic should have changed tack so sharply after defending Dalí's scene designs

153

Tales of Seduction

for the ballet *Tristán el loco* (Tristan the Mad). The theme of the misuse of public money runs through this attack.[104]

In 1964, Dalí seemed to free himself from whatever restraints had been holding him back in the 1949 version and put forward his vision for a radical reworking of his designs. This production featured '*un televisor en las escenas de la cena y del cementerio*' (a television in the dinner and cemetery scenes), and '*una gran calavera compuesta con el guarismo 50477 que según Dalí será el "gordo" de Navidad*' (a great skull adorned with the figure 50,477, which, according to Dalí, was the winning number for the lottery), as well as '*un Comendador que atraviesa muros y otras extravagancias cuya explicación se confía a la fantasía particular de cada espectador*' (a Comendador who passed through walls, and other extravagances for which explanations are confined to the private fantasies of each spectator).[105]

Yet, by now the production enjoyed none of the polemic attached to previous versions, even when Dalí himself appears in the audience, drawing the number 50,477, which gradually turned into a skull throughout the first act at the play's première, before announcing to the audience that next year he would produce a '*Tenorio a base de helicópteros y submarinos*' (Tenorio with helicopters and submarines).[106]

Critics of the reconstructive staging in 2003 approached the production with nostalgia. Eduardo Haro Tecglen, who had also attended the earlier productions, wrote of the '*rescoldo de una emoción*' (embers of an emotion) the production provoked for him.[107] He noted that '*los escenarios se han quedado anticuados y pobres, los figurines son espectaculares y bellos pero sin novedad*' (the set designs look old fashioned and poor, the costumes are spectacular and beautiful but without novelty) while the '*audacias escénicas*' (audacious scenery design) had now been overtaken by other scenographers of greater calibre.[108] Javier Villán expresses a nostalgic desire to have attended the first productions:

Repetition Compulsion: Redoing the Tenorio

confieso que me hubiera gustado ver la textura, la materialidad de estos telones dalinianos, primorosamente reconstruidos por modernas técnicas. ... Confieso que me hubiera gustado ver la mano de Dalí en el 49 (María Guerrero) y el 50 (Teatro Español) y no sólo el espíritu fervorosamente aspirado en esta ocasión por Burmann y Pedro Moreno bajo la batuta de Fernández Montesinos. (I confess that I would have liked to have seen the texture, the material nature of those Daliesque curtains, exquisitely reconstructed modern techniques. I confess that I would have liked to have seen the hand of Dalí in 1949 (at the María Guerrero) and 1950 (Teatro Español) and not just the spirit feverishly aspired to on this occasion by Burmann and Pedro Moreno under Fernández Montesinos's direction.)[109]

'*Vistos hoy*' (seen today), writes Juan Ignacio García Garzón, '*los diseños de Dalí tienen evidente empaque aunque están lastrados por una anticuada concepción en la que priman los telones pintados frente a los elementos corpóreos. Los figurines son, en cambio, primorosos e imaginativos*' (Dalí's designs are imposing although they are weighed down by an antiquated conception in which painted curtains outweigh corporeal elements. The costumes, by contrast, are exquisite and imaginative.)[110] Once more, critics sought 'firstness' in a sense of awe and wonder (in this case at Dalí's beautiful designs). Haro Tecglen mentions the 'escándalo' associated with the production. However, as we have seen, and in Jesús Rubio Jiménez's document of the event, the scandal appeared to be reduced to dissension over how the text ought to be interpreted.

Haro Tecglen cites one of the main reasons for going to see the production as '*la de la recuperación de una cultura que andaba a empujones*' (the recuperation of a culture that was struggling to survive).[111] For him, attending the

Tales of Seduction

performance transports the spectator back to an age when cultural production was struggling in the face of political opposition. Its nostalgia is for a time when culture was clearly drawn along ideological lines and theatre going (even 'mainstream' theatre going) could be seen as an act of resistance to fascism.

Of course, Haro Tecglen is also suggesting that to attend the production was to celebrate the richness of Spanish theatre since the conservative 1950s. But a year before the Dalí centenary, this production celebrated two great stalwarts of Spanish heritage brought together on stage once more – Dalí (the enduring symbol of Spanish surrealism) and Zorrilla (the canonical writer of prestige).

5. EMPTY PROMISES: OPERA AND THE AESTHETICS OF CULTURAL CONSUMPTION

A great house, a strange one, in the heart of the city. Nightfall, going to the opera. Changing worlds. Trading the working world for one of fantastic, fleeting leisure. Climbing giant staircases. Bronze women proffer fake torches, ceilings full of goddesses and gods watch with indifference; evening cloaks trail their velvet hems with old-fashioned grace on the marble floor; bit by bit a dull roar swells the festive house. ...

Entering the opera. Passing one by one through the gates of ritual; buying tickets, presenting them, letting oneself be guided by a woman who opens the doors, penetrating the heart. The immense room, red and gold, white and gold, blue and gold: always the gold of the balconies, the garlanded gold. In this architecture can be read a whole, no longer existent world. The ghosts of a society wander here in a dream. ... Opera is the place for intrigues, love affairs, glances that intersect and never meet again.

Tales of Seduction

> ... Theatre house and stage are a match for each other, reflecting the same golden image: the long gowns, the pomp of festive bourgeois in search of a forgotten nobility, correspond to the brilliant spectacle and the stage costumes. ...
> The lights, slowly and imperceptibly go down. The noises of the crowd are hushed. A few coughs surface; these are people, after all. The orchestra tunes up, improvising; for an instant, on the horn, a sad melody from the third act lingers. ... Trompe l'oeil: the curtain goes up on a forest of gauze and wood, on a palace of cloth. Always it grows cooler when the curtain rises; a breath of air moves from the stage into the audience. And the voices begin their rise.[1]

In the above quotation Clément captures an imprint of the hushed and hallowed space repeatedly created by opera for a ritualized and leisured opulence, a night of orchestrated fantasy, where audience and stage are a mirror image of one another, both searching for a 'forgotten nobility'.[2] Against such a scene, Pierre Bourdieu's conception of 'distinction', in which opera is a marker of a 'legitimate culture', and his linkage through anthropology of the aesthetics of culture to the vulgar politics of consumption appears profane.[3]

No less profane is Calixto Bieito's 2001 version of the Mozart/Da Ponte opera *Il Dissoluto punito o sia il Don Giovanni* (hereafter, *Don Giovanni*) which was a Gran Teatre del Liceu/English National Opera/Staatsoper d'Hannover co-production. Bieito's update, I argue, is not only profoundly anti-nostalgic in terms of its *mise-en-scène*, but also stages and objectifies a politics of consumption in late capitalist society in ways that some of its audiences have found deeply transgressive.[4]

Consumption is an imprecise, slippery term, but, according to Tim Edwards, it can be pinned down in contem-

Empty Promises: Opera and the Aesthetics of Cultural Consumption

porary understanding to three broad definitions.[5] First, it is consumerism (the organized practice of consumers) and this in turn is related to shopping, or purchasing merchandise to fulfil needs or wants. Second, consumption is associated with leisure, the reception of services, cultural or leisure activities as the 'conceptual flipside' to production and work. Third, it connects with the activity of consuming itself, whether through eating and drinking, or, metaphorically, through viewing and listening.

At its simplest, consumption has to do with devouring, taking in, or (more negatively) using up or wasting. It can be strongly linked to desire and 'there is an immediate connection with the more psychoanalytic dimensions of the question of consumption and a direct parallel between desiring goods or services and wanting sexual gratification'.[6] To this heady mix, we could add that for Bourdieu, consumption (of goods, services or cultural/leisure activities) is an expression of taste (with all its connotations of the discriminatory eating of food), wherein consumption becomes an affirmation of social and economic status.

In this chapter, I explore the interconnected themes of consumption surrounding Bieito's production of *Don Giovanni*, moving between addressing consumption as a leisure activity (the commodification and reception of this opera in performance) and consumerism as a theme within the diegesis. Press reports of the reception of Bieito's operatic update in production at London's Coliseum in 2001 are read against Bourdieu's description of the aesthetics of cultural consumption. Drawing on Bourdieu and Theodor Adorno, I view opera-going as a form of cultural commodification, where class and economic status are confirmed by cultural taste.

Using cannibalism as a motif, I explore how Bieito's version may interrogate Otto Rank's analysis of the Don Juan myth, to draw parallels between Freud's primal scene of the violent act of consumption at the root of society in *Totem and Taboo* and the consumerism of late-capitalist society. Finally, moving out from the internal dynamic of the production, the reception of the London and Barcelona productions is contrasted to consider how Bieito's opera (with its postmodern, cannibalistic blend of high and low culture) has been packaged as a cultural product to attract new consumers of opera in the twenty-first century.

The Aesthetics of Cultural Consumption
The orchestra, in evening dress and led by a tuxedoed conductor, just visible above the warmly-lit pit, sends out the cathedral of sound that is Mozart's overture to *Don Giovanni*, with its traditionally unorthodox shades of *ombra* in D minor, signalling 'unusual and portentous events'.[7] The heavy curtains part to reveal a minimalist set cut up by tall street lamps that cast shadows across the stage. Bieito sets the action for his *Don Giovanni* in Barcelona's Olympic Port but here it resembles an empty car park. A car, headlights blazing, advances to centre stage. Its driver, Leporello, a dishevelled tracksuit-wearing Barça supporter and taxi driver, proceeds to trample a Real Madrid banner into the ground.[8] Donna Anna and Don Giovanni emerge from the back seat of the taxi, the latter with his trousers around his ankles, indicative of recent crude passions; the former dressed in tight black skirt and leopard-print top, suggesting a 'good time girl'.[9] When Anna's father, the Commendatore, arrives to warn off her daughter's new boyfriend, he is stabbed by Don Giovanni, blood spattering his white shirt, as he slumps against the front of the car. Donna Elvira, dressed in hooded top, trainers and carrying shopping bags, laments her broken love affair with Don Giovanni.

In a later scene, Don Giovanni has arranged a wedding feast for his friends with the intention of seducing the bride Zerlina (who will later demand oral stimulation through

Empty Promises: Opera and the Aesthetics of Cultural Consumption

13. The Wedding Feast. Bieito's Barcelona production of *Don Giovanni*.

the layers of her wedding dress). The feast is a carnivalesque riot of dressing-up and disguise and takes place in a nightclub replete with icy blue lighting, snooker table and bar stools. Ottavio (Anna's betrothed) wears a limp Superman costume, Don Giovanni sports a Mexican sombrero and wheels himself around in a wheelchair, while Masetto (the groom) is resplendent in tight gold trousers, shoes and John Travolta-style wedding suit. At the end of the party, the 'wreckage of Giovanni's actions lies across the stage in chaos' as the layers of Zerlina's wedding dress, 'bottles, discarded clothes and sleepy bodies litter the floor'.[10]

In Act Two Don Giovanni swaps clothes with Leporello and dons his *'chándal de Barça'* with the intention of carrying out further seductions. The final scenes take place in Don Giovanni's filthy kitchenette/bachelor pad, where Leporello cooks stodgy food on a cramped stove and Don Giovanni sits on a stained sofa to watch a home video of

Tales of Seduction

14. An evening of wrecked stagecraft. Bieito's Barcelona production of *Don Giovanni*.

the wedding ceremony, and in turn masturbates, eats cereal with his hands (alternately stuffing it into his mouth, into Leporello's mouth and throwing it across the room), and urinates behind and on the sofa before wiping his soiled hands on Leporello's shirt and hair.

The Commendatore, who was apparently killed in Act One, emerges downstage from the boot of the car and, after attempting to stuff the starchy mass cooked by Leporello into Don Giovanni's mouth, is again stabbed by him and slumps once again, this time quite dead. In a final scene, the other characters enter, take advantage of Don Giovanni's confusion to tie him to a chair, and then take it in turns to stab him ritually to death 'à la Murder on the Orient Express'[11] as he quivers against the chair back.

Reviews by critics in the United Kingdom of the 2001 London Coliseum production were characterized in the main by censure. British critics disliked the parade of sex on

Empty Promises: Opera and the Aesthetics of Cultural Consumption

15. A reinterpretation of the 'escena del sofá'. Bieito's production of *Don Giovanni*.

stage: Michael Tanner among others was shocked by Donna Anna's copulation with Don Ottavio during the 'Non mi dir' aria, her 'coloratura flights elicited by his penetration'. 'I didn't try to keep a tally of the unzippings, the gropings', wrote Tanner in *The Spectator*, 'but it must be impressive'.[12]

In the main, critics regarded the onstage violence as overblown and out of place, recalling Tarantino's visceral cinematic excesses.[13] This was an evening of 'wrecked stagecraft' set among 'youth club culture', a 'self-indulgent wallow in coke-snorting, lager-swilling, bloodthirsty excess. It looked awful too.'[14] Critics took offence at the rubbish that littered the stage throughout the piece that 'Bieito might eventually come to realize is as apt a metaphor as possible for his own shoddy and slapdash production.'[15]

Above all, critics lamented the passing of a display of class: 'as Don Giovanni was portrayed as a lower-middle-class thug, just like the others, the theme of class divisions

163

was also ditched.'[16] Elvira was dressed, like most of the cast, 'as if by Oxfam',[17] a 'deranged bag-lady'.[18] Interestingly, the depictions of class on stage appear to cross over into the presumed target audience for this production: 'This is a Don Giovanni for Ibiza man and Essex girl.'[19] 'This is a Don Giovanni for yobbos, attaining the intellectual level of football hooligans.'[20] The production was met with 'angry scenes' in London's Coliseum, according to Bird,[21] with the audience baying 'for Bieito's blood'.[22] The director's bow was greeted with 'boos, hisses and catcalls'[23] and 'many waved programmes', while apparently some of the audience got through the performance by watching with their eyes closed.[24]

The booing and catcalling was not unanimous at the opening night of the production at London's Coliseum. A section of the audience countered the displays of disapproval with cheers, causing critic Michael Kennedy to comment that 'there's no accounting for taste, or lack of it'.[25] For Bourdieu, in his seminal work *Distinction: A Social Critique of the Judgement of Taste*, taste classifies, and it classifies the classifier. A hierarchy of the arts reflects and affirms (in *mise-en-abyme*) a hierarchy of socially stratified classes. Opera, for Bourdieu, (alongside other culturally consecrated 'legitimate' culture) presents 'an occasion for conspicuous spending', an opportunity for a 'select audience to demonstrate and experience its membership of high society in obedience to the integrating and distinguishing rhythms of the "society" calendar'.[26]

Theodor Adorno, writing in 1938, sought to bring out the links between opera and consumerism. Thus he declared that the commodities of opera (the 'gratifyingly hefty libretto booklet', audio recordings), coupled with opera-goers' obsessions with the voices of 'cult' singing star-turns, make opera listeners as 'regressive' and 'fetishistic' as those who listen to pop or 'easy-listening' music. The opera goer, writes Adorno, is nothing more than a consumer who is 'really worshipping the money that he himself has paid for the ticket to the Toscanini concert'. The commodification of opera is so much 'phony hoopla', which detracts from the music.[27]

The 'hefty libretto booklet' that accompanied Bieito's production would seem to bear out both Adorno's equation of opera with commodity fetishism, and Bourdieu's mirrored reflection between aesthetic distinction and social class (with its blend of cultural and economic capital). The programmes designed to accompany the London and Barcelona productions featured a mix of photographs of scenes from the productions, blurred scenes of clubbers on a night out, excerpts of writings on the history of the Don Juan myth and on the opera, brief biographical sketches of the performers and, in the Spanish version, a full-text version of the libretto in Italian and in translation.

Common to both booklets were glossy advertisements targeting an elite customer, what Veblen would term a 'conspicuous consumer'.[28] In the Spanish programme, alongside advertisements for perfume, in French and Italian, a lexical borrowing or language fetishism Kelly-Holmes claims is typical of pan-European intercultural advertising,[29] we also find an advert for *Zenith*, a Swiss watch, which proclaims its status as 'Class. Elite.' An advertisement for 'Brut Barroco Freixenet', a brand of Spanish champagne, draws on the distinctions of both fine art and wine tasting, while the *Lexus RX300* car runs under the caption, '*Andante, Allegro. Vivace. Tú decides cómo quieres dirigir tu vida*' (Andante, Allegro. Vivace. You decide how to conduct your life), a clear calling to the elision of lifestyle (what Bourdieu would define as the 'habitus'), cultural capital and high finances. In a series of mirrorings, the opera audience becomes a shop window for the display of conspicuous consumption, and of social class.

In his analysis of taste, Bourdieu speaks of the sacred sphere of culture where culture is consecrated by its distancing from facile pleasure.[30] In UK press reports of Bieito's production we find mention of 'vulgar abuse' and 'coarseness',[31] which caused 'revulsion', was 'disgusting', and even, reminiscent of Bourdieu's reconnection of aesthetic taste with gastronomy, featured certain 'juicy bits'.[32] Critics found Bieito's interpretation facile (recalling Bourdieu's invocation of Ortega y Gasset's rejection of the 'human'), his characters were 'caricatures' that were inappropriate to this 'enigmatic opera', and was 'terrified of depth and content to rest in the most tawdry contemporary clichés'.[33]

At the same time it portrayed the lives of ordinary people, moreover 'with no trace of ... breeding',[34] which recalls Bourdieu's observation that 'aversion to different life-styles is perhaps one of the strongest barriers between the classes; class endogamy is evidence of this'.[35] Critics also disliked the references to popular culture within opera, another example of what Bourdieu terms 'the sacrilegious reuniting of tastes which taste dictates shall be separated'.[36] 'Vulgar' works, writes Bourdieu, are an insult to 'refinement, a slap in the face to a "demanding" audience, which will not stand for "facile" offerings (it is a compliment to an artist, ... to say he "respects his audience"'.[37]

In Bieito's case, 'we're invited to sneer at how disgusting human life has become, while suspecting that the director is sneering at *us*.'[38] Finding a lack of reciprocity between the distinguished audience and their reflection on stage, the members of the audience who expressed their displeasure at the London production were playing out their membership of an upper class, searching for a 'forgotten nobility'.[39] This mismatch between audience and stage may recall Valle-Inclán's paradigm for *esperpento*, in which characters and events are not heroic and godlike, as in the age of Greek tragedy, but base and puny, with characters and events distorted by a fairground mirror of attractions.[40] In the twenty-first century, when distinctions between high and low art are thought to have been eroded, Bieito shows that cultural hierarchies remain.

'Sex Sells'

Don Giovanni (written in 1787) is the most controversial of the Mozart/Da Ponte collaborations, and the one that has attracted the most critical response.[41] Its dramatic finale of eternal damnation has been seen as curiously at odds with Enlightenment principles,[42] while its mischievous overturning of social classes has been seen as variously subversive or merely reinforcing the chaos that ensues when class hierarchies are ignored.[43] The thorny question of sexual violence stalks both the opera and its criticism.

Leporello's recanting of Don Giovanni's sexual adventures in the so-called 'Catalogue aria' is comic opera at its best, while Don Giovanni's ability to seduce is made evident in the 'Là ci darem la mano' serenade to Zerlina. But, as Kernan points out, Don Giovanni's seduction of Zerlina (the only seduction that takes place on stage), follows a trajectory from flirtatiousness to rape.[44] The offstage scream is what unites Zerlina, Elvira and Anna. 'This is the one who is the Rapist', writes Clément, 'the one who is no longer entirely "Don Juan"', signalling a move from seduction to sexual violence.[45] What may be attributed to the spirit of the age,[46] to an hysterical desire to be seduced on the part of the female characters,[47] or to a displacement through metaphor to other meanings, can also assume contemporary relevance, such as for example, Curtis, who muses on the lack of adequate theoretical background within musicology available when teaching *Don Giovanni* to female students learning in an atmosphere of 'date-rape' on US college campuses.[48]

Tales of Seduction

Yet, for many critics, music is the saviour of Don Giovanni. Kristeva writes that to strip the tale of its stylistic effects, in other words, to subtract the music, 'Don Giovanni is merely a feverish, pretentious lecher who takes advantage of the weakness of women and the common people, the more aroused as another man sidles close to his coveted mistress'.[49] But music changes everything. 'Instead of the sullen claims of the victim, the air resounds with the pure jouissance of a conqueror, but the conqueror who knows he has no object, who does not want one, who loves neither triumph nor glory in themselves, but the passing of both – the eternal return, infinitely so.'[50]

For Kristeva, the musical Don Giovanni is not narcissistic, but rather his lack of internality turns him into a 'multiplicity, a polyphony'.[51] For Kristeva, who draws on the work of Kierkegaard, Don Giovanni with music is elevated to an abstraction. In Kierkegaard, Don Giovanni's music is an example of the 'sensuous erotic'. He is the sensuous seducer. His 'inner vitality' breaks forth through the music, he effervesces like the champagne in his favourite aria: 'just as the beads in this wine, as it shimmers with internal heat, sonorous with its own melody, rise and continue to rise, just so the lust for enjoyment resonates in the elemental boiling that is his life'.[52]

The musical Don Giovanni may be abstract, but he resounds with sensuality: the jouissance of a conqueror, the elemental boiling over of the rising melody. Music itself performs a seduction. For de Certeau,[53] opera permits the expression of 'the voice of the body': 'the opera allows an enunciation to speak that in its most elevated moments detaches itself from statements, disturbs and interferes with syntax, and wounds or pleasures, in the audience, those places in the body that have no language either.' Koestenberg, less subtly, draws out the equation between operatic climaxes and the orgasm.[54]

Empty Promises: Opera and the Aesthetics of Cultural Consumption

Sex infuses Don Giovanni, both textually and musically, yet UK press reports of Calixto Bieito's 2001 production highlighted the inappropriateness of the graphic displays of sex within opera on stage. Bieito's production raises interesting questions about the representation of sex within opera.[55] Abel writes that 'opera is a sexual act played out between the performance and the audience.'[56] Bieito tests the limits of public acceptability in his graphic representations of the sexual act on stage, but Clément has shown that opera uses sex to persuade us to accept its violent vision of sexual politics. Traditionally, opera often portrays female characters as victims, as Clément elaborates, or as consumptive weak figures, mere projections of male desire, as Susan McClary and Peter and Linda Hutcheon have sought to expose. Sally Potter offers a passionate deconstruction of opera's sexual politics in her 1979 film, *Thriller*, which is itself a recasting of *La Bohème*.[57]

Interestingly, in Bieito's production, there is no rape: sex is graphic, public or furtive, but takes place between consenting adults. Bieito's females are stricken with lovesickness, and with an obsessive desire for unattainable ideals, yet they are also earthy sexual beings who seek pleasure where they can find it and are not afraid to lament loudly if a sexual partner treats them badly. Bieito's production raises the uncomfortable question of why an opera like *Don Giovanni*, with its ever-present suspicion of rape, should be more acceptable if clothed in the veneer of elaborate costumes (markers of 'history') and beautiful music rather than interpreted with graphic stage sexual scenes. Bieito's production subtly raises questions about our consumption of sex, which, when dressed in mystery and seduction, an oral and visual feast (Brecht referred to opera as 'the culinary art'), makes even the most difficult topics palatable.

Tales of Seduction

Shopping and (Fucking) with Mozart

With sex centre stage and rape removed from the scene, Bieito shifts the focus of the *Don Giovanni* tale. Desire, seduction and consumption still feature, but here Don Giovanni's sexual gratification is aligned with mass consumerism. Bieito brings *Don Giovanni* up to date, implicating us all in this story of ecstasy and waste in late capitalist society. Thus, the vacuous tale of sexual conquests is translated into the emptiness of the pursuance of commodities.

Juliet Mitchell has drawn out the atmosphere of 'wanting and wanting and wanting', alongside a culture of lying, to be found in *Don Giovanni*, a combination she finds has striking parallels with the landscape of the hysteric.[58] In Bieito's version, this atmosphere of 'wanting' is translated into varying forms of consumption, which move between images of incorporation and references to mass consumerism. The 'lie' is the promise of satisfaction the commodity offers upon its attainment: yet consumption merely sets off a never-ending chain of desire.

Bieito locates the action in the Barcelona of the smart restaurants and chic shops that moved in following the investments for the 1992 Olympic Games. According to Cester, Bieito shows a Barcelona *'en plena resaca olímpica'* (in full Olympic hangover),[59] yet the gleaming fronts of the new buildings of the Olympic Port are no more than what Augé would term a 'non-place',[60] typical of urban landscapes, a deserted space of 'furtive surveillance'.[61] This is the underside of modern commercial development: spaces devoid of community and deserted at night, the domain of gangs of youths who can find dark spaces to provide cover for acts of murder. This landscape will provide the setting for a night of *'juerga salvaje llevada al límite'* (wild partying taken to the limit),[62] an alcohol and drug fuelled binge that goes too far.

In this atmosphere of violent nihilism, Donna Anna will

develop a phantom pregnancy, symbolic of her unsatisfied desire, the awareness of emptiness where plenitude is desired. Donna Elvira, whose ritornello 'Ah! Chi mi dice mai' appears framed by the orchestra in such a way that 'she seems not to be mistress of her movements',[63] in Bieito's version is carrying shopping bags after a spree – retail therapy to assuage a broken heart. She binges on chocolate, evidence of an eating disorder propelled, perhaps, by the images of femininity conjured up by the improbable vital statistics of the Barbie dolls that litter the stage in the final scenes. Bieito's production is filled with the phantoms of lost desires.

With the class boundaries removed from Bieito's version, clothing becomes not a marker of social class but of allegiances (Leporello wears the *Barça* stripe); occasion (Zerlina's wedding dress), or else displays varying degrees of 'bling bling' ostentatiousness. 'Masetto's snugly fitting gold trousers, shoes and flamboyant wedding shirt and jacket confirm the dictum that money shouts and wealth whispers.'[64] Don Giovanni puts on Leporello's tracksuit to gain confidences and avoid retribution. Identity becomes a commodity that can be bought and sold with a new suit.

Bieito's Don Giovanni is neither a nobleman nor seductive rogue, but rather a sordid drug pusher: his charisma with the other characters comes from dependency (there are suggestions that Leporello is hooked on drugs) and the flashy display of wealth and power. Don Giovanni is the arch conspicuous consumer. He (who is traditionally 'empty' musically)[65] is here revealed to be bolstered by petty iconography: as Bieito has remarked, *'se cree alguien porque tiene una pistola y cuatro tarjetas de crédito'* (he thinks he is somebody because he has a gun and four credit cards).[66] The Barbie dolls scattered around Don Giovanni's apartment are a reference to the many women he seduces, outlined in the 'catalogue aria', an operatic *buffa* in which

Tales of Seduction

Leporello enumerates Giovanni's conquests from peasants to countesses, punctuated by the fanfare '*Ma in Spagna son gia mille tre*' (in Spain the number is already one thousand and three).

The aria may be an ironic take on the catalogue of ships that set sail to conquer foreign lands in *The Iliad*, but here the catalogue is a reference, through Giovanni's sexual conquests, to consumption: an accumulation of markers to display his success. Barbie is an ironic take on the shop-window mannequin, an equation that links Don Giovanni's serial conquests with shopping. The hedonism of a heartless seducer is here linked to the pleasures of consumerist acquisition. Barbie, after all, with her endless catalogue of accessories, home furnishings and bewildering changes in life-styles (changeable with the purchase of new commodities) is the 'plastic princess of conspicuous consumption',[67] and here Don Giovanni's never ending desire for the next woman is compared with the consumerist desires of a little girl, for whom one Barbie doll is never enough. Sexual desire and consumerism, both based on 'wanting and wanting and wanting', are neatly aligned in a visual pun.

A production of *Don Giovanni* in Salzburg in 2002 drew out the relationship between sexual lust and the desire for commodities by specularizing the fantasy played out by the visual language of advertising: beautiful women in tights stalked across the stage, which became as phantasmagorical as a shop window. The action was set in an airport: the perfect setting for the elision of casual sex and shopping. The accompanying programme, with prose in German, highlighted headings in English – 'Sex Sells', 'Permanent Prada'.

Bieito's production, meanwhile, acts to expose commodity fetishism as reification: his focus is the waste that is the underside of the allure of consumption. Rachel Bowlby has written that shopping is 'at once ecstasy and waste'. There are 'exorbitant private pleasures' writes Bowlby, 'to

Empty Promises: Opera and the Aesthetics of Cultural Consumption

be got from sniffing and seeing and touching', the packaging surrounding a purchase, pleasures linked to the memories of childlike expectation.[68] But waste can also be the tired reminder of the short-lived thrill and anticipation of the purchase. By focusing attention on the discarded packaging that we normally choose to ignore, Bieito enacts a carnivalesque move that is shocking in its combination of ordinariness and incongruity: this is an aspect of modern living we would choose to ignore.

The litter some UK critics were so disgusted to see filling the stage is nothing more than the debris of modern consumerism: empty packets, convenience foods, bits and pieces of clothing, a hypermarket shopping trolley, durable goods, TVs, fridges, video cameras which, when scattered around the stage, become just so much rubbish. Thus where Don Giovanni discards women in his haste to consume, Bieito's production is trailed with images of rubbish: a conspicuous consumer is measured by the volume of waste that remains as a residue of his or her squandering. Bieito's production is carnivalesque in that it focuses attention on an aspect of consumption we would choose to ignore – the rubbish that is a by-product. Waste, in Bieito's production, is the grim, anti-nostalgic underside of the mass consumption in which we are all implicated.

Dying of Consumption

Of all Mozart's operatic finales, none has drawn more criticism than the second act finale of *Don Giovanni*. After a scene in which Don Giovanni descends into Hell, we find that, 'having sorted out their marital and other affairs in a matter of fact way as though Don Giovanni's demise is good riddance to bad rubbish, the other characters conclude by taking the high ground in their "Questo è il fin di chi fa mal"'.[69] Described as a trivialization,[70] and 'woefully inappropriate',[71] the final scene was omitted in nineteenth-century productions,[72] leaving directors who choose to produce the work with the option of two endings.

Bieito takes liberties with Da Ponte's libretto. He recasts the traditional scene of the walking, talking Stone Guest, the Commendatore, who returns from the dead to drag Don Giovanni down into the earth, as a scene borrowed from a cinematic gangster plot, where the corpse, who has been shot, blood spattered and bundled into the boot of a car, is discovered not to have died at all, but emerges again, *'detrás de un coche, lleno de sangre como en una película de Scorsese'* (from behind a car, full of blood like in a Scorsese film). Bieito has commented that, *'mi aparición no es una estatua porque pensaba, con una estatua mi niño de un año se ríe porque no se lo cree y debe provocar terror'* (my apparition is not a statue because I thought that my one year-old son would laugh at a statue because it is not believable and it ought to provoke terror).[73]

In Bieito's version, the other characters will round on Don Giovanni, stabbing him ritually on stage to take their revenge. Bieito chose a newspaper story as the basis for the twist to his plot, the so-called, *'Crimen de la Villa Olímpica'* (Crime of the Olympic Village) in which a gang of youths stabbed another to death seemingly without motive.[74] In Bieito's anti-nostalgic vision, home is a Godless place where group murders take place on the city streets.

While Baker has found the significance of the Stone Guest in tomb sculpture in the eighteenth century,[75] Otto Rank in 1922 traced the origins of the stone statue through myth to the legend of the 'flesh-eating Demon of Death who avenges the primal crime'.[76] Rank notes that the demon is a ghostly apparition representative of the pangs of conscience, but he emphasizes the metaphor of devouring in the early myth. The demon 'returns from the grave to devour the guilty'.

Trying to find a parallel for the Don Juan story in the writings of Sigmund Freud, who, famously, never wrote about the Don Giovanni myth, Rank locates the myth in Freud's reconstruction of a primal history in *Totem and Taboo* (1913).[77] Taking up Darwin's notion of a primal horde, Freud constructs a mythical story to account for universal exogamy. Freud mentions a 'violent and jealous father who keeps all the females for himself and drives away his sons as they grow up'.[78] One day, the brothers who have been driven away, return to kill and devour the father, 'and so made an end to the patriarchal horde'. Their hatred satisfied, and their wish to identify with him achieved, then, a 'sense of guilt made its appearance',[79] thereby installing a taboo against eating the totem (the taboo on cannibalism) and against having sexual relations with the other women of the horde (taboo against incest). Rank finds a correlation between the avenging ghost who returns to devour the guilty in the Don Juan myth, and Freud's tale of primal patricide. Furthermore, the totemic meal will find its counterpart in the Stone Guest's metaphorical 'swallowing' of the body of Don Juan (the grave itself, *sarcophagus*, means flesh-eater in Greek).[80] The gang of women should be substituted for the gang of brothers: the women conspire with Don Juan to kill the primal father.[81]

Bieito's secular version removes the guilt that pervades the scene: this is a godless universe. An absinthe and drug-fuelled binge (the excesses of consumption) may fuel Don Giovanni's confusion, but the Commendatore's viscerality is confirmed by his blood-spattered shirt and by the fact that he attempts to stuff the stodgy food that Leporello has been cooking into Don Giovanni's mouth. Rather than arriving to devour Don Giovanni, he is metaphorically devoured once more. This scene of devouring, links the contemporary to the mythical, flashing up like Benjamin's memory of the past 'at a moment of danger', a revenant that returns from an age that is apparently dead and gone.[82] But here it is Don Giovanni who is killed, ritually

Tales of Seduction

16. The Commendatore stuffs food into the mouth of Don Giovanni. Bieito's production of *Don Giovanni*.

served up by the primal horde (the other characters in the Da Ponte libretto).

We remember that, according to Freud, the primal father was the one who 'had all the women', and Elizabeth Wright reminds us that 'only the pre-totemic father of the primal horde ... could really be said to *jouir* in the sense of profiting exclusively from the collective wealth of the community, or in the sense of the enjoyment of the women of the horde'.[83] A morality tale about the dangers of conspicuous consumption forms the basis of both Freudian theories of the primal construction of society and Bieito's update on the Don Giovanni tale. Marx's *Capital*, drew on a range of imagery of devouring, from cannibalism to vampirism, to express the spirit of capitalism.[84]

Freud shows us that conspicuous consumerism lies at the society's primal origins. In Bieito's update, Don Giovanni is set upon by the characters who resent his showy display of

Empty Promises: Opera and the Aesthetics of Cultural Consumption

wealth, and who literally carve him up for their pleasure. This tale of contemporary consumption, through its imagery of devouring, links past with present: Don Giovanni is not a scapegoat for Bieito, whose removal will restore peace, but a *'producto de una sociedad enferma'* (product of a sick society),[85] the centre of a cyclical pattern of consumption and greed that finds its roots in society's structures.

Selling the Bieito Product

Two advertising posters were circulated for Bieito's *Don Giovanni*. In the first, which accompanied the London production, a photograph by Andy Whale shot through a red and yellow tinted filter of a goatee-bearded Garry Magee stares up into the camera, sweat beading his brow, bare-chested and with one arm outstretched towards us. Around him is a flurry of red and yellow effects, suggesting movement, as if he were hurtling down into the depths of the blackness that surrounds him.

The poster speaks of an evening of hellfire and damnation, of overwrought emotions and tempestuous music. It promises a set design with painterly effects (the photograph suggests the texture of a painting) and gauzy costumes, the incarnation, perhaps, of what Adorno suggested ought to be the setting for opera: the mystery and 'aura of disguise', perhaps, even, the magical, childlike fantastical air he found in operatic music.[86] All this is very far from Bieito's production, in which flights of fantasy are exposed as fallacies, and allure and seduction appear cheap in his grim and gaudily melancholic present.

The second poster, which advertised the production at Barcelona's Gran Teatre del Liceu in 2002, is quite different in tone and texture. Designed by Josep Bagà Associats and shot by Hugo Menduiña, it depicts a mauve-on-yellow large-scale photograph of a Barbie doll, dressed in gaudy disco wear, her blond hair plaited and swept back, her arms outstretched.

Tales of Seduction

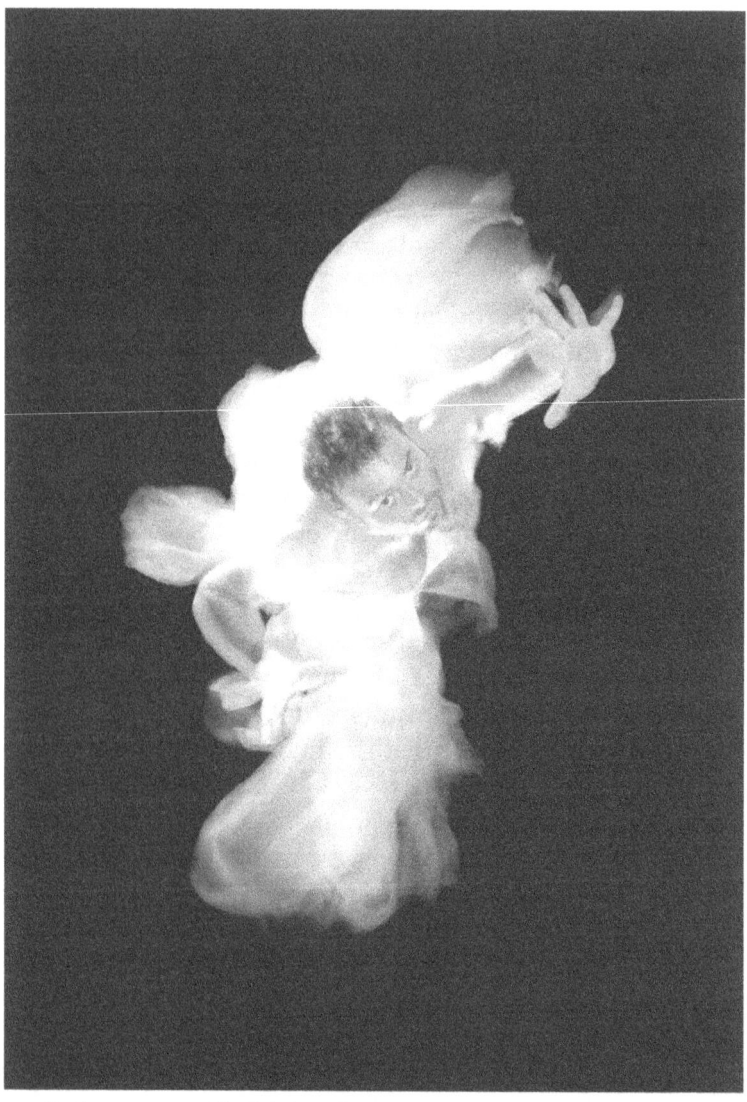

17. An evening of hell-fire and damnation. A poster to accompany Calixto Bieto's production of *Don Giovanni* at the London Coliseum. Featuring Gary Magee as Don Giovanni.

Empty Promises: Opera and the Aesthetics of Cultural Consumption

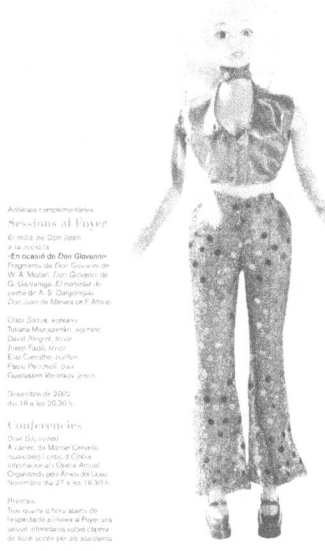

18. Barbie: postmodern diva. A poster to accompany Calixto Bieito's production of *Don Giovanni* at the Gran Teatre del Liceu, Barcelona.

This is no uncanny and sinister play on the human form, but rather a visual conceit, a reference to the many women Don Giovanni allegedly seduces, outlined in the opera in the 'Catalogue Aria'.

Barbie hints at the theme of consumerism that runs throughout the production. As an icon on an advertising poster, Barbie is a suitably postmodern replacement for the operatic diva, the trademark of opera, the fat lady, whose iconic gargantuan frame suggests both the 'glorious plenitude' and the 'embarrassing excess' of opera.

Opera, according to Sam Abel, is the 'conspicuous consumer of high culture' in Wagner's utopian *Gesamtkunstwerk*, it consumes every other art form in an 'aesthetic consumerist fantasy'. 'Opera', writes Abel, 'consumes more resources than any other art form, and revels in its excess'.[87] Simultaneously, as it attempts to compete with other art forms, opera seeks out new audiences. If *Don Giovanni* is a marker for the epitome of bourgeois culture, then Barbie is the icon for a more accessible (mass-directed) opera in the twenty-first century.[88] The Barbie poster promises the postmodern update that Bieito's production delivers.

Bieito's production is an exhilarating blend of high and low culture. As such, it not only cannibalistically consumes other art forms in the way Abel suggested, but also, because it blends high culture and popular entertainment, it transgresses the class hierarchies that Bourdieu so eloquently set out. In opera, the question of 'fidelity' to a canonical high culture text is ever present, for the audience member sits with a copy of the libretto in the accompanying handbook and has access to a translated version in the surtitles that frame the stage action. Mozart's music retained its untouchable, canonical status in Bieitos's production (although at times the physical theatre actively worked against the sound).[89]

Bieito's production, however, is spattered with visual references to popular culture. This move is not so different from the artistic style of Mozart, who included intertextual snatches from popular operas of the day.[90] Bieito does not change Mozart's music, but in the wedding feast scene three of the female characters stand in line to perform the actions to a well-known Spanish pop hit 'Aserejé' by *Las Ketchup* (itself a Spanglish version of the Sugar Hill Gang's 1979 hit 'Rapper's Delight') in a joyous accompaniment to the musical score. Many of Bieito's references are cinematic.

María Delgado has shown how the number plate on Leporello's car 'CO-TORE' is a premonition of the arrival of the Commendatore, but also is a reference to 'Torrente', Leporello's taxi-driving precedesor, from Santiago Segura's offensive protagonist of late 1990s Spanish cinema.

Critics have drawn parallels between Bieito's use of violence on stage and the cinematic excesses of Quentin Tarantino, a relation that Bieito is anxious to dispel: his violence owes more to Scorsese, while he cites Stanley Kubrick's *Barry Lyndon* as a source of inspiration for the blend of visuals and musical effects[91] and Alex de la Iglesia's *El día de la bestia* in which a group of young people have diabolical hallucinations for the production's finale.[92]

This cannibalization of different art forms leaves a trail of intertextual references that emerge like a cacophony of styles, an 'overstimulating ensemble' when set against Mozart's music.[93] For Mullighan, writing in *Sx Magazine*, Bieito's blend of visuals and sound was highly successful, producing an 'electrifying contrast' between the 'detritus-strewn stage and Mozart's sublime music'.[94] Bieito has remarked that the contrast between the 'desperate' staging of his production and the *'sublimes momentos de expansión'* (sublime moments of expansion) in Mozart's music create a sense of the passing of a world that never existed: *'son mero recuerdo de un mundo que no existe, no ahora ni en tiempos de Mozart/Da Ponte'* (they are the mere memory of a world that does not exist, not now nor in Mozart/Da Ponte's time).[95]

The nostalgia this contrast between visuals and sound evokes is immediately undercut as Bieito displays the violence, mass consumption and sexual debauchery he has found in the Da Ponte's libretto and in Mozart's music. Bieito remarks that he finds his inspiration in the libretto itself: '*De Don Giovanni. Está hablando del sexo continuamente. El lenguaje es muy vulgar. Y Don Giovanni es un personaje violento. Don Giovanni intenta fomentar sexo y violencia*' (From Don Giovanni. He is talking about sex the whole time. The language is very vulgar. And Don Giovanni is a violent person. Don Giovanni tries to foment sex and violence).[96]

Referring to the so-called 'Champagne aria', Bieito remarks that '*hay un aria que está dedicada toda al alcohol, está claro, está en la obra*' (there is an aria that is completely dedicated to alcohol, it is clear, it is in the work).[97] Sex, violence and alcoholic binges are thus not inventions of Bieito, but can be found within Mozart/Da Ponte. The effect of Bieito's production is thus not one of 'nostalgia for the present',[98] but rather one of anti-nostalgia, where libretto and music reveal not a more innocent age, but rather the visuals deconstruct and reinterpret the sound, bringing the past aggressively into the present.[99]

Moreover, in its contrasting blend of visuals and music, Bieito's production offers a reflection on genre, taste and consumption. What is acceptable in Tarantino, Kubrick or de la Iglesia is regarded as inappropriate for opera. Furthermore, following Bourdieu, we could suggest that this blend of high and low cultural references requires a new type of knowledge, a new blend of educational capital. An audience member ideally should be as versed in high art forms as in those derived from popular culture. Bieito's production contains the potential to seek out new audiences for his postmodern operatic form.

In an article entitled, 'Opera and the long-playing record', Adorno warned that opera is a 'fading anachronism, kept on life support in opera houses catering to a culture-vulture bourgeoisie by one of two means':[100] either period-piece confections (his example is *Figaro* in a rococo setting that resembles 'a praline box'), or modernizing updates that feature characters dressed in 'sweat-suits' (*Turnanzügen*) in productions 'where one cannot avoid asking, What's the point? Why even bother doing it on stage?' He recommends that the audience simply stay at home, free from distractions, and listen to the music on a long-playing record.[101] Kierkegaard, meanwhile, maintained that:

> it is often disruptive to have to use the eyes a great deal at the same time as the ears are being used. Therefore, one is inclined to shut the eyes when listening to music. This is more or less true of all music, and *in sensu eminentiori* [in an eminent sense] of *Don Giovanni*.[102]

These views on the distracting nature of the visuals in opera may chime with press reports that some of the London audiences at Bieito's production closed their eyes better to concentrate on the music. Yet, despite this negative reporting, Bieito's production was successful in increasing the accessibility of opera in that it found new markets for its product. Publicity in London capitalized on Bieito's reputation, with the words: '"sexually explicit", "shocking", "disgraceful" or "just brilliant". You decide' – and tickets starting at an accessible £6. Following savage critiques on its opening night, Bieito's production went on to achieve 75 per cent attendance at the ENO, of which 85 per cent were non-regular attenders with 29 per cent new bookers to ENO (figures from ENO). Reception of the production in Hanover was reportedly favourable with rapturous applause from its audiences.[103]

Press reports in Barcelona warned that the production '*sorprenderá al público del Liceo*' (will surprise the public of the Liceo), remarking that the production abroad had left '*un rastro de polémica*' (a trail of polemic) in its wake.[104] An article in *La Vanguardia* reported the negative reception in the London press, but made it clear that it was recommended by *Time Out*, quoting that '*es teatro musical, no un amable espectáculo para la jet set. ... Si vuestro marco de referencia es Tarantino y Kubrick, id a verla*' (it is musical theatre, not a pretty spectacle for the jet-set. ... If your points of reference are Tarantino and Kubrick, go to see it) and reported that in London '*el montaje tuvo una buena acogida de público*' (the production was warmly received by the public),[105] thereby implying a distinction between conservative critics and popular reception.

As a result of complaints about Bieito's earlier productions (both in Spain and abroad), coupled with a desire to attract new audiences for opera, the Gran Teatre del Liceu removed the production from its subscription list, and simultaneously reduced prices (a stunning move that worked to gain audiences outside its traditional remit). This unusual combination of widening access and unusual staging, coupled with the suggestion in the press that to purchase tickets for this opera was a 'patriotic tool' (for supporting local talent in the shape of the production's director and orchestra) was successful in attracting audiences: 80 per cent of its tickets had sold by the opening night [106] and the Gran Teatre del Liceu declared the production a financial success.[107]

Nevertheless, the reception was not unanimously warm in Barcelona's Liceu. *El País* reported that while the singers, conductor and orchestra were warmly received, there was some booing when the director came on stage, and the audience,

> *que al no ser, en su mayoría abonado de la temporada del Liceu y desconocer los rituales de la opera, dejó súbitamente de aplaudir y abuchear. El desconcierto cundió. Ni aplausos, ni abucheos, ni cantantes en escena y*

Empty Promises: Opera and the Aesthetics of Cultural Consumption

las luces de la sala todavía apagadas ... en uno de los finales operísticos de Liceo más insólitos de los últimos tiempos (who in the main were not season-ticket holders of the Liceu and were unused to the rituals of opera, suddenly stopped applauding and booing. There was general uneasiness. Neither applause, nor boos, nor singers on stage, and the lights still dimmed ... in one of the most unusual opera finales of the Liceu of recent times).[108]

Negative reactions were therefore explained away as the result of the audience being unused to the rituals of opera. On the whole, Spanish critics took time to reflect on the meaning of the operatic production, with much more favourable result than the knee-jerk reactions of the UK critics. Spanish critics used judgements such as *'una fiesta cutre'* (a seedy party) and *'un vestuario feísta'* (a studiously ugly wardrobe) rather than *'fea'* (ugly), *'hortera'* (naff) and *'un arribista sin chispa'* (a lacklustre nouveau-riche), referring to Masetto, and calling Donna Elvira *'una pija deprisiva'* (a stuck-up depressive). In general, rather than expressions of taste, they provided insights into the symbolism of the piece.[109] Thus, they wrote that this *Don Giovanni 'llega para cuestionar la moral de la sociedad actual'* (comes to question the morality of contemporary society),[110] and that Bieito was exploring *'el mundo de la violencia juvenil'* (the world of juvenile violence)[111] in a Spanish and European context.

Bieito is gaining a reputation for his bold reinterpretations of European classics. A Catalan born in Castile, he 'works across different languages and genres in Catalonia, within Spain and abroad'. He 'has rejected both a monolingual and homogenous theatre in favour of a theatrical discourse that probes the very nature of what cultural exchange is'. He prefers working with classics (as opposed to new writing for the theatre) because 'with a classic you have to reinvent everything, you are effectively a kind of author'.[112] Bieito has remarked that opera is a conservative genre, compared, for example, with photography and art.[113] He cites Picasso's *Las meninas (After Velázquez)* (1957), which is not a copy but a version of Velázquez's painting: Bieito wants to do the same with theatre and opera.[114]

He is fast gaining a reputation as an *enfant terrible*.[115] He is '*el más vanguardista y transgresor director de escena español*' (the most avant-garde and transgressive director of the Spanish stage)[116] and yet he insists that his work is 'not about provoking an audience',[117] an opinion confirmed by Sir Brian McMaster, director of the Edinburgh Festival, who has remarked that the provocative reviews are 'not part of his appeal'.[118] Yet, Bieito's provocation is what makes his work exciting. Bieito is interesting precisely because he makes troubling or disquieting what canonization over time has tamed and ossified, removing all risk. His work also reveals that there may be fault lines that mark a change in public taste.

Bieito's work is archaeological in that he excavates old texts and then brings out new interpretations. At the same time, while Bieito cites Glenn Gould and Peter Sellars as inspiration for his *Don Giovanni*, he also proudly displays his peculiarly Spanish cultural heritage, citing Valle-Inclán's esperpentic vision and Buñuel's maxim: 'you can be anything but boring' as his artistic forerunners.[119] The Don Giovanni myth is traditionally about transgression, about the drawing and crossing of social boundaries. Bieito shows that Don Giovanni can still transgress in Europe in the twenty-first century. By exploring the innumerable paradoxes of consumption and the limits of cultural taste, Bieito reveals himself to be one of the most exciting stage directors of the new millennium.

CONCLUSION: BETWEEN LIMITS

Two exhibitions took place in Madrid in 2004. The first of these, *Tres mitos españoles: La Celestina, Don Quijote, Don Juan* (Three Spanish Myths: La Celestina, Don Quijote, Don Juan), a state-sponsored exhibition held from February to April at the *Centro Cultural Conde Duque*, gathered together cinematic, theatrical and painterly renditions of the eponymous male seducer in Spain throughout the ages.[1] With its stills and posters from cinematic renditions, reproductions of oil paintings, costumes and sketches and early photographs from theatre productions, it reminded the viewer that Don Juan has no respect for the borders of media and genres and has appeared in innumerable transformations over time.

It provided viewers with the chance to see some of the most iconic uses to which Don Juan has been put in the twentieth century. Thus, Dalí's landmark production of the play was cited, as was Sáenz de Heredia's filmic *Don Juan*. Sketches from repeated 'mainstream' performances of Zorrilla's Don Juan jostled for attention alongside paintings rarely given airings, such as, for example, José Llaneces's *Don Juan*. This exhibition reminded us of the volume of Don Juan renditions, and the great names associated with

Tales of Seduction

the figure. This was a celebration of Don Juan as a 'national treasure', in which Spanish national heritage was on display. Don Juan's sixteenth-century dress in this context represents both heritage (the seductions of the resonances of empire are implicit) and tradition. Don Juan (sandwiched between La Celestina and Don Quixote) represents literary and artistic greatness as well as cultural tradition. Visitors to the exhibition were admiring a figure with resonance the world over, but one that is generally acknowledged to be Spanish. This was Don Juan as literary, cultural and historical heavyweight.

In July, a small space across town, the Sala de exposiciones de la Consejería de Cultura y Deportes, in Madrid was showing the work of Basque-born Naia del Castillo (1975–) in an exhibition of her photographic compositions entitled, *Trampas y seducción* (Traps and Seduction). Although no explicit mention is made of Don Juan in her work, on visiting the exhibition I was nevertheless struck by del Castillo's 2002 composition, *Seductor* (Seducer). It depicts the faceless torso of a figure dressed in what at first sight appears to be the attire (black trousers, white shirt and white cummerbund) of a male flamenco dancer. Its title, denoting the male seducer, and its peacock pose seemed to me a fitting and tantalizing riposte to the parade of incarnations of the Don Juan figure throughout time (many of which were gathered in *Tres mitos españoles*).

Del Castillo's photograph appears to draw ironically on the tradition of the 'effeminacy' of Don Juan (as displayed for example in Elías Salaverría's 'effeminate' Don Juan in his oil painting *Don Juan Tenorio en el panteón* of 1927). It also indexes the gender switching of the theatrical parodies *Doña Juana Tenorio* and *Tenorio feminista* as well as invoking the female Don Juan, Lady Ontiveros of Sáenz de Heredia's film among other *femme fatales*. However, the figure in the photograph beneath the supposedly male attire and bear-

Conclusion: Between Limits

19. *Seductor* (Seducer), Naia del Castillo, 2002.

ing the title of a male seducer is unmistakably female, as evidenced by the female nipple that peeps through the lace of the shirt. A panel has been cut out from the shirt in the shape of two doves and covered over with lace: the nipple is the point of contact between the lovebirds that meet in perfect symmetry.

While the components of the image are not shocking in themselves, the composition as a whole is arresting. The nipple functions as the 'punctum' ('sting, speck, cut, little hole')[2] of this photograph: its force and energy and our understanding of it derives from our noticing this small

Tales of Seduction

detail. The lace serves as a veil, giving us the impression that we are viewing illicitly. From here we are led on a playful dance through the instability of sartorial signs and their reading of gender differences. With its sartorial éclat and mocking of the signs of gender, del Castillo's photograph appeared to me to present an ironic and tantalizing reference to the eponymous Spanish seducer while simultaneously, like the rest of her work, pointing the way towards an interrogation of seduction for the twenty-first century.[3]

Del Castillo describes herself more as a sculptor than a photographer: she creates the object first and then builds her photographic compositions. She trades in 'impossible' objects that testify to their presence in an overdetermined manner.[4] These objects, and the bodies within or beside them, 'were there', we are assured, as is often confirmed by the presence of the object itself on display in a glass case beside the photograph. These photographs proudly display the stigmatum of 'having been there', evoking a form of embodied vision.[5]

Seductor seems to present a visual story, the story of vision in Western culture. While the body depicted with its male attire and female breast is coded as androgynous, and may evoke the guilty pleasures of cross-dressing, nevertheless the 'masculine' elements of this body are modestly covered, while the female breast peeps through the lace, the epitome of the female as object for the enjoyment of a (male) voyeur. This is an eroticization of vision through which gender is itself constructed. In an overdetermined fashion, *Seductor* questions gendered viewing positions and the relationship between signs and gender.[6]

The viewer of the nipple may be male or female, the faceless body referents a form of androgyny that resists the taking up of easy viewing positions. Yet, there is something taboo about the image in a way that goes beyond the guilty pleasures of cross-dressing. While this is a story about vision, I suggest that it is embodied vision, a form of touch that provides the image with its power. Touch is indexed by the hand, which appears to the bottom right of the frame. The guilty pleasure of this photograph encourages a desire not merely to look at the nipple, which peeps beneath the textured lace and beautifully shaped decoupage, but a desire to touch it. But the hand in the photograph is thrust deep into the pocket of the trousers, suggesting a prohibition (in this form of embodied vision) on both looking and touching. The desire to touch in this photograph becomes a guilty pleasure.

I suggested earlier that the nipple provided the 'punctum' of this photograph, the detail that reveals its import. Barthes writes that the punctum is 'that accident which pricks me but also bruises me, is poignant to me'.[7] The shock of this photograph is presented by the nipple, which not only looks back at the viewer like an eye, presenting a riposte to the gaze (resisting the notion of female body as spectacle), but which also leaps out and 'pricks' the viewer, in a startling break with the prohibition on touch. The photograph is then able to deconstruct the gaze, allowing us to engage with the narrative of the instability of gender signs and gendered spectatorial positions.

These two examples show the very different ways that Don Juan can be employed as an icon. In the first, Don Juan represents tradition, heritage and literary, cultural (and, implicitly, national) greatness. But, despite his ability to cross borders between media and genres, meaning is generally closed down: there is nothing left to discover in the taxonomy of images of the first exhibition. Naia del Castillo, meanwhile, presents us with Don Juan as a player at the limits. The limits revealed here are those between vision and touch, between male and female spectatorial positions, between active and passive, between the seductions of the visual medium and resistance to it. Del Castillo's work also reminds us of the binary oppositions that make up our world, the way that signifiers threaten constantly to collapse into their opposite. This is Don Juan as a trickster, refusing to be pinned down, leading us on a textual dance through our cultural worlds.

In the examination of Don Juan in Spain in this volume, Don Juan seems to vacillate between the liberatory trickster and an agent of conservatism. In all but the last chapter he presents a rather conservative vision of nationhood (in Chapter 5 Spanish nationhood is riddled with Bieito's Catalan status, the dialectic between London and Barcelona stagings, and the international cultural references in the text and accompanying programme). De los Ríos's Don Juan appears to represent degeneracy, but she is seduced by his attractions and he becomes the standard-bearer for a view of Spain's future that imaginatively denies the loss of its colonies. Marañón tries to eschew the dissolute Don Juan in favour of a more conservative view of Spanish masculinity, of service to the nation. Sáenz de Heredia's Don Juan leads the life of a libertine but then conforms to national Catholicism in a move from the profane to the sacred. The theatrical Don Juan of Chapter 4 at once represents theatrical tradition and theatrical innovation.

If Don Juan tends towards conservatism, this is partly to do with the imaginative potential he attracts. Spain's thinkers are often keen to enlist him to their cause and it is precisely his capacity to seduce that makes him useful to intellectuals and ideologues who wish to persuade the Spanish public of their point of view. Don Juan is so popular that he can engage with the social order. Given the way in which he has taken root in the national psyche, it is hardly surprising that he should have been used for a variety of ideologies. Don Juan's capacity for seduction (through language) also makes him seem at home in a

Conclusion: Between Limits

variety of different theories. Is it not the task of every theory to persuade us to its point of view? An intriguing idea that Don Juan puts forward in this book is that, despite his potential for liberatory freedoms, he in fact offers us only the fantasy of resistance to conservative ideas.

Undoubtedly, Don Juan's conservatism in this volume has as much to do with my selection of material as with the history of Spain. It would be possible to write a very different history of the figure of Don Juan in Spain if one focused entirely on examples of Don Juan breaking taboos or transgressing limits. I began my study by wishing to focus merely on the intersections of myth with other branches of theoretical study. Increasingly, however, I found that Don Juan was too unstable an icon to press into service for any argument. He threatens constantly to collapse into his opposite, which makes him a fascinating and productive, if volatile, field for study. This means that de los Ríos can both attack the figure for his base instincts and corruption of the bloodline, yet allow him to rise again in her vision over Spain's relations with its former colonies, to become a noble father to a new race of invigorated Spaniards.

It also means that Marañón can attempt to use Don Juan conservatively (stressing his negative potential for gender relations) yet allow him to be received as a way of opening up restrictive gender paradigms. Where the intention of Don Juan's creator is to use him conservatively, he can be received in a very different sense. This is also the case of the implied spectator of Sáenz de Heredia's *Don Juan* of Chapter 3, who may resist the ideological infrastructure of fascism in favour of private and liberatory visual pleasures. It means that (in Chapter 4) where Don Juan is pressed into service as a symbol of aggressive newness (Dalí's innovations for the stage) critics can also see him as a melancholic symbol of the passage of time. This also allowed theatre practitioner Bieito to summon connotations of history and highbrow culture before dismantling them before the eyes of the spectator.

Don Juan is a volatile icon, but it is precisely his capacity to unite antinomies within a single figure that endows him with the capacity for seduction. It is his status as the 'lord of the border' (Janus-faced, looking both ways) that gives him endless rejuvenatory capacities, revealing the limitations of any cultural system, but at the same time, endlessly seeking out new conquests. We need figures like Don Juan to restore our faith in the ability of culture to engage with the social order, rather than merely to reflect it. Working perpetually at the interface between old and new, between tradition and innovation, Don Juan is a site for the exploration of limits within any culture, a productive icon with which to explore the ideas, fantasies and chimeras of the past, and also with which to negotiate the new.

NOTES

Introduction

1. 'I am: A Casanova. Personal Style: elegant. Occupation: seeking a challenge. Interests: Eating and drinking. I listen to: classical music and opera. I am looking for: a date in real life.' Personal advertisement from http://www.love.lycos.es. Accessed 11 August 2004. All translations are my own unless otherwise stated.
2. David Crystal, *Language and the Internet* (Cambridge: Cambridge University Press, 2001) p. 286.
3. Aaron Ben-ze'ev, *Love Online: Emotions on the Internet* (Cambridge: Cambridge University Press, 2004) p. 150.
4. Quote by Antonio Piedra, 'Don Juan, ¿el fin de un mito?' in Gonzalo Santoja (ed.) *Don Juan, genio y figura* (Madrid: España Nuevo Milenio, 2001) p. 100. See Román Gubern, *El Eros electrónico* (Madrid: Taurus, 2000) and Claudia Springer, *Electronic Eros: Bodies and Desire in the Postindustrial Age* (London: Athlone, 1996).
5. Crystal, *Language and the Internet*, p. 28. Chat, or Internet Relay Chat (IRC) was developed by Jaikko Oikarinen in the late 1980s.
6. Shoshana Felman, *The Scandal of the Speaking Body: Don Juan with J. L. Austin, or Seduction in Two Languages* (Stanford: Stanford University Press, 1980).
7. Spanish versions of the Don Juan myth, Tirso de Molina's *El burlador de Sevilla y convidado de piedra* and Zorrilla's *Don Juan Tenorio* can be read in a similar vein. See also Luis Fernández Cifuentes, 'Don Juan y las palabras', in Luis Fernández Cifuentes

Notes (Introduction)

      (ed.) *José Zorrilla: Don Juan Tenorio* (Barcelona: Crítica, 1993a) pp. 38–59.
8. Felman, *The Scandal*, p. 28.
9. Felman, *The Scandal*, p. 31.
10. Ibid.
11. Stella Koh, 'The real in the virtual: speech, self and sex in the realm of pure text', *Asian Journal of Social Science*, 30 (2) 2002, p. 231.
12. Koh, 'The real in the virtual', p. 224.
13. Springer, *Electronic Eros*, p. vii. Felman notes that the body is important in two ways: in the sense that a body utters a speech, and in the sense that the body suggests the unconscious. The scandal of the speaking body is that the 'I' who speaks can never fully represent the body. A similar process operates in chat, where a body (with an unconscious) produces chat through electronic means, but the 'speech' displayed on screen is often unrepresentative or an incomplete representation of the body that produces it.
14. C. Richard King, 'The siren screams of telesex: speech, seduction and simulation', *Journal of Popular Culture*, 30 (3) 1996, p. 95.
15. For Felman, the scandal of the speaking body lies in the fact that the performative is always to some extent unknowing about what it performs (p. 67). The same function is true of chat, which relies on imagination and interactivity.
16. Piedra, 'Don Juan, ¿el fin de un mito?', p. 99.
17. Rafael de Santa Ana, *Manual del perfecto mujeriego* (Madrid: Imprenta helénica, 1919).
18. Gustavo Pérez Firmat, *Literature and Liminality: Festive Readings in the Hispanic Tradition* (Durham, NC: Duke University Press, 1986) p. 6.
19. Paul Radin, *The Trickster: A Study in American Indian Mythology* (New York: Schocken Books, 1956).
20. William G. Doty and William J. Hynes, 'Historical overview of theoretical issues: the problem of the trickster', in William J. Hynes and William G. Doty (eds) *Mythical Trickster Figures: Contours, Contexts and Criticisms* (Tuscaloosa: University of Alabama Press, 1993) p. 14.
21. The *burla*, as defined by the Real Academia Española's *Diccionario de la lengua española* (Madrid: Espasa Calpe, 1992, pp. 334–5) is a trick, lie or deception.
22. Doty and Hynes, 'Historical overview'.
23. C. W. Spinks, *Semiosis, Marginal Signs and Trickster* (London: Macmillan, 1991) and C. W. Spinks, *Trickster and Ambivalence: The Dance of Differentiation* (Madison: Atwood Publishing, 2001).
24. Spinks, *Trickster and Ambivalence*, p. 8.

Notes (Introduction)

25. Spinks, *Trickster and Ambivalence*, p. 10.
26. Spinks, *Trickster and Ambivalence*, p. 9.
27. For an interesting discussion of this play, see Raymond Conlon, 'Sexual passion and marriage: chaos and order in Tirso de Molina's *El vergonzoso en palacio*', *Hispania*, 71 (1) 1988, pp. 8–13. The rather two-dimensional female characters of *El burlador* are likewise contrasted with the spectrum of female sexual types offered up by *El vergonzoso en palacio*, as detailed by Raymond Conlon, 'Female psychosexuality in Tirso's *El vergonzoso en palacio*,' *BCom*, 37 (1) 1985, 55–69.
28. See Joan Ramón Resina who, in an excellent article on Zorrilla's play ('The time of the king: gift and exchange in Zorrilla's *Don Juan Tenorio*', *Diacritics*, 30 (1) 2000, p. 49) writes, 'There is something paradoxal about José Zorrilla's revision of the Don Juan legend, a certain contradiction between the play's structure and the logic of the action. The character of the protagonist, the form and implications of Don Juan's salvation, the strategies and temporality of seduction, even the play's generic status – all come under the law of self-cancellation'. For Denis de Rougement, it is the infinitely contradictory nature of Don Juan that constitutes his appeal. Denis de Rougement, *Love in the Western World*, Translated by Montgomery Belgion (New York: Pantheon, 1965) p. 209.
29. Piedra, 'Don Juan, ¿el fin de un mito?', p. 100. This is Don Juan as sexual predator, using the Internet to seduce his innocent victims. According to an EU study of the Internet in Spain, 34 per cent of the population in Spain use the Internet, while there are 15 per cent more male than female *usuarios* (see Anon, 'Las españolas navegan menos: España supera la media de 'brecha digital' entre hombres y mujeres', *El País*, 2005). Online edition, 14 February 2005 <http://www.elpais.com/articulo/internet/espanolas/navegan/elpeputec/20050211elpepunet12/Tes> Accessed 10 May 2007.
30. José Manuel Losada, *Bibliography of the Myth of Don Juan in Literary History* (Lewiston: The Edwin Mellen Press, 1997).
31. Leo Weinstein, *The Metamorphosis of Don Juan* (Stanford: Stanford University Press, 1959).
32. Takayuki Yokota-Murakami, *Don Juan East West: On the Problematics of Comparative Literature* (Albany: State University of New York Press, 1998) pp. 187–211.
33. According to Ramiro de Maeztu (*Don Quijote, Don Juan y la Celestina: ensayos en simpatía*, Madrid: Espasa-Calpe, 1926, p. 72), Molière's *Don Juan* is a Spanish Don Juan with a variation, Byron's version is a burlesque fantasy in which Don Juan figures little, Mozart's Don Giovanni is representative of the Spanish Don Juan.

197

Notes (Introduction)

     Jo Labanyi ('Political readings of Don Juan and romantic love in Spain from the 1920s to the 1940s', in Luisa Passerini, Liliana Ellena and Alexander C. T. Geppert (eds) *New Dangerous Liaisons: Discourses on Europe and Love in the Twentieth Century* (Oxford: Berghahn Books, forthcoming) notes that the Spanish Don Juan has nothing to do with the European tradition of courtly love. Furthermore, that a key factor in the northern European 'misreading' of Don Juan is the 'dissemination of Golden Age literature by the German Romantic critic, August Wilhelm von Schlegel, for whom it represented a primitive energy untamed by classicism'.

34. Otto Rank, *The Don Juan Legend* (Princeton: Princeton University Press, 1975) pp. 61–77 relates Don Juan's prehistory to the myth of avenging death in folklore. See Victor Saíd Armesto, *La leyenda de Don Juan: orígenes poéticos de 'El burlador de Sevilla y convidado de piedra'* (Madrid: Espasa-Calpe, 1908) for Don Juan's prehistory in Spain.
35. Ian Watt, *Myths of Modern Individualism: Faust, Don Quixote, Don Juan, Robinson Crusoe* (Cambridge: Cambridge University Press, 1996) p. 92.
36. For an accessible introduction to questions of the authorship of *El burlador de Sevilla*, see James A. Parr, 'El burlador de Sevilla: authorship and authenticity', in James Parr (ed.) *Don Quijote, Don Juan and Related Subjects: Form and Tradition in Spanish Literature, 1330–1630* (Selinsgrove: Susquehanna University Press, 2004) pp. 138–63. James B. Mandrell, *Don Juan and the Point of Honour: Seduction, Patriarchal Society and Literary Tradition* (Pennsylvania: Penn State University Press 1992) p. 2n notes that the questions of authorship, of date of publication and of textual priority continue to be pressing issues facing critics and literary historians.
37. Francisco de Goya, *Scene from 'El convidado de piedra'*, 1797–8, location unknown since the sale of the possessions of the bankrupt Osuna family in 1896. I am grateful to Nigel Glendinning for drawing my attention to this painting. A black and white photograph of the painting appears in Juliet Wilson-Bareau and Manuela Mena Marqués, *Goya: Truth and Fantasy: The Small Paintings* (New Haven: Yale University Press, 1994) p. 220. Goya is thought to have attended a performance of Zamora's play at the Teatro de la Cruz, 1797, by the Luis Navarro theatre company. The painting is thought to belong to his series on themes of witchcraft. Wendy Bird, 'Oh monstrous lamp! Special effects in Goya: a scene from El Hechizado por fuerza', *Apollo*, 159 (505) 2004, p 14 traces the relationship between phantasmagoria and Goya's work, claiming

Notes (Introduction)

that the painting appears to depict a magic lantern surrounding the figure of the stone statue.
38. Julia Kristeva, 'Don Juan, or loving to be able to', in Julia Kristeva (ed.) *Tales of Love* (New York: Columbia University Press, 1987) p. 192.
39. Jesús Rubio Jiménez, 'Don Juan Tenorio en versión de Luis Escobar y Salvador Dalí', in Andrés Peláez Martín (ed.) *Luis Escobar y la vanguardia* (Madrid: Comunidad de Madrid, 2001) p. 55.
40. David T. Gies, *From Myth to Pop: Don Juan, James Bond, and Zelig* (Greensburg, PA: Eadmer Press, 1992) p. 195.
41. Ann Davies, *The Metamorphoses of Don Juan's Women: Early Parity to Late Modern Pathology* (Lewiston: The Edwin Mellen Press, 2004) p. 1.
42. Mandrell, *Don Juan and the Point of Honour*, p. 15.
43. Watt, *Myths of Modern Individualism*.
44. Davies, *The Metamorphoses*, pp. 19–20.
45. Moyra Haslett, *Byron's Don Juan and the Don Juan Legend* (Oxford: Clarendon Press, 1997) p. 8.
46. Haslett, *Byron's Don Juan and the Don Juan Legend*, pp. 8–9.
47. Davies, *The Metamorphoses*, p. 19.
48. Mandrell, *Don Juan and the Point of Honour*, p. 17.
49. Mandrell, *Don Juan and the Point of Honour*, p. 15.
50. I am grateful to Dru Dougherty for this observation.
51. Mandrell, *Don Juan and the Point of Honour*, p. 16.
52. Davies (*The Metamorphoses*, pp. 15–19) is surely correct to note that the sexual sphere was important in the seventeenth century also, a period she links to Foucault's genealogy of a discourse of sexuality.
53. Gies, *From Myth to Pop*, p. 183.
54. Mandrell, *Don Juan and the Point of Honour*.
55. Carlos Feal, *En nombre de Don Juan: estructura de un mito literario* (Amsterdam: John Benjamins, 1984).
56. Ignacio-Javier López, *Caballero de novela: ensayo sobre el donjuanismo en la novela española moderna 1880–1930* (Barcelona: Puvill Libros, 1986).
57. Andrew Ginger, Huw Lewis and John Hobbs, *Selected Interdisciplinary Essays on the Representation of the Don Juan Archetype in Myth and Culture* (Lewiston: Edwin Mellen Press, 2000).
58. Ana Sofía Pérez-Bustamante, *Don Juan Tenorio en la España del siglo XX* (Madrid: Cátedra, 1998).
59. Luis Miguel Fernàndez, *Don Juan en el cine español: hacia una teoría de la recreación fílmica* (Santiago de Compostela: Universidade de Santiago de Compostela, 2000).
60. Yokota-Murakami, *Don Juan East West*.

Notes (Introduction/Chapter 1)

61. Elena Soriano, *El donjuanismo femenino* (Barcelona: Ediciones Península, 2000).
62. Richard A. Cardwell, 'Specul(ariz)ation on the other woman: Don Juan Tenorio's Inés', in Richard A. Cardwell and Ricardo Landeira (eds) *José Zorrilla 1839–1993: Centennial Readings* (Nottingham: University of Nottingham Monographs in the Humanities, 1993) pp. 41–57.
63. Davies, *The Metamorphoses*.
64. Roberta Johnson, 'The domestication of a modernist Don Juan', in *Gender and Nation in the Spanish Modernist Novel* (Nashville: Vanderbilt University Press, 2003) pp. 90–119.
65. Labanyi, 'Political readings'. See also Jo Labanyi, 'Impossible love and Spanishness: adventures of Don Juan (Sherman, 1949) and Don Juan (Sáenz De Heredia, 1950)', in Federico Bonaddio and Xon de Ros (eds) *Crossing Fields in Modern Spanish Culture* (Oxford: Legenda, 2003) pp. 146–54.
66. Jean Baudrillard, *Seduction* (London: Macmillan, 1990) pp. 60–71. See Moyra Haslett's gloss on Baudrillard in her excellent book, *Byron's Don Juan*, p. 275. Haslett cites Kristeva's statement, 'the baroque game (Don Juan, Casanova) can – and must –cease' as affirmation that the fixation with 'psychic interiority' is confirmed by the nineteenth-century psychological novel. See Julia Kristeva, 'The adolescent novel', in John Fletcher and Andrew Benjamin, *Abjection, Melancholia and Love* (London: Routledge, 1990).
67. Mandrell, *Don Juan and the Point of Honour*.
68. Freud makes references to Don Juan, as will be seen in various discussions in this book, but he devotes no full-length study to the figure, a notable absence given his enthusiasm for using literary and mythical figures as subjects of study. Mitchell, in *Mad Men and Medusas: Reclaiming Hysteria and the Effects of Sibling Relations on the Human Condition* (London: Allen Lane and Penguin Books, 2000) pp. 252–3, 265 attributes this to Freud's own hysteria.
69. Rank, *The Don Juan Legend*.

1. Opposites Attract: An Intellectual, Don Juan and Nation in Early Twentieth-century Spain

1. Frederick B. Pike, *Hispanismo 1898–1936: Spanish Conservatives and Liberals and their Relations with Spanish America* (Notre Dame: University of Notre Dame Press, 1971) p. 48.
2. Christopher Britt Arredondo, *Quixotism: The Imaginative Denial of Spain's Loss of Empire* (Albany: State University of New York Press, 2005).

3. As well as expressing Spanish 'essence', the return to national models may have been a response to France's cultural hegemony during the Spanish Restoration. See Dru Dougherty, 'Theatre and culture, 1868–1936', in David T. Gies (ed.) *The Cambridge Companion to Modern Spanish Culture* (Cambridge: Cambridge University Press, 1999) p. 216.
4. Britt Arredondo (p. 177) argues that 'Quixotism' sowed the seeds for the later national–Catholic ideology of the fascists in Spain, as well as perceiving a relationship with Aznar's external policy over Iraq.
5. Ramón Menéndez Pidal, 'Sobre los orígenes del "convidado de piedra" (1906)', *Estudios Literarios* (Buenos Aires: Espasa-Calpe, 1968); Saíd Armesto, *La leyenda*.
6. De los Ríos edited the journal from its inception in 1919 until it disappeared in 1926. María Luisa Solano ('Una gran escritora española: Doña Blanca de los Ríos de Lampérez', *Hispania*, XIII, 1930, p. 393) writes of the journal, '*Nos atrevemos a decir que en España es única en su género, no sólo por los fines que la guían, sino también por ser la inspiradora y editora una mujer*' (we go so far as to state that in Spain it [the journal] is unique in its genre, not only because of the principles that guide it, but also because its inspiration and editor is a woman). It contained essays from thinkers of the day on the question of Spain's relations with Spanish America. As Nieves Vázquez Recio, 'Las hijas de don Juan (1907) de Blanca de los Ríos: fin de siglo y una mirada femenina', in Ana Sofía Pérez Bustamante (ed.) *Don Juan Tenorio en la España del siglo XX* (Madrid: Cátedra, 1998) p. 380 points out, it can be seen as '*fiel reflejo de cierta actitud paternalista surgida en España con la pérdida de las colonias*' (a faithful reflection of a certain paternalistic attitude that arose in Spain with the loss of the colonies).
7. Solano, 'Una gran escritora', p. 390. Solano ('Una gran escritora', p. 391) writes that she was a '*conferenciante de alto vuelo, de palabra galana y con el raro don de despertar y retener hasta el fin el interés de sus oyentes*' (a great speaker, articulate and with the rare gift for capturing and retaining the interest of her listeners until the end).
8. Scholars have made the case for female writers such as Rosa de Chacel to be included within literary canons. See, for example, Teresa Bordons and Susan Kirkpatrick, 'Chacel's Teresa and Ortega's Canon', *Anales de la literatura española contemporánea*, 17,

Notes (Chapter 1)

(1992) pp. 283-99. Britt Arredondo (*Quixotism*) meanwhile, who deals exclusively with male writers, makes the case for the 'Generations' to be ignored altogether. The generation of 1898, in particular, is seen by him as a conservative construct (pp. 5-15).
9. *Las hijas de don Juan* was first published as part of the *El cuento semanal*, series, 18 October 1907 (Madrid: Imp. José Blas y Cía). Here I refer to its reprinted version by Ángela Ena Bordonada (ed.) *Novelas breves de escritoras españolas (1900–1936)* (Madrid: Castalia/Instituto de la Mujer) pp. 67–125. Roberta Johnson includes de los Ríos alongside other women writers who have 'domesticated' the image of Don Juan. See her excellent book, *Gender and Nation in the Spanish Modernist Novel*. The play *Don Juan no existe* (1924) by the Condesa de San Luis has now been lost (see note 27 of Chapter 4) but her talks on feminism suggest that this may have been an interesting work. On *Las hijas de don Juan*, see also Kathleen Glenn, 'Demythification and denunciation in Blanca de los Ríos' Las hijas de don Juan', in John P. Gabriele (ed.) *Nuevas perspectivas sobre el 98*, Madrid: Iberoamericana, 1999) pp. 223–30; Reyes Lázaro, 'El "Don Juan" de Blanca de los Ríos y el nacional-romanticismo español de principios de siglo', *Letras Peninsulares*, XIII (part 2) 2000, pp. 467-83; and Vázquez Recio, 'Las hijas de don Juan'. For a full list of her published works on Don Juan, see Nieves Vázquez Recio, 'Las hijas de Don Juan', p. 382n. For an account of her life, see María Antonieta González López, *Aproximación a la obra literaria y periodística de Blanca de los Ríos* (Madrid: Fundación Universitaria Española, 2001).
10. Lázaro, 'El "Don Juan" de Blanca de los Ríos', p. 475.
11. Glenn, 'Demythification', p. 224 notes the absence of de los Ríos's text from Ignacio-Javier López's excellent work *Caballero de novela*, as well as from James Mandrell's *Don Juan and the Point of Honour*.
12. González López, *Aproximación a la obra*, pp. 34–5.
13. De los Ríos claimed to have found Tirso's birth certificate in the Iglesia de San Ginés in Madrid and developed a theory according to which Tirso was the bastard son of the Duque de Osuna. scholars later questioned these findings (González López, *Aproximación a la obra*, p. 38).
14. De los Ríos would go on to become a member of the executive committee for the third centenary of the death of Cervantes; she was a member of the Academias de Buenas Letras of Barcelona and Sevilla, the Academia de Ciencias Históricas in Toledo and the Real

Notes (Chapter 1)

Academia Hispanoamericana de Ciencias y Artes, Madrid. In 1924 she received the Gran Cruz de Alfonso XII, which had never before been awarded to a woman. She also received homage from the Academia de Jurisprudencia in Madrid. In 1926, she became a member of the National Assembly of the Primo de Rivera government, alongside María de Maeztu and María Echarri. None of this was enough to permit her to be allowed to enter the Real Academia de la Lengua, despite her name being put forward more than once. Solano writes, in 1930, '*a pesar de no haber triunfado, a doña Blanca le corresponde el honor de la primacía en esta lucha por romper un absurdo prejuicio más contra el sexo, que, en nuestra época de demolición de injustificadas barreras, no podrá resistir mucho tiempo sin desaparecer por anacrónico*' (although she was not successful, Doña Blanca has the honour of being the first in this fight to break one more absurd prejudice against gender, which, in our age of destroying unjustified barriers, cannot last for much longer before disappearing as an anachronism) (Solano, 'Una gran escritora', p. 392). See also González López, *Aproximación a la obra*; and Vázquez Recio, 'Las hijas de don Juan'.
15. Both quotations from Blanca de los Ríos, 'Las hijas de don Juan', in Angela Bordonada (ed.) *Novelas breves de escritoras españolas (1900–1936)* (Madrid: Castalia/Instituto de la Mujer, 1989) p. 68.
16. Blanca de los Ríos, *Los grandes mitos de la edad moderna: Don Quijote, Don Juan, Segismundo, Hamlet, Fausto* (Madrid: Oficinas del Centro de Cultura Hispanoamericana, 1916) p. 8.
17. De los Ríos, *Los grandes mitos*, p. 9.
18. Emilia Pardo Bazán, 'La última ilusión de Don Juan', in Emilia Pardo Bazán (ed.) *Obras completas* (Madrid: Biblioteca Castro, 2004) vol. 8, p. 381.
19. See Ignacio-Javier López's excellent, *Caballero de novela* for a fascinating discussion of the ways in which authors offered a critique of the legendary Don Juan in their writing. His frame of reference is 1880 to 1930.
20. De los Ríos, 'Don Juan en la literatura', n.p.
21. See, for example, de los Ríos, *Los grandes mitos*, p. 8.
22. Robert Ter Horst, 'Epic descent: the filiations of Don Juan', *MLN*, 111 (2) 1996, pp. 255–74.
23. Exceptions to this rule include María Martinez Sierra's play *Don Juan de España* (1921) in which there is a suggestion of Don Juan's attempt to seduce his own daughter. The same is true of Valle-Inclán's Don Juanesque Marqués de Bradomín in his *Sonatas*.
24. Ibsen's *Ghosts* was not performed in Castillian (*Espectros*) in Madrid until 1906, but in Barcelona it was performed from the 1890s. See

Notes (Chapter 1)

Halldan Gregersen, *Ibsen and Spain* (Cambridge: Harvard University Press, 1936). Playwright María Teresa Borragán used Ibsen's work as inspiration for her 1924 drama, *La Voz de las sombras* (The Voice of Shadows), which deals with '*la fatal herencia patológica de la prole de un degenerado alcohólico*' (the fatal pathological inheritance of the offspring of a degenerate alcoholic) (Pilar Nieva de la Paz, 'El teatro de Maria Teresa Borragán: una contribución al feminismo reformista de preguerra', *Estreno*, 23 (2) 1997, p. 28). The work focuses on the effect of venereal diseases on the wives of unfaithful husbands as well as offering a justification for female adultery.
25. Glenn, 'Demythification', p. 225.
26. Laura Otis, *Organic Memory: History and the Body in Late Nineteenth and Early Twentieth Centuries* (Lincoln: University of Nebraska Press, 1994) p. 50.
27. Francis Galton, *Inquiries into Human Faculty and its Development* (London: Macmillan, 1883) pp. 24–5.
28. Angelique Richardson, *Love and Eugenics in the Late Nineteenth Century: Rational Reproduction and the New Woman* (Oxford: Oxford University Press, 2003) p. 2. Eugenics was 'the science of improving stock, which is by no means confined to questions of judicious mating, but which, especially in the case of man, takes cognisance of all influences that tend in however remote a degree to give to the more suitable races or strains of blood a better chance of prevailing speedily over the less suitable than they would otherwise have had' (Galton, *Inquiries into Human Faculty*, p. 25).
29. *Galton Papers*, 57, cited in Richardson, *Love and Eugenics*, p. 2.
30. Mary Nash, 'Social eugenics and nationalist race hygiene in early twentieth century Spain', *History of European Ideas*, 15 (4–6) 1992, p. 742. Nash notes that eugenics was a social reform movement in Spain that gained momentum among the liberal progressives in 1920s and 1930s Spain. See also Raquel Álvarez Peláez, 'Origen y desarrollo de la eugenesia en España', in José Manuel Sánchez Ron (ed.) *Ciencia y sociedad en España: de la ilustración a la guerra civil* (Madrid: El arquero, 1988) pp. 179–204.
31. Cesare Lombroso's *The Criminal Man* (1885) took theories of degeneracy and atavism so far as to suggest that criminals be studied as a separate race. See Cesare Lombroso, *Los criminales* (Barcelona: Centro Editorial Presa, 1911).
32. Richard A. Cardwell, 'The mad doctors: literature and medicine in finesecular Spain', *Journal of the Institute of Romance Studies*, 4 (1996) pp. 167–96.
33. Don Juan had already been parodied in theatrical renditions (see

Notes (Chapter 1)

Chapter 4) and in the late nineteenth-century novel. See López, *Caballero de novela*.
34. Both quotations are from de los Ríos, 'Las hijas de don Juan', p. 68.
35. Lázaro, 'El "Don Juan" de Blanca de los Ríos', p. 470.
36. Rafael Huertas, 'Madness and degeneration, I. From "fallen angel" to "mentally ill"', *History of Psychiatry*, 3 (1992) pp. 391–411.
37. For an explanation of the complex theories of degeneration in Spain, including Magnan and Legrain's modification of the 'fallen angel' thesis to a theory of 'a progressive movement from a more perfect state to a less perfect state', see Ricardo Campos Marín and Rafael Huertas, 'The theory of degeneration in Spain (1886–1920)', *Boston Studies in the Philosophy of Science*, 221 (2001) pp. 171–87. Cf. Richardson's (*Love and Eugenics*, p. 3) discussion of eugenics as a modification of Darwin's evolutionary theory of descent through modification ('Man had not fallen from Grace, but risen from the swamps').
38. Lázaro, 'El "Don Juan" de Blanca de los Ríos', p. 473.
39. Laura Otis (*Organic Memory*) develops a theory by which acquired characteristics such as memory were thought to be able to be inherited at the turn of the century.
40. De los Ríos, 'Las hijas de don Juan', p. 191.
41. De los Ríos, 'Las hijas de don Juan', pp. 97–8.
42. See Eugene Talbot's *Degeneracy: Its Causes, Signs and Results* (London: Walter Scott Ltd, 1898, p. 108) where he argues that inter-marriage between 'inferior' – that is, degenerate – races (rather than classes in de los Ríos's case) and 'superior' races further along in the evolutionary process 'would tend to degeneracy' (cited in Stephanie Bower, 'Dangerous liaisons: prostitution, disease and race in Frank Norris's fiction', *Modern Fiction Studies*, 42 (1) 1996, pp. 31–60).
43. Max Nordau, *Degeneration* (Lincoln: University of Nebraska Press, 1993) pp. 7–15.
44. De los Ríos, 'Las hijas de don Juan', p. 89. See Angelique Richardson's (*Love and Eugenics*, p. 9n) remarks about 'rational reproduction' in her discussion of love and eugenics, which circulated from the 1880s onwards (her example is the United Kingdom). Don Juan's marriage to Concha does not even enjoy the romantic suggestion of love – they married out of spite on Don Juan's part – and is couched in disapproving terms.
45. J. M. Escuder, in his book *Locos y anómalos* (Madrid: Establecimiento tip. 'Sucesores de Rivadeneyra', 1895) p. 198 writes '*herencia no se transmite estereotipándose íntegramente en el sucesor, sino que al mezclarse los dos elementos que forman el embrión, la herencia*

205

Notes (Chapter 1)

se modifica y transforma, presentando en cada ser un aspecto de sus variadas metamorfosis' (inheritance is not transmitted integrally in the successor, but rather, when the two elements that form the embryo are mixed, the inheritance is modified and transforms, presenting in each being an aspect of its various metamorphosis) (cited in Ricardo Campos Marín, 'La teoría de la degeneración y la clínica psiquiátrica en la España de la Restauración', *Dynamis*, 19, 1999, p. 437). The biological decadence of the race featured openly in explanations of Spain's political downfall, as Nash notes. She explains that this became a focal point in *En defensa de la raza* (1918), a well-known work by the prominent eugenicist Martinez Vargas. 'Deeply embedded was the notion that the "national vitality" of Spain had suffered constant deterioration through the organic and social decadence of numerous national groups (Nash, 'Social eugenics', p. 742). See also I. Valentí Vivó, *La sanidad nacional: eugenesia y biometría* (Barcelona: La neotipia, 1910).
46. Johnson, *Gender and Nation*, p. 129.
47. The duality of Santa Teresa's ecstasy (famously rendered in Bernini's statue) is explored by Jacques Lacan, *On Feminine Sexuality: The Limits of Love and Knowledge. Book XX: Encore, 1972–1973* (New York: Norton, 1998). Alison Weber, *Teresa of Avila and the Rhetoric of Femininity* (Princeton: Princeton University Press, 1996) pp. 98–122 describes *Interior Castle* as an exercise in which the language of erotic spirituality is obfuscated by rhetoric. Notwithstanding, de los Ríos avoids mentioning eroticism in her extended discussion of the influence of Santa Teresa's mysticism on Spanish art. She refers to Bernini's statue only to say that '*no podía con la grandilocuencia y teatralismo del arte italiano de la decadencia expresar la mística, españolísima figura de Teresa de Jesús*' (with the grandiloquence and theatricality of Italian decadent art [Bernini] could not express the mystical, peculiarly Spanish figure of Teresa de Jesús) (Blanca de los Ríos, *Influjo de la mística, de Santa Teresa singularmente, sobre nuestro grande arte nacional*, Madrid: Imprenta de los Hijos de M. G. Hernández, 1913, p. 56n).
48. De los Ríos, 'Las hijas de don Juan', p. 124.
49. De los Ríos, 'Las hijas de don Juan', p. 125.
50. Campos Marín and Huertas, 'The theory of degeneration', p. 120.
51. Ricardo Campos Marín and Rafael Huertas, 'El alcoholismo como enfermedad social', *Dynamis*, 1 (1991) pp. 263–86.
52. Rafael Cervera Barat, *Alcoholismo y Civilización* (Valencia: A. Cortés, 1896) p. 22.
53. B. González Álvarez, 'Higiene profiláctica del niño respecto de la herencia', *El Siglo Médico*, 183 (5) 1903, cited in Campos Marín and

Notes (Chapter 1)

Huertas, 'The theory of degeneration', p. 183. Tuberculosis was a key factor in this debate: 'Purifying the blood of parents is an official duty of the State', claimed lawyer G. Doval in 1912 (cited in Campos Marín and Huertas, 'The theory of degeneration', p. 183).
54. De los Ríos, 'Las hijas de don Juan', p. 70.
55. De los Ríos, 'Las hijas de don Juan', p. 72.
56. De los Ríos, 'Las hijas de don Juan', p. 93.
57. Ibid.
58. Noël Valis, *Reading the Nineteenth Century Spanish Novel: Selected Essays* (Newark: Juan de la Cuesta, 2005) p. 63.
59. Blanca de los Ríos, *Afirmación de la Raza: porvenir Hispanoamericano*, (Madrid: Imprenta de Bernardo Rodríguez, 1911) p. 21.
60. Blanca de los Ríos, *De la mística y la novela contemporánea* (Madrid: Imprenta Ibérica, 1909).
61. De los Ríos, *De la mística*, p. 28.
62. Miguel de Unamuno, *Del sentimiento trágico de la vida en los hombres y en los pueblos* (Madrid: Prudencio Pérez de Velasco, 1913).
63. Miguel de Unamuno, *En torno al casticismo* (Madrid: Alianza, 1986).
64. De los Ríos, 'Las hijas de don Juan', p. 93.
65. Robert Koch had refuted the prevailing notion of tuberculosis resulting from inheritance in 1882 when he announced the discovery of the *Mycobacterium tuberculosis*, which showed that the condition was in fact an infectious disease.
66. De los Ríos, 'Las hijas de don Juan', p. 108.
67. Johnson, *Gender and Nation*, p. 129.
68. Ibid.
69. De los Ríos, 'Las hijas de don Juan', p. 76.
70. De los Ríos, 'Las hijas de don Juan', p. 95.
71. De los Ríos, 'Las hijas de don Juan', p. 83.
72. De los Ríos, 'Las hijas de don Juan', p. 82. The relationship between reading and identity is made explicit throughout. Fontibre turns to morphine after having read a serial story entitled *El paraíso de un morfinómano* (The Paradise of a Morphine Addict). Reading cheap literature is seen as a seductive activity parallel to drug-taking: '*el gozador decrépito halló su anhelo refugiado, sensorial, voluptuoso, en el novelesco* hatchis *sugeridor de* euforia *morbosa, de artificiales delicias, en el pérfido alcaloide que diluye en la sangre el jugo maldito de todas las flores del mal*' (the decrepit philanderer found his hidden, sensorial and voluptuous longing in the novelesque hashish suggestive of morbid euphoria, of artificial delights, in the treacherous alkaloid that dilutes in the blood the damned juice of all the flowers of evil). Bordonada notes the reference to *Les fleurs du mal* and Baudelaire's attempt to evade reality through the artificial paradise created by

Notes (Chapter 1)

      drugs and alcohol (de los Ríos, 'Las hijas de don Juan', p. 118n).
73. De los Ríos, 'Las hijas de don Juan', p. 99.
74. In an essay entitled 'Don Juan y sus avatares', *Revista Nacional de Educación*, 77 (8) 1948, p. 41, de los Ríos notes that, '*en manos de Zorrilla, Don Juan, trocado en fanfarrón de libertinaje y homicidios, muerto impenitente y salvado por la herética doctrina de la rendención por el amor profano, perdió su nimbo de ejemplaridad católica, pero envuelto en un torrente de arrogancia y de poesía, nos arrebata el aplauso frenético y vuelve anualmente a nuestra Escena como una efemérides nacional. El fuego interno que anima la creación de Tirso sigue prendiendo en perennes avatares*' (in Zorrilla's hands, Don Juan, transformed into a braggart of libertinism and homicides, impenitent on death and saved by the heretical doctrine of redemption by profane love, lost his halo of Catholic exemplariness, but enclosed in a torrent of arrogance and poetry, he attracts our frenetic applause and returns annually to our Stage like a national celebration. The fire within which animates Tirso's creation continues to kindle perennial avatars).
75. Johnson (*Gender and Nation*, p. 130) notes that, 'the narrator understands that *fin de siècle* literary trends like decadentism, which emphasizes sexual perversion, were extremely damaging to women.' The association between popular erotic fiction and Don Juan is made explicit in the magazine, *El Don Juan*, from 1910, a *periódico galante*, a Barcelona based weekly publication that was directed at the man about town, and that featured piquant jokes, salacious short fiction and advertisements for pornographic novelettes on the back page. The first edition dates to 19 November 1910, edited by Enrique Godó. The Hemeroteca in Madrid stocks only two copies of this magazine, making it difficult to discern how long the publication remained in print.
76. Kirsty Hooper, 'Extranjera en mi patria: gender and nation in the pre-1914 writings of Sofía Casanova (1861–1958)', University of Oxford dissertation, 2003, p. 167.
77. Lázaro, 'El "Don Juan" de Blanca de los Ríos', p. 475.
78. Hooper points out that, although the genre was tainted with associations of femininity in comparison with the literary heavyweight, the realist novel, the number of women writers was nevertheless small compared with the stories written by male writers. Hooper, 'Extranjera en mi patria', pp. 169, 171–5. A short story by Catelle Méndes that appears in *El Don Juan* is a slightly racy tale of a girl whose mother wishes to remarry and chooses a younger man. Her daughter gets her own back by tempting him with her blouse open, showing '*las tintas de nieve y los matices de*

Notes (Chapter 1)

rosa' (the snowy tints and shades of pink) of her *'delicado seno'* (delicate breast) until he kisses her.
79. Lázaro, 'El "Don Juan" de Blanca de los Ríos', p. 475; Glenn, 'Demythification, p. 229.
80. Glenn ('Demythification, p. 229) who cites Maryellen Bieder's excellent article entitled 'Woman and the twentieth century Spanish literary canon: the lady vanishes', *Anales de la literatura española contemporánea*, 17 (1992) pp. 301–24.
81. See the controversy that surrounded Brieux's play *Les Avariés*, which tackled the conspiracy of silence surrounding syphilis. Despite having been endorsed by George Bernard Shaw in 1905, it was banned in England until it eventually appeared in 1911. See also Lesley A. Hall, *Sex, Sin and Suffering: Venereal Disease and European Society since 1870* (London: Routledge, 2001). It seems likely that de los Ríos saw it as taboo to mention venereal disease explicitly.
82. Anne McClintock, *Imperial Leather: Race, Gender and Sexuality in the Colonial Contest* (London: Routledge, 1995) p. 47 draws together a link between female sexuality, degeneration and contagion in the context of Victorian England when she explains that, 'the image of bad blood was drawn from biology but degeneration was less a biological fact than it was a social figure. Central to the idea of degeneration was the idea of *contagion* (the communication of disease, by touching, from body to body) and central to the idea of contagion was the peculiarly Victorian paranoia about boundary order. ... Body boundaries were felt to be dangerously permeable and demanding continual purification, so that sexuality, in particular woman's sexuality, was cordoned off as the central transmitter of racial and hence cultural contagion.'
83. See Susan Sontag's portrait of the disease in *Illness as Metaphor* (Harmondsworth: Penguin, 1977) pp. 25–6.
84. Sontag, *Illness as Metaphor*, p. 42. Robert Koch discovered the *Mycobacterium tuberculosis* responsible for contagion in 1882.
85. Lázaro, 'El "Don Juan" de Blanca de los Ríos', p. 472.
86. De los Ríos, 'Las hijas de don Juan', p. 73. The *guayabera* is a loose shirt, typically from Cuba, while the *mantón*, a Manila shawl, was shipped to Spain from China via the port of Manila. The *mantón* was traditionally worn by the *chula*, a working-class woman from Madrid.
87. Philip W. Silver, *Ruin and Restitution: Reinterpreting Romanticism in Spain* (Nashville: Vanderbilt University Press, 1997); Inman Fox, *La invención de España: nacionalismo liberal e identidad nacional*, (Madrid: Cátedra, 1998).
88. Labanyi, 'Political readings', n.p.

Notes (Chapter 1)

89. De los Ríos, 'Las hijas de don Juan', p. 73.
90. Pike (*Hispanismo 1898–1930*, p. 51) who goes on to say that others turned to Europeanization (advancing links with Europe to compete with the machines, industries, banks and money of the United States) or else to regionalism. Thinkers such as Unamuno and Maeztu started out turning to Europe as a solution to Spain's problems, but increasingly saw Spanish America as providing a greater hope for Spain's future. Scholars have noted how the Americas were part of the forging of Spanish identity only after 1898. Carlos Serrano, *El nacimiento de Carmen: símbolos, mitos y nación* (Madrid: Taurus, 1999) pp. 77–131 demonstrates how Spain 'rediscovered' the Americas post-1898 in a series of monuments and commemorations. See also Christopher Schmidt-Nowara, *The Conquest of History: Spanish Colonialism and National Histories in the Nineteenth Century* (Pittsburgh: University of Pittsburgh Press, 2006); and Eric Storm, 'The problems of the Spanish nation building process around 1900', *National Identities*, 6 (2) 2004, pp. 143–56.
91. Pike, *Hispanismo 1898–1936*, p. 55.
92. Miguel de Unamuno, 'La raza ibero-americana en la gran raza latina', *Unión Ibero-Americana* (special issue) 1904, cited in Pike, *Hispanismo 1898–1936*, p. 60.
93. See Pike's chapter on 'The Spanish raza and Spain's mission in America', in Pike, *Hispanismo 1898–1936*, pp. 128–45.
94. De los Ríos, *Afirmación de la Raza*.
95. De los Ríos, *Afirmación de la Raza*, p. 10.
96. De los Ríos, *Afirmación de la Raza*, p. 14.
97. De los Ríos, *Afirmación de la Raza*, p. 11.
98. Maeztu, *Don Quijote*, p. 72.
99. Maeztu, *Don Quijote*, p. 74.
100. Maeztu, *Don Quijote*, p. 88.
101. Britt Arredondo, *Quixotism*, pp. 152–3.
102. Pike, *Hispanismo 1898–1936*, p. 295.
103. De los Ríos, *Afirmación de la Raza*, p. 9. Motherhood was seen as the main role for women in the early part of the twentieth century. See Mary Nash, 'Un/contested identities: motherhood, sex reform and the modernization of gender identity in early twentieth-century Spain', in Victoria Loree Enders and Pamela Beth Radcliffe (eds) *Constructing Spanish Womanhood: Female Identity in Modern Spain* (Albany: State University of New York Press, 1999, pp. 25–49).
104. The narrator uses language to evoke questions of taste. Thus, her text is scattered with language used as value judgement (*selezta*), the use of the Madrid accent to denote the lower-class status of the Corderos; the scattering of French words *toilette* to suggest Lita's

Notes (Chapter 1)

seduction by the decadent Garba; the *guayabera* to evoke the exotic provenance of the clothes worn by the lower classes in church). She also invents words of her own, '*diminutivar, femenizando, piltrafería*' as Glenn, 'Demythification, p. 228 points out.
105. De los Ríos, *Afirmación de la Raza*, p. 15.
106. De los Ríos, *Los grandes mitos*, p. 11.
107. Blanca de los Ríos de Lampérez, 'Hispanismo', in Blanca de los Ríos de Lampérez (ed.) *Nuestra raza es española (ni Latina ni Ibera)* (Madrid: Imprenta E. Maestre, 1926) p. 14.
108. De los Ríos de Lampérez, 'Hispanismo', p. 15.
109. De los Ríos de Lampérez, 'Hispanismo', p. 16.
110. Ibid.
111. Ernesto Giménez Caballero, *Los toros, las castañuelas y la virgen*, (Madrid: Caro Raggio, 1927) p. 118.
112. From *Genio de España*, cited in Jo Labanyi, 'Internalisations of empire: colonial ambivalence and the early Francoist missionary film', *Discourse*, 23 (1) 2001, p. 28.
113. Ernesto Giménez Caballero, *Genio de España: exaltaciones a una resurrección nacional y del mundo* (Barcelona: Ediciones Jerarquía, 1939) p. 160.
114. Labanyi, 'Political readings', n.p. An alternative to this fascist view of Don Juan's role in Europe is provided by Salvador de Madariaga, also cited by Labanyi, whose radio play of 1948 *La Don-Juanía o Seis Don Juanes y una Dama* (*Don-Juanism or Six Don Juans and a Lady*), written for the BBC Latin American Service for broadcast to Latin America on Halloween, brought together six different European versions of Don Juan (Byron's English Don Juan, Pushkin's Russian, Tirso and Zorrilla's Spanish, Molière's Frenchman and Mozart's Italian Don Giovanni) whose rivalry (an implicit allegory of the Second World War) is stopped by a veiled Doña Inés, who declares herself to be the eternal feminine. As Labanyi notes, 'Only Zorrilla's Romantic Don Juan is capable of appreciating her message of redemption through love. ... It is the Spanish Don Juan and Doña Inés who offer a model of redemptive love that brings peace to Europe' (Labanyi, 'Political readings', n.p.). See Salvador de Madariaga, 'La don-juanía o seis don Juanes y una dama', in Salvador de Madariaga (ed.) *Teatro en prosa y verso* (Madrid: Espasa-Calpe, 1983) pp. 419–48.
115. Labanyi, 'Political readings', n.p.
116. González López, *Aproximación a la obra*, p. 11.
117. Labanyi, 'Internalisations of empire', p. 29.
118. See Anne McClintock's discussion of colonialism and race in Victorian Britain in which 'controlling women's sexuality, exalting

maternity and breeding a virile race of empire-builders were widely perceived as the paramount means for controlling the health and wealth of the male imperial body politic' (McClintock, *Imperial Leather*, p. 47).

2. Performance Anxieties: Don Juan in the Consulting Room

1. Nash, 'Un/contested identities'.
2. Alison Sinclair, 'Love, again: crisis and the search for consolation. The *Revista de Occidente* and the creation of a culture, 1923–1936', in Laura Passerini et al. (eds) *New Dangerous Liaisons* (forthcoming) notes that Marañón's work for 'sexual reform suggests that his views might be generally liberal in character, but his interest in eugenics places him (and others) in markedly prescriptive positions. The apparent mismatch between his role as leader of sexual reform, and the nature of his theories is arguably characteristic of Spain at the time, rather than exceptional and puzzling', n.p.
3. See for example, Francisco Agustín, *Don Juan en el teatro, en la novela y en la vida* (Madrid: Editorial Peláez, 1928); Arturo Farinelli, *Don Giovanni* (Turin: Ermanno Loescher, 1896); Gérard Gendarme de Bévotte, *La légende de Don Juan* (Paris: Hachette, 1911); Gonzalo Lafora, *Don Juan, los milagros y otros ensayos* (Madrid: Biblioteca Nueva, 1927); Ramiro de Maeztu, *Don Quijote, Don Juan y la Celestina: ensayos en simpatía* (Madrid: Espasa-Calpe, 1925); Menéndez Pidal, 'Sobre los orígenes'; José Ortega y Gasset, 'Introducción a un Don Juan', in José Ortega y Gasset (ed.) *Obras completas* (Madrid: Revista de Occidente, 1921) vol. 6, pp. 121–37; Ramón Pérez de Ayala, *Las máscaras* (Madrid: Calleja, 1919); Otto Rank, *Don Juan et le double* (Paris: Payot, 1913); and Saíd Armesto, *La leyenda*. This list is not exhaustive. For an excellent bibliography, see Pérez-Bustamente, *Don Juan Tenorio*.
4. Nerea Aresti, *Médicos, donjuanes y mujeres modernas: las ideales de feminidad y masculinidad en el primer tercio del siglo XX* (Bilbao: Universidad del País Vasco, 2001) p. 182.
5. Margarita Nelken, *La mujer ante las cortes constituyentes* (Madrid: Castro, 1931) citing Eleuterio Mañueco Villapadierna, in a report on *Sociedad española de higiene* of 1914, cited in Nerea Aresti's excellent study of the period (*Médicos, donjuanes y mujeres modernas*) p. 181. Ricardo Royo-Villanova Morales, 'Notas para una nueva biología

Notes (Chapter 2)

de Don Juan', *Revista Española de Medicina y Cirugía*, 14 (November) 1931b) p. 573 cites a work by J. Moneva Pujo entitled, *La posición moral y la posición jurídica ante el donjuanismo*, which was apparently published in Madrid in 1929.

6. Ramón Pérez de Ayala, *Las máscaras* (Madrid: Austral, 1940) p. 337.
7. Michel Foucault, *The History of Sexuality* (London: Penguin Books, 1990) p. 119.
8. Gregorio Marañón, *Don Juan: ensayos sobre el origen de su leyenda*, (Madrid: Espasa-Calpe, 1942) VIII, p. 349.
9. Marañón, *Obras completas*, VIII, p. 347.
10. Sexual continence is exemplified for Marañón in the figure of Henri Frederic Amiel. See my forthcoming article 'The Reluctant Don Juans: Marañón, Lorca, Amiel', in *Anales de la literatura española contemporánea*, 32 (2) 2007, pp. 447–61.
11. This term is taken from Ludwik Fleck's ground-breaking analysis, *Genesis and Development of a Scientific Fact* (Chicago: University of Chicago Press, 1979) of the way pre-scientific notions enter into science and may later be proved as fact. His example is syphilis, which for years was associated with 'bad blood' before the Wasserman test confirmed this as fact. First published in 1935, his work was largely ignored by the scientific community until its reprinting in 1979.
12. Diana Long Hall, 'Biology, sex hormones and sexism in the 1920s', *Philosophical Forum*, 1 (2) 1973, pp. 80–3.
13. Mitchell, *Mad Men and Medusas*, p. 252.
14. Foucault, *History of Sexuality*. It would be left to Otto Rank (*The Don Juan Legend*) to fill in the gap left by Freudian psychoanalysis. Rank's theory draws on Sigmund Freud's 'Totem and taboo', *The Standard Edition of the Complete Psychological Works of Sigmund Freud* (London: Vintage, 2001, first published 1913) vol. 13, pp. 1–162, to posit Don Juan's homosexuality.
15. Mitchell, *Mad Men and Medusas*, p. 38. Gonzalo Rodríguez Lafora, *Don Juan and Other Psychological Studies* (London: Thornton Butterworth, 1930) p. 43, like Mitchell, notes the tendency to tell lies as one symptom of male hysteria, alongside 'fickleness or inconstancy of character', the tendency to 'go in for exaggeration and play acting', 'exaggerated boastfulness and false chivalry'. Rodríguez Lafora's explanation of male hysteria remains under theorized.
16. Rodríguez Lafora, *Don Juan*, pp. 42–3.
17. Mitchell, *Mad Men and Medusas*, pp. 251–67.
18. From an unpublished manuscript at the Fundación Gregorio Marañón, Madrid.

Notes (Chapter 2)

19. 'Notas para una biología de Don Juan', *Revista de Occidente*, Año 11, vol. VII (January 1924) pp. 15-53 and in Gregorio Marañón, *Obras completas*, vol. 4, pp. 75-93. 'Psicopatología del donjuanismo' (a reprinting of this article under a different name) appears in *Obras completas*, vol. 3, pp. 75-94.
20. Marañón, *Obras completas*, III, p. 76.
21. Ibid.
22. Marañón, *Obras completas*, VIII, p. 340.
23. Marañón, *Obras completas*, III, p. 177.
24. Marañón, *Obras completas*, III, p. 76.
25. Marañón, *Obras completas*, III, p. 77.
26. Ibid.
27. Marañón, *Obras completas*, III. p. 76.
28. Marañón, *Obras completas*, III, p. 77.
29. Juliet Mitchell, *Mad Men and Medusas*, p. 95 writes that, 'as the "talking cure" grew in popularity, so did the hysterical ability to imitate it. Lying has always been noted as a characteristic of hysteria.'
30. Of course, hysteria also has bodily symptoms that are 'read' from the body.
31. Marañón, like most neurologists, relied on visual processes for the execution of his work. He used histology to chart the flow of internal secretions, and photography to aid his classification of morphological types.
32. Letter from Santiago Ramón y Cajal to Gregorio Marañón, March 1928, from the archives of the Fundación Marañón, Madrid. There is no correspondence in Cajal's files to suggest that any journalists or newspaper editors actively thwarted him in his choice of topics.
33. Marañón, *Obras completas*, III, p. 78.
34. Marañón's comments on dissecting Don Juan to '*tiempos más lejanos*' (far distant times) may suggest a concern about the possible atavism of sexual traits and degenerationist theories. For example, within the theory of atavism, the homosexual was considered an ancestral throwback. Michel Foucault, *The History of Sexuality*, volume 1, *An Introduction* (Harmondsworth: Penguin, 1990) p. 118 writes on the theory of 'degenerescence': 'it explained how a heredity that was burdened with various maladies (it made little difference whether these were organic, functional or psychical) ended by producing a sexual pervert (look into the genealogy of an exhibitionist or a homosexual: you will find a hemiplegic ancestor, a phthisic parent, or an uncle afflicted with senile dementia).'
35. Marañón, *Obras completas*, III, p. 78. The assertion of the privileged position of the doctor was one echoed by Lafora (*Don Juan*);

Notes (Chapter 2)

Hernani Mandolini, 'Psicopatología del Don Juan', *Revista de Criminología, Psiquiatría y Medicina Legal*, May–June (1926) pp. 332–30; Royo-Villanova y Morales, 'Notas para una nueva biología de Don Juan' and others who attempted to diagnose Don Juan's symptoms. Rodríguez Lafora attributes part of Don Juan's psychosexual make-up to the peculiar situation for young men in Spain, where 'owing to Oriental and Arab historical influences, the separation of the sexes is stricter than in countries of central Europe, the youthful adolescent commonly takes his first steps in sexual life in the brothel, and so gets accustomed to a kind of carnal or physical love without a grain of idealism and without any psychological concomitants' (Rodríguez Lafora, *Don Juan*, p. 47). Sexual intercourse 'made easy for men by prostitution, is apt to turn the sexually inclined young man into what the German pathologists (amongst them Hirschfeld) call a "sexual athlete", whose tireless eroticism is encouraged by premature undue excitement of the endocrine glands' (Rodríguez Lafora, *Don Juan*, p. 48). He describes the clinical case of a Don Juan, a 'well-to-do bachelor of thirty-four years of age' whose misadventures lead to a mistress falling pregnant: 'our Don Juan, influenced partly by the idea of having a son of his own, partly by the increased beauty he now discovered in his melancholy and troubled mistress, fell in love with her.' But he was terrified of her leaving him as he had left so many women. 'Madly the lovers met in cinemas and theatres, risking possible discovery, and surrendering themselves to emotional rapture. Don Juan was being reformed. Sentimental complications on the screen or the stage made them weep together like children' (Rodríguez Lafora, *Don Juan*, p. 69). In the end he turned to religion to ease his pain.
36. Corpus Barga, 'Don Juan y los doctores', *El Sol*, 19 December 1926, p. 1, writes, *'Don Juan no ha sido un hombre natural; ha sido, en el estricto sentido se la palabra, un prejuicio literario'* (Don Juan has never been a natural man; he has been, strictly speaking, a literary device). Mandolini, in his study, gets around the problem of Don Juan's literary status by claiming that by Don Juan he is not referring to the *'archiconocido símbolo del espadachín inmoral y aventurero que nació de la leyenda y cursó las tablas desde Tirso de Molina hasta Zorrilla'* (infamous symbol of the immoral and adventurous swordsman, who was born of legend and tread the boards from Tirso de Molina to Zorrilla), rather, he widens the type to include historical figures such as Julius Caesar, Andronicus and Romantic seducers (Mandolini, 'Psicopatología', p. 322).
37. Marañón, *Obras completas*, VIII, p. 89.

Notes (Chapter 2)

38. In his discussion of morphology, Marañón was influenced by Ernst Kretschmer's, *Physique and Character: An Investigation of the Nature of Constitution and of the Theory of Temperament* (London: Kegan Paul, 1925) body types (which others were using to attempt to account for criminal typology). Marañón, *Obras completas*, VIII, p. 367–412 wrote a treatise on morphology entitled, 'Gordos y flacos'. See also Lombroso (*Los criminales*) for his account of 'criminaloides'. See also Antonio Molero Asenjo, *Observaciones antropológicas de las anomalías en los criminales* (Guadalajara: Daniel Ramirez, 1910) pp. 18–19 who writes '*Morfológicamente, se evidencian distintivos caracteres en estos criminales, apreciándose precoz sinóstesis, desarrollo pronunciado de los senos frontales, gran desarrollo del temporal y de las mandíbulas.*' (In morphological terms, different characteristics are evidenced in these criminals, exhibiting sinostosis praecox, pronounced development of the frontal breasts, greatly developed temple and jaws.)
39. Marañón, *Obras completas*, VIII, p. 89.
40. Unfortunately all records of Marañón's case histories of patients have apparently been lost. Certainly, the Fundación Marañón is unaware of their whereabouts. Gonzalo Torrente Ballester, writing in 1960, notes, '*carecemos de estadísticas, de datos, de encuestas. Aquí nadie ha intentado nada parecido al "informe Kinsey"*' (we lack statistics, data, surveys. Here no-one has tried anything similar to the 'Kinsey Report').
41. Barga, 'Don Juan y los doctores', p. 1.
42. James J. Bono, 'Science, discourse and literature: the role/rule of metaphor in science', in Stuart Peterfreund (ed.) *Literature and Science: Theory and Practice* (Boston: Northeastern University Press, 1990) pp. 59–89.
43. Lisa Cartwright, *Screening the Body: Tracing Medicine's Visual Culture* (Minneapolis: University of Minnesota Press, 1995) writes persuasively of the importance of visual media in medicine.
44. Thomas F. Glick, 'The naked science: psychoanalysis in Spain, 1914–1948', *Comparative Studies in Society and History*, 24, 1982, pp. 533–71.
45. Marañón (*Obras completas*, VIII, p. 618 n.3) seems to attempt to marry psychology with biology, but repeatedly he returns to the organism to explain pathology. Most significantly, his theories, unlike those of psychoanalysts, find no place for unconscious fantasies. His definition of fetishism, in 1930, for example, is that it is caused by a system of conditioned reflexes, a theory he derives from I. P. Pavlov's *Los reflejos condicionados* (Madrid: Morata, 1929).
46. Michel Foucault, 'The discourse on language', in Michel Foucault

Notes (Chapter 2)

translated by A. M. Sheridan-Smith, *The Archaeology of Knowledge* (New York: Irvington Publishers, 1972) pp. 215–37.
47. For further discussion on the role of metaphor as a medium of exchange between discourses in science, see Bono, 'Science, discourse', pp. 59–89.
48. Nelly Oudshoorn, *Beyond the Natural Body: An Archaeology of Sex Hormones* (London: Routledge, 1994) p. 22.
49. Gregorio Marañón, 'Sesión de 6 de octubre de 1928', *Anales del servicio de patología médica del Hospital General de Madrid* (Madrid: Compañía Ibero-Americana de Publicaciones, 1928–9) vol. 4, pp. 3–4.
50. Oudshoorn, *Beyond the Natural Body*, p. 24.
51. Marañón, *Obras completas*, III, p. 83.
52. Ibid.
53. Dale Pratt, *Signs of Science: Literature, Science and Spanish Modernity Since 1868* (West Lafayette: Purdue University Press, 2001) pp. 1–14 has written of the perceptions within Spain of its own backwardness in the field of science at this time.
54. Diana Long Hall, 'Biology, sex hormones', p. 85 citing Geddes, Thompson and Heape. In the Spain of the 1920s and 1930s there was little discussion of 'bisexuality' in the sense that we might use it, although *'ambisexualidad'* was used occasionally. Bisexuality meant *'bisexualidad inicial del organismo'*, the germs of either sex within the embryo.
55. Marañón, *Obras completas*, III, p. 79.
56. Marañón, *Obras completas*, III, p. 81. José Ortega y Gasset, 'Amor en Stendhal', *El sol*, 24 August 1926, p. 6 is of the same opinion: *'Don Juan no es el hombre que hace el amor a las mujeres, sino el hombre a quien las mujeres hacen el amor'* (Don Juan is not the man who makes love to women, but rather the man to whom women make love).
57. Presumably, for this reason Marañón finds no irony in his own succumbing serially to the seductions offered by Don Juan's psychosexual make-up. In his pursuit of the aetiology of Don Juan's condition, he pursues the masculine stance of questor and adventurer.
58. Marañón, *Obras completas*, VIII, p. 325.
59. Marañón, *Obras completas*, VIII, p. 345.
60. See, for example, Anon. 'Los experimentos del Sr Voronoff', *El Sol*, 25 February 1926, p. 4; and F.H., 'El doctor Cardenal ensaya los métodos de Voronoff', *El Sol*, 26 February 1926, p. 4.
61. Pedro Muñoz Seca, *Las inyecciones o el doctor Cleofás Uthof vale más que Voronoff* (Madrid: Zaballos, 1927).
62. Thomas Glick, 'Trials of a preparadigmatic science: gerontology in Spain, 1910–1935', unpublished article, n.d., p. 9.

217

Notes (Chapter 2)

63. Marañón, *Obras completas*, I, pp. 437–44.
64. Glick, 'Trials of a preparadigmatic science', p. 12.
65. Ibid.
66. E. Bonilla, 'La lucha contra la vejez', *El Sol*, 1927, p. 7.
67. Chandak Sengoopta, 'Glandular politics: experimental biology, clinical medicine, and homosexual emancipation in fin-de-siècle central Europe', *Isis*, 89, 1998, p. 454.
68. Sengoopta, 'Glandular politics', p. 471.
69. Marañón, *The Evolution of Sex and Intersexual Conditions*, translated by Warre B. Wells (London: George Allen & Unwin Ltd, 1932) p. 169n.
70. Marañón, *The Evolution of Sex*, p. 169n.
71. Sengoopta, 'Glandular politics', p. 471.
72. Sengoopta, 'Glandular politics', p. 472.
73. Pedro Muñoz Seca and Pedro Pérez Fernández, *La plasmatoria: farsa cómica en tres actos* (Madrid: La Farsa, 1936) p. 46.
74. Jorge de la Cueva, 'La plasmatoria', *El Debate*, 1935, p. 4.
75. Thomas Alva Edison, *The Diary and Sundry Observations of Thomas Alva Edison* (New York: Philosophical Library, 1948) p. 234.
76. Ralph D. Blumenfeld recorded attending a séance with Conan Doyle in the 1920s and viewing the photographs afterwards: 'the double photograph showed between us what was said to be ectoplasm. To me it was like a cloudy smudge.' Quoted in Ronald Pearsell, *Conan Doyle: A Biographical Solution* (London: Weidenfeld & Nicholson, 1977) p. 232.
77. Muñoz Seca and Pérez Fernández, *La plasmatoria*, p. 43.
78. The painting is currently held at the Museo de Teatro in Almagro, Spain.
79. Muñoz Seca and Pérez Fernández, *La plasmatoria*, p. 46.
80. Barco Teruel, *Elogio y nostalgia de Gregorio Marañón* (Barcelona: Barça, 1961) p. 41.
81. Bernadino de Pantorba, *El pintor salaverría: ensayo biográfico y crítico* (Madrid: Espasa-Calpe, 1948) p. 25. See Aresti, *Médicos, donjuanes y mujeres modernas*, p. 137.
82. See Aresti, *Médicos, donjuanes y mujeres modernas*, p. 137; *El liberal* (Bilbao) 12 November 1927, p. 4. Dictionary references are in *Diccionario de la Real Academia Española* (Madrid: Real Academia, 1992 Madrid: Real Academia, 1992).
83. *Diccionario de la lengua española* (Madrid: Real Academia, 1992 Madrid: Real Academia, 1992) p. 1223.
84. The shooing motion presumably refers to effeminate mannerisms. In 1930 Marañón, *Don Juan*, VIII, p. 556 n.2 cites '*el gesto de la mano*' (gesturing with the hand), '*un gesto de adorno*' (gesturing as adornment) as characteristic of femininity. He also writes that '*estas*

Notes (Chapter 2)

actitudes o gestos del hombre homosexual no corresponden exactamente a los de la mujer' (these attitudes or gestures of the homosexual man do not correspond exactly to those of the woman), they are, so to speak, *'más estilizados'* (more stylized), *'llegando a veces a caricaturizarlos, por eso son tan fáciles de imitar'* (at times becoming caricatured, for this reason it is so easy to imitate them) (Marañón, *Obras completas*, VIII, p. 613). Yet he also makes it clear that not all homosexuals exhibit intersexual secondary sexual characteristics. *'Ladeao'* suggests the English term 'bent', which can, according to the 1992 edition of *Collins English Dictionary*, p. 139 mean 'sexually deviant, homosexual'. Meanwhile *'que si sí, que si no'* suggests indecision over sexual object choice.

85. Alan Sinfield, *The Wilde Century: Effeminacy, Oscar Wilde and the Queer Moment* (London: Cassell, 1994) p. 37 writes that 'up to the time of the Wilde trials – far later than is widely supposed – it is unsafe to interpret effeminacy as defining of, or as a signal of, same-sex passion'.
86. Marañón (*Obras completas*, VIII, p. 615 n.1) provides an explanation of his use of the term: *'al hablar de homosexuales, me refiero, naturalmente, sólo a aquellos en los que la inversión del instinto es un fenómeno evidente, hayan o no tenido relaciones homosexuales'* (on speaking of homosexuals, I am referring, naturally, only of those in whom the inversion of instinct is an evident phenomenon, whether or not they have had homosexual relations). He speaks of a *'secreto e inconsciente fondo homosexual'* (secret and unconscious homosexual inclination).
87. Paul Julian Smith, *The Theatre of García Lorca: Text, Performance, Psychoanalysis* (Cambridge: Cambridge University Press, 1998) p. 13.
88. Marañón, *Obras completas*, VII, p. 213.
89. Richard Cleminson, 'The review "Sexualidad" (1925–28), social hygiene and the pathologisation of male homosexuality in Spain', *Journal of Iberian and Latin American Studies*, 6 (2) 2000, pp. 119–29. The *Diccionario de la lengua española* cites *'dicho de un hombre homosexual'* (said of a homosexual man) as the third meaning of *'afeminado'* (effeminate). The dictionary did not acquire this third meaning until 1992, but our evidence from *La plasmatoria* suggests that equating effeminacy with homosexuality goes back much further. Furthermore, Gary Keller, whose book is the most thorough work on Marañón to date, writes that, 'the belief that Marañón implacably diagnosed Don Juan as a homosexual has entrenched itself so widely and deeply as to have become a topical assumption'. In the examples chosen by Keller from 1959 and 1960

Notes (Chapter 2)

of critical commentaries on Don Juan, we likewise find a switching between 'effeminacy' and 'homosexuality' as if they are synonymous. See Gary D. Keller, *The Significance and Impact of Gregorio Marañón: Literary Criticism, Biographies and Historiography* (New York: Bilingual Press, 1977) p. 237 n.75.

90. Marañón, *Obras completas*, VII, p. 213.
91. Ibid.
92. Letter from Cajal to Marañón, 1929, from the archives of the Fundación Marañón, Madrid.
93. Marañón, *Obras completas*, VIII, p. 627.
94. Marañón, *Obras completas*, VII, pp. 225-7.
95. Marañón, *Obras completas*, VIII, p. 616.
96. Marañón, *Obras completas*, VIII, p. 360.
97. Jean-François Lyotard, *The Postmodern Condition: A Report on Knowledge* (Manchester: Manchester University Press, 1989) pp. 27-8 writes that 'the state spends large amounts of money to enable science to pass itself off as epic', yet while scientists 'play by the rules of the narrative game' they simultaneously reject narrative as an inferior form of knowledge representation. Elizabeth Leane, 'Popular cosmology as mythic narrative: a site for interdisciplinary exchange', in Julie Scanlon and Amy Waste (eds) *Crossing Boundaries: Thinking Through Literature* (Sheffield: Sheffield Academic Press, 2001) pp. 84-97 applies Lyotard's theories to a discussion of the popularization of the work of Stephen Hawking.
98. The references are to Chris Rojek's definitions in *Celebrity* (London: Reaktion Books, 2001) of the 'celeactor' in the present day. Celeactors are fictional characters who are either momentarily ubiquitous or become an institutionalized feature of popular culture. They 'embody desire and galvanize issues in popular culture, dramatize prejudice, affect public opinion and contribute to identity formation' (Rojek, *Celebrity*, pp. 21, 26).
99. George Chauncey, *Gay New York: The Making of the Gay Male World, 1890-1940* (London: Harper Collins, 1994) p. 5. Smith, *The Theatre of García Lorca*, p. 19 has commented on the homophobic reporting of a 'strange brotherhood' that flocked to see Garcia Lorca's *Yerma* in 1934, 'shrieking in the intervals and archly gesturing with "their finger on their cheek"'. I have found no reporting of the presumed sexuality of audience members at *La plasmatoria*, although the end of the first act apparently caused laughter that lasted for five minutes (Gonzalo LaTorre, 'La plasmatoria', *La Nación*, 19 December 1935, p. 14).
100. Gaylin Studlar, *This Mad Masquerade: Stardom and Masculinity in the Jazz Age* (New York: Columbia University Press, 1996) pp. 78-9.

Notes (Chapter 2)

101. Ricardo Royo-Villanova Morales, 'La medicina y los médicos a la cabecera de Don Juan', *Revista Española de Medicina y Cirugía*, 14 (June) 1931, p. 281.
102. Marañón, *Obras completas*, VIII, p. 345.
103. Marañón, *Obras completas*, VIII, p. 325.
104. For an interesting analysis of the attempts of clinicians visually to trace blood's fluidity, see Cartwright, *Screening the Body*, p. 82.
105. Laura Otis, *Membranes: Metaphors of Invasion in Nineteenth-Century Literature, Science, and Politics* (Baltimore: The Johns Hopkins University Press, 1999) pp. 64–89, 90–118 writes persuasively of the metaphors of contagion and bacteriology in the work of Conan Doyle and of Santiago Ramón y Cajal.
106. José Ortega y Gasset, 'Para una psicología del hombre interesante', in José Ortega y Gasset (ed.) *Obras completas* (Madrid: Revista de Occidente, 1987) vol 4.
107. F. Oliver Brachfeld, *Polémica contra Marañón* (Barcelona: Europa, 1933) p. 32. Ricardo Royo-Villanova Morales, *Los médicos donjuanes: el nuevo donjuanismo* (Madrid: Imprenta Castellana, 1930) uses Marañón's theories of Don Juan to launch an attack on the medical establishment, declaring, that '*los medicos donjuanes*' (Don Juanesque doctors) pursue the profession for its prestige, and in order to be surrounded by women.
108. Carmen de Burgos, *La entrometida* (Madrid: La novela corta, 1921).
109. Miguel Ángel Lozano Marco, 'Introducción', in Ramón Pérez de Ayala (ed.) *Tigre Juan: el curandero de su honra* (Madrid: Espasa-Calpe, 1990) p. 36.
110. Andrés Franco, *El teatro de Unamuno* (Madrid: Insula, 1971).
111. Sarah Wright, 'Ethical seductions: a comparative reading of Unamuno's *El hermano Juan* and Kierkegaard's *Either/Or*', *Anales de La Literatura Española Contemporánea*, 29 (2) 2004, pp. 119–34.
112. Sarah Wright, 'The Reluctant Don Juans: Lorca, Amiel, Marañón', *Anales de la literatura española contemporánea*, 32 (2) 2007, pp. 447–61.
113. A reactionary contrast to these liberatory paradigms is the discussion of Don Juan provided by Giménez Caballero in his *Los toros, las castañuelas y la virgen* (The Bullfight, Castanets and the Virgin). After elaborating a theory by which Don Juan caused Marianism (women, for Don Juan are too close, too easy to seduce, leading to a need to distance them, adore them as in the case of the Virgin), he goes on to suggest contemporary gender paradigms of masculinized women – '*el pelo lamido de cosmético, en peinado equívocamente viril. ... Un poco más y se les ve caer en el homosexualismo. En fuerza de cultivar el cuerpo viril, sobrepasaron toda la apetencia de feminidad, hasta reducirse al esquema a que han llevado la*

de la actual mujer, incitándola a virilizarse' (the hair smoothed down with cosmetics, in an equivocally virile style. ... Just a bit further and they fall into homosexuality. As a result of cultivating a virile body, they go past all desire for femininity, until they are reduced to the schemata that represents contemporary woman, inciting her to masculinize herself). Giménez Caballero, *Los toros*, pp. 191, 192).

3. Screen Seductions: Negotiating Theatricality in Don Juan Films

1. Julia Kristeva, 'Ellipsis on dread and the specular seduction', *Wide Angle*, 3 (3) 1979, p. 46.
2. For Otto Rank (*The Don Juan Legend*, p. 41), 'the many women [Don Juan] must always replace anew represent to him the *one* irreplaceable mother.' For Otto Fenichel, *The Psychoanalytic Theory of Neuroses* (London: Routledge & Kegan Paul, 1946) pp. 243–4, 'Don Juan's behaviour is no doubt due to his Oedipus complex. He seeks his mother in all women and cannot find her. ... It is due to the archaic nature of the typical Don Juan's Oedipus complex that he is so little interested in the personality of his objects. He has not passed the pre-stages of love. His sexual activities are primarily designed to contradict an inner feeling of inferiority by proof of erotic "successes". After having "made" a woman, he is no longer interested in her, first because she too, has failed to failed to bring about the longed-for relaxation, and second because his narcissistic need requires proof of his ability to excite women; after he knows he can exite a specific woman, his doubts rise concerning other women whom he has not yet tried'. J. Flugel, *Men and their Morals* (London: Routledge & Kegan Paul, 1934) p. 108, in similar fashion, relates Don Juan's perpetual seductions to his search for an ideal that no one can live up to. Jacques Lacan, meanwhile, writes that Don Juan is a feminine dream of a man who is lacking nothing. See Roberto Harari, *Lacan's Seminar on 'Anxiety': An Introduction,* translated by Jane C. Lamb-Ruiz (New York: Other Press, 2001) pp. 154–5.
3. Mary Ann Doane, *Femmes Fatales: Feminism, Film Theory, Psychoanalysis* (London: Routledge, 1996) p. 1.
4. The grand opening of the film also featured a brief filmed speech by Will Hays, head of the Motion Picture Producers and Directors of America. See Aristides Gazetas, *An Introduction to World Cinema* (Jefferson: Mcfarland & Company, 2000) p. 95.
5. Palmira González López, 'Don Juan Tenorio 1910', in Julio Pérez

Notes (Chapter 3)

Perucha (ed.) *Antología crítica del cine español 1906–1995: flor en la sombra* (Madrid: Cátedra, 1997) pp. 28–30.
6. Several versions of the 1922 version circulate. Luis Miguel Fernández, 'Don Juan en imágenes: aproximación a la recreación cinematográfica del personaje', in Ana Sofía Pérez-Bustamante (ed.) *Don Juan Tenorio en la España del Siglo XX* (Madrid: Cátedra, 1998) p. 518 also mentions a version from 1921 to which sound was added during the Spanish Civil War and was released in 1943 under the title *El castigador castigado* (The Punisher Punished). The 1910 version had a humorous text added by Antonio Sau in the style of Enrique Jardial Poncela's *'celuloides rancios'* (rancid celluloids) and was released in 1942 under the title *Vida privada de Don Juan* or *Don Juan en píldoras* (Private Life of Don Juan or Doses of Don Juan). I am working from the copy housed at the Filmoteca de Catalunya, Barcelona. It opened on 27 October 1922 in Barcelona. The *Parodia del Tenorio*, also named *Tenorio Porno* (date unknown) is also attributed to the de Baños. A description of its risqué content (including nude masturbation scenes) is provided by Fernández (*Don Juan en el cine*, pp. 196–7).
7. González López, 'Don Juan Tenorio 1910', p. 30.
8. Fernand Léger, 'A critical essay on the plastic qualities of Abel Gance's film The Wheel', in Edward Fry (ed.) *Functions of Painting* (London: Thames & Hudson, 1973) p. 21 cited in Tom Gunning, 'The cinema of attractions: early film, its spectator and the avant-garde', in Thomas Elsaesser (ed.) *Early Cinema: Space, Frame, Narrative* (London: British Film Institute, 1990) p. 56.
9. Jean Mitry, *Histoire du cinéma* (Paris: Editions Universitaires, 1967) p. 370 cited in André Gaudreault, 'Theatricality, narrativity, and trickality: reevaluating the cinema of Georges Méliès', *Journal of Popular Film and Television*, 15 (3) 1987, p. 112.
10. Mitry, *Histoire du cinéma*, p. 400.
11. Juan Francisco de Lasa, *Los hermanos Baños* (Madrid: Filmoteca Nacional de España, 1975) p. 13.
12. Andrew Ginger, 'Dashing on the silver screen: Don Juan Tenorio (1922) Dir Ricardo de Baños (based on the play of the same title by José Zorrilla (1844)', in Andrew Ginger, Huw Lewis and John Hobbs (eds) *Selected Interdisciplinary Essays on the Representation of the Don Juan Archetype in Myth and Culture* (Lewiston: Edwin Mellen Press, 2000) pp. 187–213. I am very grateful to Andrew Ginger for discussion and materials relating to the film.

Notes (Chapter 3)

13. It is interesting to note that both Ricardo, the director, and his brother Ramón, the cameraman, are afforded equal importance.
14. As an aside, it was the double exposure technique in Rye's *The Student of Prague*, used to create the double who emerged from the mirror, that led Otto Rank to conceive of his theory of the double, a theory that would later emerge in his thesis that Leporello is Don Juan's double, or alter ego. See Otto Rank, 'Der Doppelgänger', *Imago: A Journal for the Application of Psychoanalysis to the Human Sciences*, 3 (1914) pp. 97–164; and Rank, *The Don Juan Legend*.
15. Gaudreault, 'Theatricality, narrativity, and trickality'.
16. Gunning, 'The cinema of attractions'.
17. X. Theodore Barber, 'Phantasmagorical wonders: the magic lantern ghost show in nineteenth-century America', *Film History*, 3 (1989) p. 76 relates the history of the magic lantern show, seeing the 'phantasmagoria' as the forerunner of the trick-shot in cinema. They included, in one show by Etienne Gaspard Robertson in the USA, a phantom known as the Bleeding Nun, derived from the Gothic novel *The Monk* by Matthew Lewis.
18. For Kristeva, 'Ellipsis on dread', p. 46, it is the role of cinema to capture terror and restore it to the symbolic order (her example is Christian art, viewed in the 'penumbra of churches').
19. Tom Gunning, 'An aesthetic of astonishment: early film and the (in)credulous spectator', in Linda Williams (ed.) *Viewing Positions: Ways of Seeing Film* (New Brunswick: Rutgers University Press, 1997) p. 117 describes the 'aesthetic of astonishment' deriving from the awe and wonder audiences felt at early cinema, but suggests it involved an intellectual disavowal – I know, but yet I see – rather than a fear or incredulity at the images projected. Barber, 'Phantasmagorical wonders, p. 78 suggests that phantasmagoria had more to do with a fascination with science than with fear of the afterlife.
20. Fernández, *Don Juan en el cine*, p. 143. The *destape* (literally 'taking the lid off'): 'a partial relaxation in the censorship laws during the mid-1970s produced a "boom" in the publication of soft porn and films that included sexualized or soft-porn scenes' (Núria Triana-Toribio, *Spanish National Cinema*, London: Routledge, 2003, p. 179).
21. In 1988 Fernando Guillén had played the role of the playboy boyfriend in Pedro Almodóvar's *Mujeres al borde de un ataque de nervios*.
22. Javier Hernández Ruiz, 'La Celestina, don Juan y el Quijote en las pantallas: luces y sombras de sus recreaciones audiovisuales', in *Ties Mitos españoles: La Celestina, Don Quijote, Don Juan* (Madrid: Sociedad estatal de commemoraciones culturales, 2004) p. 147

Notes (Chapter 3)

23. John Berry was in exile after making *The Hollywood Ten* (1950) during the McCarthy witch hunts.
24. The film stars famous comic actresses Veronica Forqué and Rossy de Palma.
25. See Roger Mortimore, 'Buñuel, Sáenz de Heredia and filmófono', *Sight and Sound*, 44 (1975) pp. 180-2 for Sáenz de Heredia's early collaborations with Buñuel.
26. Sáenz de Heredia was the cousin of the martyred founder of the Falange, José Antonio Primo de Rivera.
27. Javier Memba, 'José Luis Sáenz de Heredia: El Leni Riefhsteald [sic] de Franco', *El Mundo*, 5 November 1992, p. 10.
28. Ángel Fernández Santos, 'Muere José Luis Sáenz de Heredia, el máximo cineasta del franquismo militante', *El País*, 1992, p. 36.
29. Susan Martín Márquez, *Feminist Discourse and Spanish Cinema: Sight Unseen* (Oxford: Oxford University Press, 1999) p. 89.
30. Cinematography was by Alfredo Fraile, music by Manuel Parada, script by Carlos Blanco and José Luis Sáenz de Heredia.
31. The Cine Avenida, Avda. de José Antonio, now Gran Vía, opened in 1928 as a theatre and 1929 as a cinema with 1632 seats (later reduced to 1576). See Pascual Ceballada and Mary G. Santa Eulalia, *Madrid y el Cine* (Madrid: Comunidad de Madrid, 2000) p. 239.
32. Triana-Toribio, *Spanish National Cinema*, p. 51.
33. The year 1553 places the setting within the empire of the reign of Carlos V, grandson of the 'Catholic Monarchs' Ferdinand and Isabella. It was the date of Bartolomé de las Casas's 'Treatise Confining the Sovereign Empire and Universal Princedom that the Kings of Castile and Leon pursue over the Indians'. The year 1553 was also the date of publication of the first Spanish Old Testament, the Ferrara Bible.
34. Luis de Pedrola, 'La legendaria figura de Don Juan en una magnífica película española', *Cámara*, 186 (1950) p. 10. It is worth noting that the cast is international, including the film's protagonist, Vilar, who is Portuguese, but repeatedly referred to in press publicity as 'Iberian'.
35. A. P., 'Don Juan, el personaje español famoso en todo el mundo, en una grandiosa superproducción nacional', *Cámara*, 187 (1950) p. 44.
36. Anon., '"Don Juan", realización cumbre de Sáenz de Heredia, triunfa en el cine Avenida', *Ya*, 17 October 1950, p. 6. For a comparison of Sáenz de Heredia's *Don Juan* and the Errol Flynn vehicle, see Labanyi ('Impossible love') who notes that Sáenz de Heredia's film was a direct riposte to Sherman's epic and contains many references to the other film.
37. A pamphlet entitled, *The Spanish Cinema* (Madrid: Diplomatic

Notes (Chapter 3)

Information Office, 1950) advertises the strong film-making talent to be found in Spain, and encourages foreign film makers to make films in Spain, foregrounding the high quality films made on low budgets and highlighting the production of *Valca*, a Spanish-made raw film.

38. Censorship laws would not be formalized until 1964, but the regulations of 1964 state quite clearly that adultery and illicit sexual relations must not be portrayed in any way as justified. See the 'Normas de censura cinematográfica', 8 March 1963, *Boletín Oficial del Estado*, No. 58. I would like to thank Catherine O'Leary for providing me with a copy of this material.
39. Now generally used as a pejorative term to refer to Spanish films that focus on local customs, folklore and stereotyped characters within an Andalusian setting. Triana-Toribio (*Spanish National Cinema*) pp. 62–5 provides an excellent discussion of the debates for and against the *españolada* during the 1940s and 1950s in Spain. For some commentators, *españolada* came to connote low quality film-making in Spain. According to her definitions, *Don Juan* could be seen as a 'highbrow *españolada*. The trampling of a red carnation into the ground by Don Juan could be seen as the perceived triumph of literary over folkloric 'Spanishness' as presented in this film.
40. Miriam Hansen, *Babel and Babylon: Spectatorship in American Silent Film* (Cambridge, MA: Harvard University Press, 1991) p. 3.
41. Hansen, *Babel and Babylon*, p. 253.
42. Ernesto Giménez Caballero, *El cine y la cultural humana* (Bilbao: Tipografía Hispano-Americana, 1944) p. 29.
43. In an attempt to account for spectatorship in the 1950s, I include material in my study dating from 1944 to 1960.
44. Miguel Siguan, *El cine, el amor y otros ensayos* (Madrid: Editora Nacional, 1956) p. 15.
45. Ernesto Gutiérrez del Egido ¡*Conquistemos el cine! Hacia una solución total y acertada del problema cinematográfico* (Ávila: Gloria, 1946) p. 17.
46. Siguan, *El cine*, p. 15.
47. Siguan, *El cine*, p. 19.
48. José Manuel Vivanco, *Moral y pedagogía del cine* (Madrid: Ediciones Fax, 1952).
49. José Luis García Escudero, *El cine y los hijos* (Madrid: Esse, 1959).
50. Juan García Yagüe, *Cine y juventud* (Madrid: Consejo superior de investigaciones científicas, 1953) p. 191.
51. Siguan, *El cine*, p. 32.
52. Anon. ¿*Sabes ir al cine?* (Madrid: Talitha, 1960) p. 7.
53. Anon. ¿*Sabes ir al cine?* p. 3.

Notes (Chapter 3)

54. Juan Gil-Albert, *Contra el cine* (Valencia: Tip. Artística, 1955) p. 14.
55. García Escudero, *El cine y los hijos*, p. 83.
56. Siguan, *El cine*, p. 23.
57. Anon. *¿Sabes ir al cine?* p. 1.
58. Anon. *¿Sabes ir al cine?* p. 41.
59. Ibid.
60. A. Garmendía de Otaola, *Estética y ética del cine: guía para cines y cineclubs* (Bilbao: Gráficas Ellecuria, 1956)
61. Anon. *¿Sabes ir al cine?* p. 1.
62. Ibid.
63. Ibid.
64. Anon. *¿Sabes ir al cine?* p. 5.
65. My reading of Don Juan's masquerade is indebted to Mary Ann Doane's (1996) study of the *femme fatale*.
66. Homi Bhabha, 'The other question', *Screen*, 24 (6) 1983, pp. 18-36.
67. Marañón was famous for his description of the ageing Don Juan. See, for example, Gregorio Marañón, 'La vejez de Don Juan', in Gregorio Marañón (ed.) *Obras completas* (Madrid: Espasa-Calpe, 1966) vol. 1, pp. 437-44
68. Marañón (*Obras completas*) classified Don Juan on the 'feminine' scale of his schema of intersexuality – he possesses 'feminine' traits, which chimes with Rivière's interest in 'intermediate types' in her discussion of the masquerade. See Joan Rivière, 'Womanliness and the masquerade (1929)', in Victor Burgin, J. Donald and Cora Kaplan (eds) *Formations of Fantasy* (London: Routledge, 1986) pp. 35-44. While Rivière speaks only of 'womanliness' as masquerade, she introduces the possibility of masquerading homosexual men. Chris Holmlund, 'Masculinity as multiple masquerade: the "mature" stallone and the stallone clone', in Steve Cohan and Ina Rae Hark (eds) *Screening the Male: Exploring Masculinities in Hollywood Cinema* (London: Routledge, 1993), pp. 213-29, reminds us that Lacan states that men can 'have' the phallus just as little as women can ever 'be' it, advances the theory of male masquerade.
69. Sáenz de Heredia remarks, '*Marañón me dijo absolutamente que no, que no le gustaba. Y yo le contesté que ni el suyo a mí*' (Marañón told me absolutely that he did not like it. I answered that I did not like his version either) (Juan Julio Abajo de Pablo, *Mis charlas con José Luis Sáenz de Heredia*, Valladolid: Ourion Ediciones, 1996, p. 58).
70. Anon., 'El personaje que Usted ha interpretado en el cine ¿sería en la segunda mitad del siglo igual que ha sido antes?' *Primer Plano*, 31 December 1950, n.p.
71. Anon., 'Primer desafío a sangre de Don Juan con su navaja de afeitar', *Primer Plano*, 23 April 1950, n.p.

Notes (Chapter 3)

72. Anon., 'Barba va, barba viene', *Primer Plano*, 18 March 1950, n.p.
73. Publicity on *Primer Plano*, of 23 and 28 May 1950, n.p.
74. Anon. *Primer Plano*, 29 October 1950, n.p.
75. Hansen, *Babel and Babylon*, p. 282.
76. Gina Marchetti, 'Action-adventure as ideology', in Ian Angus and Sut Jhally (eds) *Cultural Politics in Contemporary America* (New York: Routledge, 1989) pp. 182–97.
77. For a useful summing up of the debate over *suture*, see Susan Hayward, *Key Concepts in Cinema Studies* (London: Routledge, 1996) pp. 371–9.
78. Hansen, *Babel and Babylon*, p. 246.
79. My thanks to Graeme Hayes for drawing my attention to this.
80. Mary Ann Doane, in *Femmes Fatales*, finds the deceptive cinema as the perfect medium for her discussion of the masquerade.
81. Walter Benjamin, 'The work of art in the age of mechanical reproduction', in Leo Braudy and Marshall Cohen (eds) *Film Theory and Criticism: Introductory Readings*, (Oxford: Oxford University Press, 1999) p. 742.
82. Hansen, *Babel and Babylon*, p. 246.
83. Hansen, *Babel and Babylon*, p. 249.
84. Carmen Martín Gaite, *Usos amorosos de la postguerra española* (Barcelona: Editorial Anagrama, 1987) p. 33.
85. Luis Miguel Fernández (*Don Juan en el cine*, p. 106) studies the alternating *ménage à trois* created by posters for the film.
86. Sáenz de Heredia has described Lady Ontiveros as 'a female Don Juan' ('*una Doña Juana*') (Abajo de Pablo, *Mis charlas*, p. 58).
87. Anon., '"Guitarras, aceitunas y el talento publicitario de Iturbi y Dalí, faltaron en la fiesta española de Venecia", declara Annabella', *Primer Plano*, 1 October 1950, n.p.
88. Kristeva, 'Don Juan', p. 191.
89. Fried, *Absorption and Theatricality*, p. 104.
90. Ibid.
91. Ibid.
92. Ibid.
93. Ciutti is pivotal in Don Juan's redemption: in an impassioned speech during the kidnapping of Doña Inés he reveals that for the first time, he believes Don Juan to have gone too far. The move of the ideal spectator therefore mirrors the position of Ciutti: from ironic observation of serial seductions, to outrage at Don Juan's kidnap of Doña Inés, and finally, to grief at his death.
94. A point made by Joan Copjec, 'More! From melodrama to magnitude', in Janet Bergstrom (ed.) *Endless Night: Cinema and*

Notes (Chapter 3/Chapter 4)

Psychoanalysis, Parallel Histories (Berkeley: University of California Press 1999) p. 251.
95. Jean-Pierre Oudart, 'Cinema and suture', *Screen*, 18 (1) 1977, pp. 35–47.
96. Such as, for example, the Columbus monument in Barcelona by Rafael Atché built for the Universal Exhibition of 1888.
97. For an excellent study of the roles of Spanish heroines, see Jo Labanyi, 'Feminizing the nation: women, subordination and subversion in post-Civil War Spain', in Ulrike Sieglohr (ed.) *Heroines Without Heroes: Reconstructing Female Identities in European Cinema, 1945–51* (London: Cassell, 2000) pp. 163–84.
98. See Alejandro Yarza's excellent article, 'The petrified tears of General Franco: kitsch and fascism in José Luis Sáenz de Heredia's *Raza*', *Journal of Spanish Cultural Studies*, 5 (1) 2004, pp. 41–55, which analyses the use of Catholic imagery in Sáenz de Heredia's *Raza* and advances the theory of a brand of fascist aesthetic kitsch (that relies on petrification for its impact). For Yarza, camp was a strategy adopted in the post-Franco years as a way to offer a revision of this kitsch aesthetic.
99. Kristeva, 'Ellipsis on dread', p. 47 writes, 'the film actor … but also the discrepancy or conflict between sound and image, discourse and representation, or the "impious fracturing of projection" possible in camera movement itself (Godard, Bresson), hold the spectator, still inside a phantasm, but at a distance from his own fascination.'
100. Michael Fried, *Absorption and Theatricality: Painting and Beholder in the Age of Diderot* (Berkeley: University of California Press, 1980) p. 45.
101. Carmen Martín Gaite, *The Back Room* (San Francisco: City Lights Books, 2000) p. 61.
102. For Lacanian *jouissance*, see B. Benvenuto and R. Kennedy, *The Works of Jacques Lacan: An Introduction* (New York: St Martin's Press, 1986) pp. 185–93.

4. Repetition Compulsion: Redoing the Tenorio

1. Sigmund Freud, 'Extracts from the Fliess papers', in J. Strachey (ed.) *The Standard Edition of the Complete Psychological Works of Sigmund Freud* (London: Hogart, 1886–99) vol. 1, p. 209 wrote, in a letter to Fliess in 1924, that 'every collector is a substitute for Don Juan Tenorio and so too is the mountaineer, the sportsman and such people'.

Notes (Chapter 4)

2. Nuria Espert's rendition of Don Juan was seen at once to break with the tradition of Don Juan being played by a male actor, as well as to present a homage to theatrical Doña Juanas.
3. Neither Zorrilla's play nor that of Tirso de Molina has caught on in quite the same way abroad. For Benjamin Bridges Gunter, *Don Juan Plays the USA: (El burlador de Sevilla and tan largo me lo fiais) for Twenty-First Century Performances in the United States* (Tallahassee: Florida State University dissertation, 2005) this has to do in part with translation difficulties into English, although chicano versions, such as Carlos Morton's *Johnny Tenorio* (1983), written in a mixture of Spanish, English and caló (Mexican slang) have been successful.
4. Timothy Mitchell, *Violence and Piety in Spanish Folklore* (Philadelphia: University of Pennsylvania Press, 1988) p. 170.
5. Rank, *The Don Juan Legend*, p. 64.
6. Saíd Armesto, *La leyenda*, pp. 100–1.
7. Hans Mattauch, *La implantación del rito del Tenorio en Madrid (1844–1877)*, Actas del Congreso sobre José Zorrilla, Una nueva lectura, (Universidad de Valladolid, 1995) p. 411.
8. Mattauch, *La implantación del rito*, p. 412.
9. J. L. Abellán, 'Don Juan: interpretación y mito', *Horizontes*, 5 (1962) p. 8.
10. Francisco Nieva (ed.) 'Introducción', in José Zorrilla, *Don Juan Tenorio*, (Madrid: Espasa-Calpe, 1995) p. 9.
11. Qualifying this, however, is the interesting fact that while the figure of Don Juan is an export on a par with flamenco and the bullfight, Zorrilla and Tirso are less well-known than, for example, the creator of *Don Quijote*, Miguel de Cervantes. Might this have to do with the proliferation of 'foreign' versions of Don Juan, as well as the presence of two texts within Spain (by Tirso and Zorrilla), making it difficult to assign authorship? Possibly the vogue for Don Juan within Spain may have had something to do with a patriotic attempt to reclaim a figure who had been appropriated abroad by the likes of Byron and Mozart.
12. David T. Gies, *Don Juan contra Don Juan: apoteosis del romanticismo español*, Actas del séptimo Congreso de la Asociación Internacional de Hispanistas (Venice: Bulzone Editore, 1980)
13. Donald L. Shaw, *Historia de la literatura española* (Barcelona: Ariel, 1978).
14. José Alberich, 'La popularidad de Don Juan Tenorio', in José Alberich (ed.) *La popularidad de Don Juan Tenorio y otros estudios de*

Notes (Chapter 4)

literatura española moderna, (San Antonio de Calonge, Gerona: Aubí, 1982) pp. 13–24.
15. Eamonn Rodgers, 'Zorrilla's Don Juan Tenorio as cultural paradigm', in Andrew Ginger, Huw Lewis and John Hobbs (eds) *Selected Interdisciplinary Essays on the Representation of the Don Juan Archetype in Myth and Culture* (Lewiston: Edwin Mellen Press, 2000) p. 162, who notes the fictionalization of the profound impact on individuals of attending a performance of Zorrilla's Don Juan in Leopoldo Alas's *La Regenta* (The Magistrate's Wife) of 1885 in which the protragonist, Ana Ozores, is enraptured by a performance.
16. Mitchell, *Violence and Piety*, p. 170.
17. James Mandrell, 'Nostalgia and the popularity of Don Juan Tenorio: reading Zorrilla through Clarín', *Hispanic Review*, 59 (1) 1991, pp. 37–55.
18. Luis Fernández Cifuentes, 'Prólogo', in José Zorrilla, *Don Juan Tenorio*, (Barcelona: Crítica, 1993) p. 25.
19. This may account for the different fortunes within Spain and abroad. Performance within Spain led to its popularity nationally.
20. Jesús Rubio Jiménez, 'Don Juan Tenorio: drama de espectáculo, plasticidad y fantasía', *Cuadernos de Investigación Filológica*, XV (1–2) 1989, p. 7.
21. Parodies of Golden Age texts were common during the turn of the century but it is striking to note the sheer proliferation of parodies of Zorrilla's text. David Thatcher Gies, *The Theatre in Nineteenth Century Spain* (Cambridge: Cambridge University Press, 1994) calls Zorrilla's work 'one of the key plays – if not *the* key play – of the nineteenth century'. He attributes the 'cottage industry' of parodies to its 'deep spirituality, its heightened theatricality, and the fact that its audiences knew whole scenes by heart' (p. 286).
22. José Ortega y Gasset, 'La estrangulación de Don Juan', in José Ortega y Gasset, *Obras completas* (Madrid: Revista de Occidente, 1935) vol. 5, pp. 238–46.
23. Andrés Peláez Martín, 'Tres personajes en los escenarios españoles en el último siglo: La Celestina, don Quijote y don Juan', in José Luis Díez, *Tres mitos españoles: La Celestina, don Quijote, don Juan*, (Madrid: Sociedad Estatal de Conmemoraciones Culturales, 2004) p. 102.
24. Javier Villán, 'Don Juan Tenorio, historia de un mito', *El Mundo*, 30 October 2002.
25. César Oliva, 'Trayectoria escénica del Tenorio', in Ana Sofía Pérez-Bustamante (ed.) *Don Juan Tenorio en la España del siglo XX*, (Madrid: Cátedra, 1998) p. 33.
26. Oliva, 'Trayectoria escénica del Tenorio', p. 32.

Notes (Chapter 4)

27. It is now generally accepted that Gregorio was the one who put on plays, while María Martínez Sierra (now known also as María Lejárraga) did most of the writing. The letters of María to the composer Manuel de Falla concerning the play seem to back up the suggestion that she wrote the text. See Laura Dolfi, 'Falla y el Don Juan de España (1921) de Martínez Sierra', in Ana Sofía Pérez Bustamante (ed.) *Don Juan Tenorio en la España del siglo XX* (Madrid: Cátedra, 1998) pp. 95–127. Alda Blanco, 'Introducción', in María Martínez Sierra (ed.) *Una mujer por los caminos de España* (Madrid: Castalia, 1989) pp. 7–42 sees the voluntary renunciation of authorship by María as an intentional and strategic move by a feminist determined to see her words in print. *Don Juan de España* takes Don Juan to Italy, Flanders and Paris before returning to Spain. The *'dama velada'* (veiled lady), a *femme fatale*, is an apparition who presages Don Juan's death. The play was originally envisaged to be accompanied with a score by Manuel de Falla, but as Dolfi ('Falla y el Don Juan') notes, it was the cause of a split between the working partnership of the composer with the Martínez Sierras. Johnson (*Gender and Nation*) pp. 47–8, 123–4 sees Martínez Sierra's *Tú eres la paz* (Thou Art Peace) as a novel that addresses Valle-Inclán's versión of the Don Juan myth.
28. Readers are referred to Maria C. Dominicis, *Don Juan en el teatro español del siglo XX* (Barcelona: Ediciones Universal, 1977). *Don Juan no existe* (1924) is noted by Pilar Nieva de la Paz, *Autoras dramáticas españolas entre 1918 y 1936* (Madrid: Consejo superior de investigaciones científicas, 1993) p. 329 who includes references to press reviews of the play. However, neither of us has managed to unearth the original play. The current Conde de San Luis believes it to be lost (from a private communication with the present Conde de San Luis).
29. For a history of the *Teatros Nacionales*, see Andrés Peláez Martín, *Historia de los Teatros Nacionales (1939–62)* (Madrid: Centro de Documentación Teatral, 1993).
30. Fernando Jiménez Placer, Francisco Cervera y Jiménez Alfaro and Antonio Sierra Corella *Centenario del estreno de 'Don Juan Tenorio' (1844–1944)* (Madrid: Instituto Nacional del Libro Español, 1944).
31. See Peláez Martín, *Historia de los Teatros Nacionales*.
32. Oliva, 'Trayectoria escénica del Tenorio', p. 36.
33. Ibid.
34. Carmen Martín Gaite, 'Prólogo', in Tirso de Molina, *El burlador de Sevilla y convidado de piedra* (Teatro Municipal General, 1988) pp. 1–7.
35. Anon., 'Presentación de "El burlador de Sevilla"', *Lanza*, 13 September 1988, p. 13.

Notes (Chapter 4)

36. Luis Vázquez, '"El burlador" de Tirso, refundido por Carmen Martín Gaite', *Ya*, 15 October 1988, p. 11.
37. From a private interview with Eduardo Vasco, Compañía Nacional de Teatro Clásico, Madrid, October 2005.
38. See Chapter 5, note 99.
39. Andrzej Wirth, 'The Don Juan myth radiantly transformed', *Performing Arts Journal*, 15 (1) 1993, p. 43.
40. With Héctor Colomé as the ageing Don Juan, María José Goyanés as Doña Inés and Amparo Soler Leal as Brígida, in a staging by the Centro Dramático Nacional.
41. The exhibition *Tres mitos españoles: la Celestina, don Quijote, don Juan*, was held at the Centro Cultural Conde Duque in Madrid in 2004.
42. Pérez de Ayala, *Las máscaras*, pp. 152–3.
43. Ibid.
44. James Mandrell, 'Don Juan Tenorio as refundición: the question of repetition and doubling', *Hispania*, 70 (1) 1987, pp. 22–30 develops the theme of doubling, that Zorrilla's Don Juan is a double of Tirso's original character, which suggests that the play should be read intertextually as a *'refundición'* (doubling) of *El burlador de Sevilla*. Timothy Mitchell (*Violence and Piety*, p. 169) writes that, 'Every one of Zorrilla's "innovations", including the abduction of a nun, Don Juan's vision of his own funeral, and his eventual salvation ... can be found before 1844 in romances, blind beggar ballads, and other popular genres.' See also Thomas A. Fitz Gerald, 'Some notes on the sources of Zorrilla's Don Juan Tenorio', *Hispania*, 5 (1) 1922, pp. 1–7.
45. Susan Stewart, *On Longing: Narratives of the Miniature, the Gigantic, the Souvenir, the Collection* (Durham: Duke University Press, 1993) p. 23.
46. James Mandrell, 'Nostalgia and the popularity of Don Juan Tenorio', sees the play as tapping into a nostalgia for the past that assigns it a place within a national literary canon, while C. Christopher Soufas, 'The sublime, the beautiful and the imagination in Zorrilla's Don Juan Tenorio', *MLN*, 110 (2) 1995, pp. 302–19 sees the play as pervaded by an aesthetic of the sublime as a critique to modernity. Cf. Susan Bennett's, *Performing Nostalgia: Shifting Shakespeare and the Contemporary Past* (London: Routledge, 1996) discussion of nostalgia in mainstream productions of Shakespeare's plays.
47. Rubio Jiménez, 'Don Juan Tenorio', p. 55.
48. Carlos Serrano, 'Don Juan y la inversión paródica: el caso de las Doña Juana', in Ana Sofía Pérez-Bustamante (ed.) *Don Juan Tenorio en la España del siglo XX* (Madrid: Cátedra, 1998) p. 56.

Notes (Chapter 4)

49. Carlos Serrano, *Carnaval en noviembre: parodias teatrales españolas de Don Juan Tenorio* (Alicante: Instituto de cultura Juan Gil-Albert, 1996) pp. 45–70.
50. Jeffrey T. Bersett, *El burlado de Sevilla: Nineteenth-Century Theatrical Appropriations of Don Juan Tenorio* (Delaware: Juan de la Cuesta, 2003) p. 8.
51. David Thatcher Gies, 'La subversión de Don Juan: parodias decimonónicas del 'Tenorio' con una nota pornográfica', *España Contemporánea*, VII (1) 1994, p. 100.
52. Gies, *The Theatre in Nineteenth Century Spain*, p. 218.
53. Bersett, *El burlado de Sevilla*, pp. 12, 13.
54. Martin Nozick, 'Some parodies of Don Juan Tenorio', *Hispania*, 33 (2) 1950, pp. 105–12 examines these two plays.
55. Serrano, *Carnaval en noviembre*, pp. 53–5.
56. Anon. 'Notas teatrales', *ABC*, 1908, p. 13.
57. Anon. 'Tenorio modernista de D. Pablo Parellada', *ABC*, 1906, pp. 14–15.
58. Ibid.
59. Antonio Paso Cano and Carlos Servet y Fortuny, *Tenorio feminista: Parodia lírica mujeriega en un acto, dividido en tres cuadros, original hasta cierto punto* (Madrid: Sociedad de autores españoles, 1907) p. 21.
60. Anon., 'Aventuras del Tenorio', *Heraldo de Madrid*, 1907, p. 4.
61. Serrano, *Carnaval en noviembre*, p. 55. Certain themes, such as bullfighting, are repeated as a motif that appears in *El Tenorio taurino* (Bullfighting Don Juan) (Maximiliano Flores) and a parody with the same title by Pepe Moros (1913) and *Tenorio torero* (Matador Don Juan) (Luis Esteso, Luis López de Haro, 1915).
62. Francisco Serrano, *El Tenorio Sarasa* (Barcelona, 1927) p. 12.
63. Serrano, *El Tenorio Sarasa*, p. 22.
64. Linda Hutcheon, *A Theory of Parody: The Teachings of Twentieth-Century Art Forms* (New York: Methuen, 1985) p. 37.
65. Angry at the copyright issues that prevented him from profiting from his most famous play, Zorrilla tried to discredit his masterpiece by producing a zarzuela version with music by Manent. However, 'this attempt to profane his own masterpiece had little success – it ran for only eight consecutive days'. He also wrote a novel called *El Tenorio bordelés* (Bordelais Don Juan), but this was not printed until 1909 (Nozick, 'Some parodies of Don Juan Tenorio', p. 105).
66. Serrano, *Carnaval en noviembre*, p. 21.
67. Fernández Cifuentes, 'Prólogo', pp. 23–4.
68. Julio Caro Baroja, 'Recuerdos valleinclanesco-barojianos', *Revista de occidente*, 4/2 (44 and 45) November–December 1966, p. 309.

69. Joaquín Montaner, *El hijo del diablo* (The Son of the Devil) (Barcelona: A. López Llausás, 1927).
70. Antonio Sánchez Romeralo, 'Un Tenorio de Buñuel ("Libreto" para una representación en la Residencia de Estudiantes)', *La Torre*, 3 (10) April–June 1989, p. 364.
71. Sánchez Romeralo, 'Un Tenorio de Buñuel', p. 366.
72. Agustín Sánchez Vidal, *Buñuel, Lorca, Dalí: El enigma sin fin* (Barcelona: Planeta, 1988) p. 115.
73. See, for example, Juan Bautista Avalle-Arce, 'La esperpentización de Don Juan Tenorio', *Hispanófila*, 7 (1959) pp. 29–40; Dru Dougherty, 'The tragicomic Don Juan: Valle-Incán's *Las galas del difunto*', *Modern Drama*, 23 (1980) pp. 44–57; and Carlos S. Feal, 'Don Juan como esperpento: *Las galas del difunto*', in Jesús Torrecilla (ed.) *La generación del 98 frente al nuevo fin de siglo* (Amsterdam: Rodopi, 2000) pp. 71–90. For a fascinating exposition of the link between Valle-Inclán's *Sonatas* and the refiguring of Don Juan by women writers, see Johnson, *Gender and Nation*, pp. 115–17.
74. José Luis Alonso de Santos, 'La sombra del Tenorio', *Primer acto*, 257 (1995) p. 67. The suggestion is that we all aspire to be Don Juans, but have to be content with being the Ciuttis of this world. Are we all merely Other, seeing ourselves reflected in the lives of another? This is *theatrum mundi* – Saturnino is nothing when he is not on stage, but when on stage he has to play the role assigned to him, rather than taking his life in his own hands, and playing the role he has always desired. Here we see him putting on the clothes of Don Juan, in an attempt to step into the role. '*Teatro, actor, público … ¿Qué hacemos todos al fin y al cabo en la vida sino una representación para que nos aplauda ese ser desconocido que nos mira desde la oscuridad? Hasta que algún día nos llegue el momento del mutis final, como le llega hoy a Saturnino … y nos caiga el telón*' (Theatre, actor, public … When all is said and done in life are we not all just playing a role to win the applause of that unknown being who looks at us from the darkness? Until one day it is time for our final exit, just as today is Saturnino's time … and the curtain falls on us) (Alonso de Santos, 'La sombra del Tenorio', p. 75). For further information on the play, see José Monleón, 'La realidad del teatro: *La sombra del Tenorio* (1994) de José Luis Alonso de Santos', in Ana Sofía Pérez Bustamante (ed.) *Don Juan Tenorio en la España del siglo XX* (Madrid: Cátedra, 1998) pp. 289–310.
75. Alberto de la Hera, 'El Tenorio de Dalí, una resurrección muy deseada', *Guía del ocio*, 28 November 2003, reproduced in César Oliva (ed.) *Seis caminos hacia el mito de Don Juan* (Madrid: Compañía Nacional de Teatro Clásico, 2004) p. 180.

Notes (Chapter 4)

76. César Oliva, 'Ángel Fernández Montesinos, director de escena: entrevista', in César Oliva (ed.) *Seis caminos hacia el mito de Don Juan* (Madrid: Compañía Nacional de Teatro Clásico, 2004) p. 171.
77. María Delgado, *'Other' Spanish Theatres: Erasure and Inscription on the Twentieth-Century Spanish Stage* (Manchester: Manchester University Press, 2003) p. 5.
78. Eduardo Haro Tecglen, 'Rescoldo de una emoción', *El País*, 25 November 2003, in César Oliva (ed.) *Seis caminos hacia el mito de Don Juan* (Madrid: Compañía Nacional de Teatro Clásico, 2004) pp. 178–9.
79. Haro Tecglen claims that rumours of homosexuality were created around Huberto Pérez de la Ossa, Igoa and Luis Escobar as reasons to disapprove of their work and to justify Escobar's and Pérez de la Ossa's subsequent removal as directors of the Teatro María Guerrero, replacing these with Alfredo Marqueríe, *'un mujeriego, diríamos con lenguaje de entonces – el cual abrió su temporada con una obra de Benavente, cuya homosexualidad conocida estaba respetada ya por el premio Nobel, y ya habían pasado suficientes años desde que le persiguiera por* rojo' (a womanizer, we would say in the language of the day – who opened his theatrical season with a work by Benavente, whose openly homosexual status was respected because he had won the Nobel prize, and enough years had passed since they were chasing him for being a *red*) (Haro Tecglen, 'Rescoldo de una emoción', p. 178). Haro Tecglen, a self-proclaimed *'rojo'*, became an object of scrutiny in 2001 for apparently having praised the Franco regime when it was in power.
80. Michel de Certeau, *The Writing of History* (New York: Columbia University Press, 1988) p. 8.
81. Gyenes was of Hungarian origin. He became a top society photographer in Spain in the 1940s, but also photographed the film and theatre world. The Biblioteca Nacional in Madrid has recently purchased his photographic archive.
82. Scenographer Wolfgang Burmann (who has worked with Pedro Almodóvar, among others) was responsible for bringing Dalí's designs to the stage in 2003. In a private interview with him on 23 October 2006, he notes that given the large quantity of documentation available on the first productions it was not such a challenging project. The greatest difficulty for him lay in getting the colours right.
83. Haro Tecglen, 'Rescoldo de una emoción', p. 178.
84. Rubio Jiménez, 'Don Juan Tenorio'.
85. Rubio Jiménez, 'Don Juan Tenorio en versión de Luis Escobar y Salvador Dalí', p. 66.
86. Rubio Jiménez, 'Don Juan Tenorio en versión de Luis Escobar y Salvador Dalí', p. 76.

Notes (Chapter 4)

87. Rubio Jiménez, 'Don Juan Tenorio en versión de Luis Escobar y Salvador Dalí', p. 70.
88. Alfredo Marqueríe, 'En el María Guerrero se estrenó una version escenográfica del "Tenorio"', *ABC* (1949) p. 19.
89. Rubio Jiménez, 'Don Juan Tenorio en versión de Luis Escobar y Salvador Dalí', p. 70.
90. Rubio Jiménez, 'Don Juan Tenorio en versión de Luis Escobar y Salvador Dalí', p. 73.
91. Lewis Kachur, *Displaying the Marvellous: Marcel Duchamp, Salvador Dalí and Surrealist Exhibition* (Cambridge, MA: MIT Press, 2003) p. 112.
92. William Tydeman and Steven Price, *Wilde: Salome* (Cambridge: Cambridge University Press, 1996) p. 131.
93. Henry Bacon, *Visconti: Explorations of Beauty and Decay* (Cambridge: Cambridge University Press, 1998) p. 52.
94. Rubio Jiménez, 'Don Juan Tenorio en versión de Luis Escobar y Salvador Dalí', p. 76.
95. Ibid.
96. Oliva, 'Ángel Fernández Montesinos', p. 170.
97. Ian Gibson, *The Shameful Life of Salvador Dalí* (London: Faber & Faber, 1997) p. 450.
98. John London, 'Twentieth-century Spanish stage design', *Contemporary Theatre Review*, 7 (5) 1998, p. 38. London cites Ros's description of the prodouction: 'Evacuated by the Reds, the soul of Calderón returned to Madrid after centuries' to show how the production confirmed the Right's newly victorious ideology (Samuel Ros, 'Un auto de Calderón en los jardines del Retiro y en el año de la victoria', *Vértice*, 25 (1939) pp. 212–13).
99. Correspondence held at the Fundación Gala-Dalí, Cadaqués.
100. Famous productions in the UK that featured innovative intersections between artist and theatre might include the 2003 Glyndebourne production of *Idomeneo* directed by Peter Sellars with set designs by Anish Kapoor, and Glyndebourne's 1975 production of Stravinksy's *The Rake's Progress*, with stage designs by David Hockney. An exhibition at the Museo Reina Sofía in 2000, *El teatro de los pintores en la Europa de las vanguardias* (Painters and Avant-garde Theatre in Europe) celebrated the collaborations between painters and theatre practitioners in Europe. In Europe, Diaghilev revitalized the stage through the Ballets Russes's collaboration with painters such as Picasso, Braque, Miró, Gris, Ernst (see Marga Paz, *El teatro de los pintores en la Europa de las vanguardias*, Madrid: Aldeasa, 2000). John London has noted that, 'the theatre world of famous Spanish painters is a striking, neglected part of theatre history'. He cites

Notes (Chapter 4)

Picasso's sets for Diaghilev's production of *Parade* and *Le Tricorne*, Dalí's work with Lorca and Adrià Gual and Joan Miró's set designs, describing these as being 'in the mainstream of European experimentalism' (see London, 'Twentieth-century Spanish stage design', p. 35). German Bauhaus, Italian Futurism and Russian Constructivism are all seen to have repercussions on European theatre of the vanguard. In Spain, however, the landscape was rather less exciting, conditioned by the social realism of Echegaray and Benavente, or the folkloric backdrop of *costumbrista sainetes*. Exceptions included Adrià Gual's L'Escola Catalana d'Art Dramàtic, the work of Gregorio Martínez Sierra (who collaborated with the painters Penagos and Ontañón and the scenographers Fontanals, Burmann and Barradas). During the Second Republic the Teatro de las Misiones Pedagógicas and Federico García Lorca's *La Barraca* were both innovative. *La Barraca* participated with Santiago Ontañón, Ramón Gaya, Ponce de León, Benjamín Palencia, Manuel Ángeles Ortiz, Norah Borges and José Caballero. Siegfried Burmann worked on the scenography for *Yerma* in 1934, on *Bodas de sangre* in 1935 and *El burlador de Sevilla* in 1936. Salvador Dalí designed the scenery for Margarita Xirgu's production of Lorca's *Mariana Pineda* in 1927, and was planning to collaborate on a version of *Amor de Don Perlimplín con Belisa en su jardín* (The Love of Don Perlimplín for Belisa in his Garden). Lorca's itinerant theatre company, *La Barraca*, collaborated with important painters of the day, such as Manuel Angeles Ortiz, Benjamín Palencia, José Caballero and Santiago Ontañón, with sets that had to be dismantled with every new touring location (London, 'Twentieth-century Spanish stage design', p. 37). The Spanish Civil War brought an end to many scenographic innovations. However, Cayetano Luca de Tena's invitation to the Third Reich's Chamber of Culture to study German theatre in 1942 led to his use of a revolving stage in his 1942 production of Calderón's *La dama duende* (The Phantom Lady) and inspired other artists (see London, 'Twentieth-century Spanish stage design', p. 43).

101. FCP, for instance, writing in *Dígame*, 7 November 1950, notes of the 1950 staging, the *'sensación de una escenografía ajena al drama'* (sensation of the scenography alien to the drama) (Rubio Jiménez, 'Don Juan Tenorio', p. 89n).
102. José Camón Aznar, 'Un año de Arte', *ABC*, 28 December 1950, p. 5.
103. José Tamayo's Don Juan Tenorio of 1956 and 1957 contrasted a *'versión de los pintores'* (painters' version) with a *'versión romántica'* (romantic version), in an allusive riposte to Dalí. Within Spain the rise of the scenographer is linked to the rise of the director, while the scenographer is arguably linked to the development of a per-

Notes (Chapter 4/Chapter 5)

formance language. Some scenographers went into exile after 1936. Ontañón and Fontanals, for example, were part of the brain drain during the Civil War and its aftermath. I am grateful to María Delgado for pointing this out. Admittedly, some of those who have gained recognition have done so in part because of the crossover with film. Andrés Peláez has written an interesting overview of some of the scenographers who have worked with Zorrilla's text. Avrial y Flores, Busato and Fernández worked on early productions of the Tenorio. See Andrés Peláez Martín, 'Breve álbum de recuerdos del Tenorio', in César Oliva, *Seis caminos hacia el mito de Don Juan* (Madrid: Compañía Nacional de Teatro Clásico, 2004) pp. 241–8.
104. According to Escobar, the production cost 50,000 pesetas (see Juan Manuel García de Vinuesa, 'El 'Tenorio número dos', de Dalí', *ABC*, 29 October 1950, p. 11). Budgets were low because of a recession and Escobar, afraid that state officials would reject the production, economized as far as he could (see Ángel Fernández Montesinos, 'Entrevista: Ángel Fernández Montesinos', in César Oliva, *Seis caminos hacia el mito de Don Juan*, Madrid: Compañía Nacional de Teatro Clásico, 2004, p. 170).
105. José de Juanes, 'Tercer "Tenorio" de Dalí, en el Español', *Arriba*, 31 October 1964, p. 22.
106. Ibid.
107. Haro Tecglen, 'Rescoldo de una emoción', p. 178.
108. Haro Tecglen, 'Rescoldo de una emoción', p. 179.
109. Javier Villán, 'La sombra de Dalí', in César Oliva (ed.) *Seis caminos hacia el mito de Don Juan* (Madrid: Compañía Nacional de Teatro Clásico, 2004) p. 177.
110. Juan Ignacio García Garzón, 'La destrucción o el amor', in César Oliva (ed.) *Seis caminos hacia el mito de Don Juan* (Madrid: Compañía Nacional de Teatro Clásico, 2004) p.176.
111. Haro Tecglen, 'Rescoldo de una emoción', p. 179.

5. Empty Promises: Opera and the Aesthetics of Cultural Consumption

1. Clément, Catherine, 'Prelude, *Opera, or the Undoing of Women* (London: Virago Press, 1988) pp. 3–5.
2. Clément, *Opera*, p. 4.
3. Pierre Bourdieu, *Distinction: A Social Critique of the Judgement of Taste* (London: Routledge, 1984).
4. The production opened at London's Coliseum in June 2001, in Hanover at the Staatsoper in January 2002 and in Barcelona at the

Notes (Chapter 5)

Gran Teatre del Liceu in December 2002. For the purposes of this chapter, I analyse a production of the opera in Italian with Catalan subtitles in Barcelona in December 2002. I also make reference to press reports from the UK and Spain.

5. Tim Edwards, *Contradictions of Consumption: Concepts, Practices and Politics in Consumer Society* (Buckingham: Open University Press, 2000) pp. 2–3.
6. Edwards, *Contradictions of Consumption*, p. 10.
7. Wye Jamison Allanbrook, *Rhythmic Gesture in Mozart: Le Nozze Di Figaro and Don Giovanni* (Chicago: University of Chicago Press, 1983) p. 197.
8. The London production featured Nathan Berg/Iain Paterson as Leporello, Garry Magee as Don Giovanni, Claire Rutter as Donna Anna, Phillip Ens as the Commendatore, Claire Weston as Donna Elvira, Paul Nilon as Don Ottavio, Linda Richardson as Zerlina and Leslie John Flanagan as Masetto and was conducted by Joseph Swenson/Noel Davis. The Barcelona production featured Wojtek Drabowicz as Don Giovanni, Kwanchul Youn as Leporello, Regina Schörg as Donna Anna, Anatoli Kotxerga as the Commendatore, Véronique Gens as Donna Elvira, Marcel Reijans as Don Ottavio, Marisa Martins as Zerlina and Felipe Bou as Masetto, and the musical direction was by Bertrand de Billy. Costumes (for both productions) were by Mercè Paloma and scenery by Alfons Flores.
9. Delgado, 'Calixto Bieito', p. 56.
10. Ian Irvine, 'Director Booed After Ibizan *Don Giovanni*', *Independent*, 1 June 2001, p. 10.
11. Martin Hoyle, 'Turn of the screw: why Don Giovanni's critics have missed the point', *Time Out*, 10 June 2001, p. 10.
12. Michael Tanner, 'Lust without love', *The Spectator*, 9 June 2001, p. 49.
13. Paul Driver, 'Reservoir Don', *Journal of Spanish Cultural Studies*, 10, June 2001, p. 21.
14. Richard Fairman, 'Don Giovanni: English National Opera at the London Coliseum', *Opera*, August 2001, pp. 1005–7.
15. Duncan Hadfield, 'Don Giovanni: London Coliseum', *What's On*, 6 June 2001, p. 25.
16. Fairman, 'Don Giovanni'.
17. Michael Kennedy, 'Mozart plumbs new depths', *Sunday Telegraph*, 3 June 2001, p. 8.
18. Michael Church, 'From tragedy to farce: Don Giovanni', *The Scotsman*, 4 June 2001, p. 15.

Notes (Chapter 5)

19. Hoyle, 'Turn of the screw', p. 10.
20. Kennedy, 'Mozart plumbs new depths', p. 8.
21. Steve Bird, 'Coke-snorting Giovanni divides the Coliseum', *The Times*, 1 June 2001, p. 5.
22. Tim Ashley, 'Don Giovanni', *Guardian*, 2 June 2001, p. 23.
23. Luke Leitch, 'Uproar as Mozart gets "Tarantino" treatment', *Evening Standard*, 1 June 2001, p. 56.
24. Bird, 'Coke-snorting Giovanni', p. 5.
25. Kennedy, 'Mozart plumbs new depths', p. 8.
26. Bourdieu, *Distinction*, pp. 6, 270, 272.
27. Theodor Adorno, 'On the fetish character in music and the regression of listening', in Theodor Adorno, *Essays in Music* (Berkeley: University of California Press, 2002) pp. 295, 296, 284.
28. Thorstein Veblen, *The Theory of the Leisure Class: An Economic Study of Institutions* (London: George & Unwin, 1899).
29. Helen Kelly-Holmes, 'Bier, parfum, kaas: language fetish in European advertising', *European Journal of Cultural Studies*, 3 (1) pp. 67–82. Kelly-Holmes draws out the use of lexical borrowing and language fetishism in pan-European advertising. Advertisements in the libretto also include Masriera jewellery, a Barcelona-based company founded in 1839. Spain, and particularly Catalonia, is well-known for its excellence in design, a positive feature of cultural competence overlooked by Kelly-Holmes, who asserts that SEAT's advertisement 'German engineering, Spanish design' demonstrates that 'Spanish cultural competence is perhaps harder to identify instantly ... it is perhaps easier to identify what it is not. ... engineering is too serious a business to leave to the Spaniards, who can be trusted with the less practical, more abstract, and "fluffy" aspects, such as design and appearance' (p. 72).
30. Bourdieu, *Distinction*, p. 32.
31. Kennedy, 'Mozart plumbs new depths', p. 8.
32. James Mulligan, 'Sorted for e's, opera and Mozart' *Sx Magazine*, 13 June 2001, p. 5.
33. Ibid.
34. Tanner, 'Lust without love', p. 49.
35. Bourdieu, *Distinction*, p. 56.
36. Bourdieu, *Distinction*, p. 57.
37. Bourdieu, *Distinction*, p. 486.
38. Andrew Clark, 'Humdrum tales of sex and violence', *Financial Times*, 4 June 2001, p. 16.
39. Clément, *Opera*, p. 4.
40. Bleito staged Vall-Inclán's *Comedias bárbaran* (Barbaric Comedies) at the Edinburgh Festival in 2000.

Notes (Chapter 5)

41. Jessica Waldoff, 'Don Giovanni: recognition denied', in Mary Hunter and James Wester (eds) *Opera Buffa in Mozart's Vienna*, (Cambridge: Cambridge University Press, 1997) p. 286.
42. Nicholas Till, *Mozart and the Enlightenment: Truth, Virtune and Beauty in Mozart's Operas* (London: Faber & Faber, 1992) p. 197.
43. Laurel Elizabeth Zeiss, 'Permeable boundaries in Mozart's Don Giovanni', *Cambridge Opera Journal*, 13 (2) 2001, p. 117.
44. Joseph Kernan, 'Reading Don Giovanni', in Jonathan Miller, *Don Giovanni: Myths of Seduction and Betrayal* (New York: Schocken Books, 1990) pp. 110–11.
45. Clément, *Opera*, p. 34.
46. Roy Porter, 'Libertinism and promiscuity', in Jonathan Miller, *Don Giovanni: Myths of Seduction and Betrayal* (New York: Schocken Books, 1990) pp. 1–20.
47. Pierre Jean Jouve, *Le Don Juan de Mozart* (Paris: Egloff, 1940).
48. Liane Curtis, 'The sexual politics of teaching Mozart's "Don Giovanni "', *Women's Studies Association Journal*, 12 (1) 2000, pp. 119–42.
49. Kristeva, 'Don Juan', p. 192.
50. Kristeva, 'Don Juan', p. 193.
51. Ibid.
52. Søren Kierkegaard, *Either/Or* (Princeton: Princeton University Press, 1987) p. 134.
53. Michel de Certeau, *The Practice of Everyday Life* (Berkeley: University of California Press, 1984) p. 192.
54. Wayne Koestenbaum, *The Queen's Throat: Opera, Homosexuality, and the Mystery of Desire* (London: Gay Men's Press, 1993) p. 43.
55. Note the indifference with which sex is received in theatrical productions of Don Juan-related texts. See Gunter, who shows how translation can be an excuse for a more ribald version of Tirso de Molina's *El burlador de Sevilla*. He cites titles as 'Playboy' (Schizzano and Mandel, 1963); 'Rogue' (O'Brien in 1963), 'Beguiler' (Oppenheimer in 1976), even 'Ladykiller' (Kidd in 2004), while Nick Dear's *Last Days of Don Juan*, commissioned for the Royal Shakespeare Company in 1990, and Kidd's *Ladykiller* choose to open the play with sexual scenes on stage. Gunter (*Don Juan Plays the USA*, p. 53) argues that, 'the problem with this strategy is that it co-opts audience expectations so completely that it can never successfully upset them.'
56. Sam Abel, *Opera in the Flesh: Sexuality in Operatic Performance* (Boulder: Westview Press, 1996) p. 101.
57. Peter Hutcheon and Linda Hutcheon, *Opera: Desire, Disease, Death* (Lincoln: University of Nebraska, 1996); Susan McClary, *Feminine Endings: Music, Gender and Sexuality* (Minneapolis: University of

Notes (Chapter 5)

Minnesota Press, 1991). I am grateful to the British Film Institute for granting me permission to view *Thriller* at its London offices.
58. Mitchell, *Mad Men and Medusas*, pp. 246–79.
59. Xavier Cester, 'Mozart con ojos contemporáneos', *Opera Actual*, 20–24 November 2002, p. 21.
60. Marc Augé, *Non-Places: Introduction to the Anthropology of Supermodernity* (London: Verso, 1992).
61. Delgado, 'Calixto Bieito's', p. 54.
62. Cester, 'Mozart con ojos contemporáneos', p. 21.
63. Allanbrook, *Rhythmic Gesture in Mozart*, p. 233.
64. Delgado, 'Calixto Bieito's', p. 56. A recent addition to the 2002 *Shorter Oxford English Dictionary*, 'bling bling' means flashy, ostentatious, conspicuous in consumption, as John Mullan writes, 'Diamond geezers: word of the week: bling bling', *Guardian*, 23 May 2003, p. 23.
65. Julian Rushton, *W. A. Mozart: Don Giovanni* (Cambridge: Cambridge University Press, 1981) p. 108 asks, 'Where is the real Giovanni?' Don Giovanni imitates a range of musical styles in order to gain confidences or seduce other characters, but no character of his own comes through strongly in the music.
66. Agustí Fancelli, 'Calixto Bieito: Don Juan es un producto de una sociedad enferma', *El País*, 30 November 2002, p. 23.
67. Jennifer King, 'Eco-Barbie: Barbie's latest accessory is a social conscience', *Utne Reader*, 39 (1990) p. 112.
68. Rachel Bowlby, *Carried Away: The Invention of Modern Shopping* (London: Faber & Faber, 2000) p. 19.
69. Michael F. Robinson, 'The alternative endings of Mozart's Don Giovanni', in Mary Hunter and James Wester (eds) *Opera Buffa in Mozart's Vienna* (Cambridge: Cambridge University Press, 1997) p. 261.
70. Rushton, *W. A. Mozart*, p. 65.
71. Wye Jamison Allanbrook, 'Mozart's happy endings: a new look at the "Convention" of the "Lieto Fine"', *Mozart-Jahrbuch*, 1984–5, p. 2.
72. Robinson, 'The alternative endings', p. 261.
73. From a private interview with Calixto Bieito, July 2002.
74. Carlos Javier Robledo, aged 22, was beaten to death on 1 April 2000 by a gang of youths in the Villa Olímpica in Barcelona. See for example, Anon, 'Tres años y medio de cárcel para dos condenados ya por el crimen de la Villa Olímpica', *El País*, 16 July 2000, sec. Cataluña, p. 4.
75. Malcolm Baker, 'Odzooks! A man of stone', in Jonathan Miller (ed.) *Don Giovanni: Myths of Seduction and Betrayal* (New York: Schocken Books, 1990) pp. 62–9.

Notes (Chapter 5)

76. Rank, *The Don Juan Legend*, p. 78.
77. Mitchell points out that *Don Giovanni* was Freud's favourite opera (p. 251), and also that in a letter to Fliess he refers to himself as a 'conquistador', and to his first published works as 'a list of all the beauties', a reference to Leporello's 'catalogue aria', from the Mozart/Da Ponte opera (p. 65).
78. Freud, 'Totem and taboo', p. 141.
79. Freud, 'Totem and taboo', pp. 141, 143.
80. Rank, *The Don Juan Legend*, p. 73.
81. Mitchell (*Mad Men and Medusas*, p. 253) writes that, 'rather straining the point, Rank suggests that the Don Juan story substitutes women for the brothers'.
82. Walter Benjamin, *Illuminations* (London: Fontana/Collins, 1992) p. 247.
83. Elizabeth Wright, *Feminism and Psychoanalysis: A Critical Dictionary* (Oxford: Blackwell, 1992) pp. 195–6.
84. Crystal Bartolovich, 'Consumerism or the cultural logic of late cannibalism', in Francis Barker, Peter Hulme and Margaret Iversen (eds) *Cannibalism and the Colonial World* (Cambridge: Cambridge University Press, 1998) pp. 204–37; John Kraniauskas, 'Cronos and the political economy of vampirism: notes of a historical constellation', in Francis Barker, Peter Hulme and Margaret Iversen (eds) *Cannibalism and the Colonial World* (Cambridge: Cambridge University Press, 1998) pp. 142–57.
85. Fancelli, 'Calixto Bieito'.
86. Theodor Adorno, 'Bourgeios opera', in Theodor Adorno (ed.) *Sound Figures* (Stanford: University of California Press, 1999) p. 16 writes that illusion is the prime referent in opera. 'Opera has reached the state of crisis because the genre cannot dispense with illusion without surrendering itself, and yet it must want to do so. Opera runs head on into the aesthetic limits of demystification.' He goes on to discuss the futility in his mind, in using abstractions to replace the mystical elements of opera, such as, for example, using a beam of light to represent the swan in *Lohengrin*: 'the premise of the entire work would be attacked to such an extent as to be rendered pointless.' Presumably Adorno would not have approved of Bieito's update of the living, breathing Commendatore to replace the Stone Guest.
87. Abel, *Opera in the Flesh*, p. 16.
88. In Claude Chabrol's film *La Cérémonie* (1995), *Don Giovanni* becomes a marker for the myopic conservatism of the bourgeoisie.
89. In the last act Leporello and Don Giovanni stuff food into their own and each other's mouths in a way that transgresses the traditional

Notes (Chapter 5)

cult of the voice in opera. The surtitles in Bieito's 2002 production of Brecht's *Threepenny Opera* (2002) did not provide a translation, but, in a stunningly original move, provided information about the stock exchange, the prices of certain goods displayed on stage, or repeated slogans from contemporary politics such as Aznar's phrase '*España va bien*' (Spain is working well).

90. Snatches from three well-known operas of the day are to be found within Mozart's opera: Martín y Soler's *Una cosa rara*; Sarti's *I litiganti* and also *Figaro* (Allanbrook, *Rhythmic Gesture in Mozart*, p. 288).
91. From a private interview with Calixto Bieito, July 2002.
92. Michael Billington, 'Sex, booze, drugs and Mozart', *Guardian*, 30 May 2001, p. 14.
93. Frederic Jameson, *Postmodernism, or the Cultural Logic of Late Capitalism* (London: Verso, 1991) p. 18.
94. Mulligan, 'Sorted for e's'.
95. Fancelli, 'Calixto Bieito'.
96. From a private interview with Calixto Bieito, July 2002.
97. Ibid.
98. Jameson, *Postmodernism*, p. 278.
99. An interesting comparison of this effect can be made with Terry Donovan Smith's study of Peter Sellars's modern-dress production (on TV) of *Don Giovanni*, set in Harlem in the 1980s, which Smith ('Shifting through space–time: a chronotopic analysis of Peter Sellars' Don Giovanni', *Modern Drama*, 34 (4) 1996, pp. 668–79) subjects to chronotopic reading using Bakhtin's theories. Apthorp, meanwhile, in an interesting article on Bieito's version of Mozart's *Die Entführung aus dem Serail* at Berlin's Komische Opera House in 2004, while musing on Bieito's use of working prostitutes for his production, argues against the current vogue for the aggressive sense of presence on stage in opera. While noting that 'sex and violence have often sold opera' (she cites, for example, Freschi's *Berenice* of 1680, which included 100 virgins) she laments the vogue for going 'that extra mile' in an attempt to make the 'audience feel something'. Jan Fabre's version of Wagner's *Tannhaüser*, in 2004 in Brussels featured naked pregnant women masturbating while Christoph Schlinensief's *Attabambi-Pornoland* (theatre, rather than opera, but infused with Wagner's *Parsifal*) in Zürich in 2004 slaughtered live piglets on stage (Apthorp, p. 37). Sandra Apthorp, 'Opera in Need of Soap', *Financial Times*, 3 July 2004, magazine, p. 37. Sellars set *Così fan tutte* in a neon-lit American diner and *Figaro* in Trump Tower. Other examples of updates of *Don Giovanni* are the famous *Donna Giovanna* played by Mexican women at the Fringe section of the 1987 Salzburg Festival and Leontyne Price's

Notes (Chapter 5)

groundbreaking performances as Elvira and Anna in the 1950s, the only African American face in an otherwise white cast. In Spain, Lluís Pasqual's production of *Don Giovanni* of 2005 at the Teatro Real with Carlos Álvarez in the title role transposed the action to 1940s Spain. The production was noted for its tones of grey, while a past-his-prime Don Giovanni is dressed in military uniform complete with dark glasses and Fascist moustache. Set designer Ezio Frigerio achieves the aesthetics of Francoism – a state funeral in muted colours, for example. The production included '*la supuesta filmación de in No-Do dirigido por el propio Don Giovanni*' (the supposed filming of a Francoist newsreel directed by Don Giovanni himself) (Roger Alier, 'Discutido pero brillante', *La Vanguardia*, 2 October 2005, p. 37). The production was greeted with alternate boos and cheers.

100. Richard Leppert, 'Commentary: culture, listening and technology', in Theodor W. Adorno, *Essays on Music* (Berkeley: University of California Press, 2002) p. 236.
101. Theodor Adorno, 'Opera and the long-playing record', in Theodor Adorno, *Essays in Music* (Berkeley: University of California Press, 2002) p. 284.
102. Kierkegaard, *Either/Or*, p. 120.
103. Nevertheless, there was one case of an audience member reporting the production to the German attorney general on the grounds of its being harmful to young people. See Cester, 'Mozart con ojos contemporáneos', p. 21.
104. C. López Rosell and M. Cervera, 'Bieito divide al público del Liceu con "Don Giovanni"', *El Periódico*, 1 December 2002, p. 52.
105. Mariano Rodríguez, 'Un estreno con poca discordia', *La Vanguardia*, 1 December 2002, p. 39.
106. López Rosell and Cervera, 'Bieito divide'.
107. Information from Gran Teatre del Liceu. Fuentes, 'Jóvenes que van de opera', p. 2 confirms the success of artists such as Bieito in attracting young audiences to opera.
108. Lourdes Morgades, 'Aplausos y broncas para Bieito en el estreno de "Don Giovanni "', *El País*, 1 June 2002, p. 9.
109. Marta Cervera and Jordi Subirana, 'Bieito carga "Don Giovanni" de sexo, drogas y violencia', *El Periódico*, 25 November 2002, p. 49.
110. P. M. H., 'El "Don Giovanni" de Bieito llega para cuestionar la moral de la sociedad actual', *ABC,* 27 November 2002, p. 60.
111. Morgades, 'Aplausos y broncas'.
112. María Delgado, 'Calixto Bieito: reimagining the text for the age in which it is being staged', *Contemporary Theatre Review*, 13 (3) 2004, pp. 59–66.

Notes (Chapter 5/Conclusion)

113. From a private interview with Calixto Bieito.
114. Ibid.
115. Fancelli, 'Calixto Bieito'.
116. Fernando Sans Rivière, 'Libertinaje marca Calixto Bieito', *La Razón*, 2 December 2002, p. 58.
117. Delgado, 'Calixto Bieito: reimagining the text'.
118. From a private interview with Sir Brian McMaster, director of the Edinburgh Festival, 2003, who has remarked that the polemical reviews are 'not part of his appeal'. For McMaster, (a gate-keeper for European cultural production and, in some sense, a 'taste-maker') Bieito's *Don Giovanni* was 'one of the most exciting pieces of opera production I have seen'. An article by Fondevila (p. 47) credits McMaster with establishing Bieito's international reputation.
119. From a private interview with Calixto Bieito, July 2002.

Conclusion: Between Limits

1. *Tres mitos españoles: La Celestina, Don Quijote, Don Juan* was sponsored by the Sociedad Estatal de Conmemoraciones Culturales, the Junta de Castilla la Mancha, and the Ministerio de Cultura.
2. Roland Barthes, *Camera Lucida: Reflections on Photography* (New York: Hill & Wang, 1981) p. 27.
3. Del Castillo cites Baudrillard's *Seduction* as a formative influence for her work. 'Seduction', writes Baudrillard (in *Seduction*, p. 2), 'never belongs to the order of nature, but that of artifice – never to the order of energy, but that of signs and rituals'. Baudrillard's nostalgia for the seduction of the eighteenth century – ritualistic, strategic, aristocratic – finds an echo in del Castillo's *Cortejo* (Courtship) (2002), which depicts two legs, wearing boots covered in *toile de jouy* with its images of pastoral romance. But, while the laced boots suggest fetishism, we see that on this site of seduction (a fur rug – the icon of the seducer's lair), the boots belong to two different females. The symmetry of their composition and their intimacy suggests self-sufficiency. The homoerotic *frisson* created in this work suggests that the female owners of these boots have no need for the seductiveness of Laclos, Casanova, Sade or even Don Juan.
4. There is a joyful playfulness about the lipsticks, these 'impossible objects' that remind one of Baudrillard's statement that cosmetics are not false, since in being falser than false, they attain instead a

Notes (Conclusion)

kind of innocence and transparency (Baudrillard, *Seduction*, p. 94). The lipstick, generally the reserve of the female seducer, the *femme fatale*, here turns the gender stereotype on its head. The lipsticks designated as 'female', peep submissively over the rims of the lipstick case, and cluster around the cockerels, reminding us that in nature it is often the male of the species who preen themselves prior to seduction. Other 'impossible' objects are the *toile de jouy* boots and, of course, the 'androgynous' body.

5. The camera, for Roland Barthes, does not merely view the world, it is touched by it. In *Camera Lucida*, Barthes writes of the 'stigmatum' of having been there: 'the photograph is literally an emanation of the referent' he writes, 'from a real body which was there, proceed radiations which ultimately touch me, who am here. ... A sort of umbilical cord links the body of the photographed thing to my gaze: light, though impalpable, is here a carnal medium, a skin I share with anyone who has been photographed' (Barthes, *Camera Lucida*, pp. 80–1). The photograph is therefore a conduit to touch through time and space, of present to past, or self to other. It is easy to see photography as a form of fetishism: the photograph is a comforting substitution for what once was there (giving the illusion of still being there, touching the subject, giving the illusion of presence in place of absence). For Geoffrey Batchen, it is this sense of touch, of embodied vision, that is at stake in the transition to digital photography. 'The digital', he writes, 'has no haptic purchase on history and declines to proffer the substitution-anxiety of the fetish. This is why digital images remain untroubled by the future anterior, the complex play of "this has been" and "this will be" that so animates the photograph' (Geoffrey Batchen, 'Carnal knowledge: artistic expression through photography', *Art Journal*, 60 (1) 2001, p. 22). The digital has no claim of authority over an original referent. Digital images are 'not so much signs of reality as signs of signs' (Geoffrey Batchen, *Burning with Desire: The Conception of Photography*, Cambridge: MIT Press, 1997, p. 213). When asked about the process of photography, Naia del Castillo is vague about the transition from analogue to digital. She claims that sometimes she uses digital, but that '*las cámaras digitales buenas son muy caras. Si el contenido de la fotografía tiene interés, el sistema no importa*' (Good digital cameras are very expensive. If the content of the photograph is interesting, the system is not important)

Notes (Conclusion)

(Eduardo Parra, 'Primero es el objeto y luego la fotografía', 20 October). See bibliography for complete reference (n.p.).
6. *Seductor* suggests Baudrillard's utopian vision of seduction, in which binary oppositions are eradicated. 'Is it to seduce, or to be seduced, that is seductive?' he asks. 'But to be seduced is the best way to seduce. It is an endless refrain. There is no active or passive mode in seduction, no subject or object, no interior or exterior: seduction plays on both sides, and there is no frontier separating them. One cannot seduce others, if one has not oneself been seduced' (Baudrillard, *Seduction*, p. 81). *Seductor* contains something of the reversibility of Baudrillard's conception of seduction, in which the line separating seducer 'active' perpetrator from 'passive' victim is indecipherable.
7. Barthes, *Camara Lucida*, p. 27.

BIBLIOGRAPHY

Abajo de Pablo, Juan Julio (1996) *Mis charlas con José Luis Sáenz de Heredia*, Valladolid: Ourion ediciones
Abel, Sam (1996) *Opera in the Flesh: Sexuality in Operatic Performance*, Boulder: Westview Press
Abellán, J. L. (1962) 'Don Juan: interpretación y mito', *Horizontes*, 5, pp. 8–19
Adorno, Theodor (1999) 'Bourgeios opera', in Theodor Adorno (ed.) *Sound Figures*, Stanford: University of California Press, pp. 15–28
—— (2002a) 'On the fetish character in music and the regression of listening', in Theodor Adorno, *Essays in Music*, Berkeley: University of California Press, pp. 287–317
—— (2002b) 'Opera and the long-playing record', in Theodor Adorno, *Essays in Music*, Berkeley: University of California Press, pp. 283–7
Agustín, Francisco (1928) *Don Juan en el teatro, en la novela y en la vida*, Madrid: Editorial Peláez
Alberich, José (1982) 'La popularidad de Don Juan Tenorio', in José Alberich (ed.) *La popularidad de Don Juan Tenorio y otros estudios de literatura española moderna*, San Antonio de Calonge, Gerona: Aubí, pp. 13–24
Alier, Roger (2005) 'Discutido pero brillante', *La Vanguardia*, 2 October, p. 37

Bibliography

Allanbrook, Wye Jamison (1983) *Rhythmic Gesture in Mozart: Le Nozze Di Figaro and Don Giovanni*, Chicago: University of Chicago Press
(1984–5) 'Mozart's happy endings: a new look at the "Convention" of the "Lieto Fine"', *Mozart-Jahrbuch*, pp. 1–5
Alonso de Santos, José Luis (1995) 'La sombra del Tenorio', *Primer Acto*, 257, pp. 64–88
Álvarez Peláez, Raquel (1988) 'Origen y desarrollo de la eugenesia en España', in José Manuel Sánchez Ron (ed.) *Ciencia y sociedad en España: de la ilustración a la guerra civil*, Madrid: El arquero, pp. 179–204
Anon. (1906) 'Tenorio modernista de D. Pablo Parellada', *ABC*, pp. 14–15
Anon. (1907) 'Aventuras del Tenorio' *Heraldo de Madrid*, p. 4
Anon. (1908) 'Notas teatrales', *ABC*, p. 13
Anon. (1926) 'Los experimentos del Sr Voronoff', *El Sol*, 25 February, p. 4
Anon. (1950a) 'Barba va, barba viene', *Primer Plano*, 18 March, n.p.
Anon. (1950b) '"Don Juan", realización cumbre de Sáenz de Heredia, triunfa en el cine Avenida', *Ya*, 17 October, p. 6
Anon. (1950c) 'El personaje que Usted ha interpretado en el cine ¿sería en la segunda mitad del siglo igual que ha sido antes?' *Primer Plano*, 31 December, n.p.
Anon. (1950d) '"Guitarras, aceitunas y el talento publicitario de Iturbi y Dalí, faltaron en la fiesta española de Venecia", declara Annabella', *Primer Plano*, 1 October, n.p.
Anon. (1950e) 'Primer desafío a sangre de Don Juan con su navaja de afeitar', *Primer Plano*, 23 April, n.p.
Anon. (1950f) *The Spanish Cinema*, Madrid: Diplomatic Information Office
Anon. (1960) *¿Sabes ir al cine?* Madrid: Talitha
Anon. (1963) 'Normas de censura cinematográfica', *Boletín Oficial del Estado*, no. 58 (8 March) n.p.
Anon. (1988) 'Presentación de "El burlador de Sevilla"', *Lanza*, 13 September, p. 13
Anon. (2000) 'Tres años y medio de cárcel para dos condenados ya por el crimen de la Villa Olímpica', *El País*, 16 July, sec. Cataluña, p. 4

Bibliography

Anon. (2005) 'Las españolas navegan menos: España supera la media de "brecha digital" entre hombres y mujeres', *El País*, 14 February, see http://www.elpais.com/articulo/internet/espanolas/navegan/elpeputec/2005021/elpepunet_12/Tes Accessed 10 May 2007

Apthorp, Sandra (2004) 'Opera in Need of Soap', *Financial Times*, magazine section, p. 37

Aresti, Nerea (2001) *Médicos, donjuanes y mujeres modernas: las ideales de feminidad y masculinidad en el primer tercio del siglo XX*, Bilbao: Universidad del País Vasco

Ashley, Tim (2001) 'Don Giovanni', *Guardian*, 2 June, p. 23

Augé, Marc (1992) *Non-Places: Introduction to the Anthropology of Supermodernity*, London: Verso

Avalle-Arce, Juan Bautista (1959) 'La esperpentización de Don Juan Tenorio', *Hispanófila*, 7, pp. 29–40

Bacon, Henry (1998) *Visconti: Explorations of Beauty and Decay*, Cambridge: Cambridge University Press

Baker, Malcolm (1990) 'Odzooks! A man of stone', in Jonathan Miller (ed.) *Don Giovanni: Myths of Seduction and Betrayal*, New York: Schocken Books, pp. 62–9

Barber, X. Theodore (1989) 'Phantasmagorical wonders: the magic lantern ghost show in nineteenth-century America', *Film History*, 3, pp. 73–86

Barga, Corpus (1926) 'Don Juan y los doctores', *El Sol*, 19 December, p. 1

Barthes, Roland (1981) *Camera Lucida: Reflections on Photography*, New York: Hill & Wang

Bartolovich, Crystal (1998) 'Consumerism or the cultural logic of late cannibalism', in Francis Barker, Peter Hulme and Margaret Iversen (eds) *Cannibalism and the Colonial World*, Cambridge: Cambridge University Press, pp. 204–37

Batchen, Geoffrey (1997) *Burning with Desire: The Conception of Photography*, Cambridge: MIT Press

—— (2001) 'Carnal knowledge: artistic expression through photography', *Art Journal*, 60 (1) pp. 21–3

Baudrillard, Jean (1990) *Seduction*, London: Macmillan

Benjamin, Walter (1992) *Illuminations*, London: Fontana/Collins

—— (1999) 'The work of art in the age of mechanical reproduction', in Leo Braudy and Marshall Cohen (eds) *Film Theory and*

Criticism: Introductory Readings, Oxford: Oxford University Press, pp. 731–51

Bennett, Susan (1996) *Performing Nostalgia: Shifting Shakespeare and the Contemporary Past*, London: Routledge

Benvenuto, B. and R. Kennedy (1986) *The Works of Jacques Lacan: An Introduction*, New York: St Martin's Press

Ben-ze'ev, Aaron (2004) *Love Online: Emotions on the Internet*, Cambridge: Cambridge University Press

Bersett, Jeffrey T. (2003) *El Burlado de Sevilla: Nineteenth-Century Theatrical Appropriations of Don Juan Tenorio*, Delaware: Juan de la Cuesta

Bhabha, Homi (1983) 'The other question', *Screen*, 24 (6) pp. 18–36

Bieder, Maryellen (1992) 'Woman and the twentieth century Spanish literary canon: the lady vanishes', *Anales de la literatura española contemporánea*, 17, pp. 301–24

Billington, Michael (2001) 'Sex, booze, drugs and Mozart', *Guardian*, 30 May, p. 14

Bird, Steve (2001) 'Coke-snorting Giovanni divides the Coliseum', *The Times*, 1 June, p. 5

Bird, Wendy (2004) 'Oh monstrous lamp! Special effects in Goya: a scene from El Hechizado por fuerza', *Apollo*, 159 (505) pp. 13–19

Blanco, Alda (1989) ' Introducción', in María Martínez Sierra (ed.) *Una mujer por los caminos de España*, Madrid: Castalia, pp. 7–42

Bonilla, E. (1927) 'La lucha contra la vejez', *El Sol*, p. 7

Bono, James J. (1990) 'Science, discourse and literature: the role/rule of metaphor in science', in Stuart Peterfreund (ed.) *Literature and Science: Theory and Practice*, Boston: Northeastern University Press, pp. 59–89

Bordonada, Ángela Ena (ed.) *Novelas breves de escritoras españolas (1900–1936)* Madrid: Castalia/Instituto de la Mujer

Bordons, Teresa and Susan Kirkpatrick (1992) 'Chacel's Teresa and Ortega's Canon', *Anales de la Literatura Española Contemporánea*, 17, pp. 283–99

Bourdieu, Pierre (1984) *Distinction: A Social Critique of the Judgement of Taste*, London: Routledge

Bibliography

Bower, Stephanie (1996) 'Dangerous liaisons: prostitution, disease and race in Frank Norris's fiction', *Modern Fiction Studies*, 42 (1) pp. 31–60
Bowlby, Rachel (2000) *Carried Away: The Invention of Modern Shopping*, London: Faber & Faber
Brachfeld, F. Oliver (1933) *Polémica contra Marañón*, Barcelona: Europa
Britt Arredondo, Christopher (2005) *Quixotism: The Imaginative Denial of Spain's Loss of Empire*, Albany: State University of New York Press
Burgos, Carmen de (1921) *La entrometida*, Madrid: La novela corta
Camón Aznar, José (1950) 'Un año de Arte', *ABC*, 28 December, p. 5
Campos Marín, Ricardo (1999) 'La teoría de la degeneración y la clínica psiquiátrica en la España de la Restauración', *Dynamis*, 19, pp. 429–56
Campos Marín, Ricardo and Rafael Huertas (1991) 'El alcoholismo como enfermedad social', *Dynamis*, 1, pp. 263–86
(2001) 'The theory of degeneration in Spain (1886–1920)', *Boston Studies in the Philosophy of Science*, 221, pp. 171–87
Cardwell, Richard A. (1993) 'Specul(ariz)ation on the other woman: Don Juan Tenorio's Inés', in Richard A. Cardwell and Ricardo Landeira (eds) *José Zorrilla 1839–1993: Centennial Readings*, Nottingham: University of Nottingham Monographs in the Humanities, pp. 41–57
(1996) 'The mad doctors: literature and medicine in finesecular Spain', *Journal of the Institute of Romance Studies*, 4, pp. 167–96
Caro Baroja, Julio (1966) 'Recuerdos valleinclanesco-barojianos', *Revista de occidente*, IV/2 (44 and 45) November–December, pp. 302–13
Cartwright, Lisa (1995) *Screening the Body: Tracing Medicine's Visual Culture*, Minneapolis: University of Minnesota Press
Cebollada, Pascual and Mary G. Santa Eulalia (2000) *Madrid y el Cine*, Madrid: Comunidad de Madrid
Certeau, Michel de (1984) *The Practice of Everyday Life*, Berkeley: University of California Press
(1988) *The Writing of History*, New York: Columbia University Press

Bibliography

Cervera, Marta and Jordi Subirana (2002) 'Bieito carga "Don Giovanni" de sexo, drogas y violencia', *El Periódico*, 25 November, p. 49

Cervera Barat, Rafael (1896) *Alcoholismo y civilización*, Valencia: A. Cortés

Cester, Xavier (2002) 'Mozart con ojos contemporáneos', *Opera actual*, 20-24 November, pp. 20-4

Chauncey, George (1994) *Gay New York: The Making of the Gay Male World, 1890-1940*, London: Harper Collins

Church, Michael (2001) 'From tragedy to farce: Don Giovanni', *The Scotsman*, 4 June, p. 15

Clark, Andrew (2001) 'Humdrum tales of sex and violence', *Financial Times*, 4 June, p. 16

Clément, Catherine (1988) *Opera, or the Undoing of Women*, London: Virago Press

Cleminson, Richard (2000) 'The review "Sexualidad" (1925-28), social hygiene and the pathologisation of male homosexuality in Spain', *Journal of Iberian and Latin American Studies*, 6 (2) pp. 119-29

Conlon, Raymond (1985) 'Female psychosexuality in Tirso's *El vergonzoso en palacio*,' *BCom*, 37 (1) pp. 55-69

—— (1988) 'Sexual passion and marriage: chaos and order in Tirso de Molina's *El vergonzoso en palacio*', *Hispania*, 71 (1) pp. 8-13

Copjec, Joan (1999) 'More! From melodrama to magnitude', in Janet Bergstrom (ed.) *Endless Night: Cinema and Psychoanalysis, Parallel Histories*, Berkeley: University of California Press, pp. 249-72

Crystal, David (2001) *Language and the Internet*, Cambridge: Cambridge University Press

Cueva, Jorge de la (1935) 'La plasmatoria', *El Debate*, p. 4

Curtis, Liane (2000) 'The sexual politics of teaching Mozart's "Don Giovanni"', *Women's Studies Association Journal*, 12 (1) pp. 119-42

Davies, Ann (2004) *The Metamorphoses of Don Juan's Women: Early Parity to Late Modern Pathology*, Lewiston: The Edwin Mellen Press

Delgado, María (2001) 'Calixto Bieito's "Don Giovanni" outrages the British critics', *Western European Stages*, 13 (3) pp. 53-8

Bibliography

(2003) *'Other' Spanish Theatres: Erasure and Inscription on the Twentieth-Century Spanish Stage*, Manchester: Manchester University Press
(2004) 'Calixto Bieito: reimagining the text for the age in which it is being staged', *Contemporary Theatre Review*, 13 (3) pp. 59–66
Doane, Mary Ann (1996) *Femmes Fatales: Feminism, Film Theory, Psychoanalysis*, London: Routledge
Dolfi, Laura (1998) 'Falla y el Don Juan de España (1921) de Martínez Sierra', in Ana Sofía Pérez Bustamante (ed.) *Don Juan Tenorio en la España del siglo XX*, Madrid: Cátedra, pp. 95–127
Dominicis, Maria C. (1977) *Don Juan en el teatro español del siglo XX*, Barcelona: Ediciones Universal
Doty, William G. and William J Hynes (1993) 'Historical overview of theoretical issues: the problem of the trickster', in William J. Hynes and William G. Doty (eds.) *Mythical Trickster Figures: Contours, Contexts and Criticisms*, Tuscaloosa: University of Alabama Press, pp. 13–32
Dougherty, Dru (1980) 'The tragicomic Don Juan: Valle-Incán's *Las galas del difunto*', *Modern Drama*, 23, pp. 44–57
(1999) 'Theatre and culture, 1868–1936', in David T. Gies (ed.) *The Cambridge Companion to Modern Spanish Culture*, Cambridge: Cambridge University Press, pp. 211–21
Driver, Paul (2001) 'Reservoir Don', *Sunday Times*, 10 June, p. 21
Edison, Thomas Alva (1948) *The Diary and Sundry Observations of Thomas Alva Edison*, New York: Philosophical Library
Edwards, Tim (2000) *Contradictions of Consumption: Concepts, Practices and Politics in Consumer Society*, Buckingham: Open University Press
Escuder, José María (1895) *Locos y anómalos*, Madrid: Establecimiento tip. 'Sucesores de Rivadeneyra'
F. H. (1926) 'El doctor Cardenal ensaya los métodos de Voronoff', *El Sol*, 26 February, p. 4
Fairman, Richard (2001) 'Don Giovanni: English National Opera at the London Coliseum', *Opera*, August, pp. 1005–7
Fancelli, Agustí (2002) 'Calixto Bieito: Don Juan es un producto de una sociedad enferma', *El País*, 30 November, p. 23
Farinelli, Arturo (1896) *Don Giovanni*, Turin: Ermanno Loescher
Feal, Carlos S. (1984) *En nombre de Don Juan: estructura de un mito literario*, Amsterdam: John Benjamins

(2000) 'Don Juan como esperpento: *Las galas del difunto*', in Jesús Torrecilla (ed.) *La generación del 98 frente al nuevo fin de siglo* (Amsterdam: Rodopi, 2000) pp. 71–90

Felman, Shoshana (1980) *The Scandal of the Speaking Body: Don Juan with J. L. Austin, or Seduction in Two Languages*, Stanford: Stanford University Press

Fenichel, Otto (1946) *The Psychoanalytic Theory of Neuroses*, London: Routledge & Kegan Paul

Fernández Cifuentes, Luis (1993a) 'Don Juan y las palabras', in Luis Fernández Cifuentes (ed.) *José Zorrilla: Don Juan Tenorio*, Barcelona: Crítica, pp. 38–59

(1993b) 'Prólogo', in José Zorrilla, *Don Juan Tenorio*, Barcelona: Crítica, pp. 1–66

Fernández, Luis Miguel (1998) 'Don Juan en imágenes: aproximación a la recreación cinematográfica del personaje', in Ana Sofía Pérez-Bustamante (ed.) *Don Juan Tenorio en la España del Siglo XX*, Madrid: Cátedra, pp. 503–38

(2000) *Don Juan en el cine español: hacia una teoría de la recreación fílmica*, Santiago de Compostela: Universidade de Santiago de Compostela

Fernández Montesinos, Ángel (2004) 'Entrevista: Ángel Fernández Montesinos', in César Oliva, *Seis caminos hacia el mito de Don Juan*, Madrid: Compañía Nacional de Teatro Clásico, pp. 169–73

Fernández Santos, Ángel (1992) 'Muere José Luis Sáenz de Heredia, el máximo cineasta del franquismo militante', *El País*, p. 36

Fitz Gerald, Thomas A. (1922) 'Some notes on the sources of Zorrilla's Don Juan Tenorio', *Hispania*, 5 (1) pp. 1–7

Fleck, Ludwik (1979) *Genesis and Development of a Scientific Fact*, Chicago: University of Chicago Press

Flugel, J (1934) *Men and their Morals*, London: Routledge & Kegan Paul

Fondevila, Santiago, 'El hombre que creó a Calixto Bieito', *La Vanguardia*, 6 November 2003, cultura section, p. 47

Foucault, Michel (1972) 'The discourse on language', in Michel Foucault translated by A. M. Sheridan-Smith, *The Archaeology of Knowledge*, New York: Irvington Publishers, pp. 215–37

(1990a) *The History of Sexuality*, London: Penguin Books

Bibliography

(1990b) *The History of Sexuality*, volume 1, *An Introduction*, Harmondsworth: Penguin

Fox, Inman (1998) *La invención de España: nacionalismo liberal e identidad nacional*, Madrid: Cátedra

Franco, Andrés (1971) *El teatro de Unamuno*, Madrid: Insula

Freud, Sigmund (1886–99) 'Extracts from the Fliess papers', in J. Strachey (ed.) *The Standard Edition of the Complete Psychological Works of Sigmund Freud*, London: Hogart, vol. 1, pp. 175–279
(1901) *The Psychopathology of Everyday Life*, London: T. Fisher Unwin
(2001) 'Totem and taboo', *The Standard Edition of the Complete Psychological Works of Sigmund Freud*, London: Vintage, vol. 13, pp. 1–162

Fried, Michael (1980) *Absorption and Theatricality: Painting and Beholder in the Age of Diderot*, Berkeley: University of California Press

Fuentes, Enrique (2002) 'Jóvenes que van de ópera', *La Vanguardia*, 23 December, Tarragona section, p. 2

Galton, Francis (1883) *Inquiries into Human Faculty and its Development*, London: Macmillan

García de Vinuesa, Juan Manuel (1950) 'El 'Tenorio número dos', de Dalí', *ABC*, 29 October, p. 11

García Escudero, José Luis (1959) *El cine y los hijos*, Madrid: Esse

García Garzón, Juan Ignacio (2004) 'La destrucción o el amor', in César Oliva (ed.) *Seis caminos hacia el mito de Don Juan*, Madrid: Compañía Nacional de Teatro Clásico, pp. 175–6

García Yagüe, Juan (1953) *Cine y juventud*, Madrid: Consejo superior de investigaciones científicas

Garmendía de Otaola, A. (1956) *Estética y ética del cine: guía para cines y cineclubs*, Bilbao: Gráficas Ellecuria

Gaudreault, André (1987) 'Theatricality, narrativity, and trickality: reevaluating the cinema of Georges Méliès', *Journal of Popular Film and Television*, 15 (3) pp. 111–19

Gazetas, Aristides (2000) *An Introduction to World Cinema*, Jefferson: Mcfarland & Company

Gendarme de Bévotte, Gérard (1911) *La légende de Don Juan*, Paris: Hachette

Gibson, Ian (1997) *The Shameful Life of Salvador Dalí*, London: Faber & Faber

Gies, David Thatcher (1980) 'Don Juan contra Don Juan: apoteosis del romanticismo español', in Giuseppe Bellini (ed.) *Actas del séptimo Congreso de la Asociación Internacional de Hispanistas*, Venice: Bulzone Editore, pp. 545–51

—— (1992) *From Myth to Pop: Don Juan, James Bond, and Zelig*, Greensburg, PA: Eadmer Press

—— (1994a) 'La subversión de Don Juan: parodias decimonónicas del 'Tenorio' con una nota pornográfica', *España Contemporánea*, 7 (1) pp. 93–102

—— (1994b) *The Theatre in Nineteenth Century Spain*, Cambridge: Cambridge University Press

Gil-Albert, Juan (1955) *Contra el cine*, Valencia: Tip. Artística

Giménez Caballero, Ernesto (1927) *Los toros, las castañuelas y la Virgen*, Madrid: Caro Raggio

—— (1939) *Genio de España: exaltaciones a una resurrección nacional y del mundo*, Barcelona: Ediciones Jerarquía

—— (1944) *El cine y la cultural humana*, Bilbao: Tipografía Hispano-Americana

Ginger, Andrew (2000) 'Dashing on the silver screen: Don Juan Tenorio (1922) Dir Ricardo de Baños (based on the play of the same title by José Zorrilla (1844)', in Andrew Ginger, Huw Lewis and John Hobbs (eds) *Selected Interdisciplinary Essays on the Representation of the Don Juan Archetype in Myth and Culture*, Lewiston: Edwin Mellen Press, pp. 187–213

Ginger, Andrew, Huw Lewis and John Hobbs (2000) *Selected Interdisciplinary Essays on the Representation of the Don Juan Archetype in Myth and Culture*, Lewiston: Edwin Mellen Press

Glenn, Kathleen (1999) 'Demythification and denunciation in Blanca de los Ríos' Las hijas de don Juan', in John P. Gabriele (ed.) *Nuevas perspectivas sobre el 98*, Madrid: Iberoamericana, pp. 223–30

Glick Thomas F. (1982) 'The naked science: psychoanalysis in Spain, 1914–1948', *Comparative Studies in Society and History*, 24, pp. 533–71

—— (n.d.) 'Trials of a preparadigmatic science: gerontology in Spain, 1910–1935', unpublished article, pp. 1–33

Bibliography

González Álvarez, B. (1903) 'Higiene profiláctica del niño respecto de la herencia', *El Siglo Médico*, 183 (5) pp. 582–5

González López, María Antonieta (2001) *Aproximación a la obra literaria y periodística de Blanca de los Ríos*, Madrid: Fundación Universitaria Española

González López, Palmira (1997) 'Don Juan Tenorio 1910', in Julio Pérez Perucha (ed.) *Antología crítica del cine español 1906–1995: flor en la sombra*, Madrid: Cátedra, pp. 28–30

Gregersen, Halldan (1936) *Ibsen and Spain*, Cambridge: Harvard University Press

Gubern, Román (2000) *El Eros electrónico*, Madrid: Taurus

Gunning, Tom (1990) 'The cinema of attractions: early film, its spectator and the avant-garde', in Thomas Elsaesser (ed.) *Early Cinema: Space, Frame, Narrative*, London: British Film Institute, pp. 56–62

(1997) 'An aesthetic of astonishment: early film and the (in)credulous spectator', in Linda Williams (ed.) *Viewing Positions: Ways of Seeing Film*, New Brunswick: Rutgers University Press, pp. 114–33

Gunter, Benjamin Bridges (2005) *Don Juan Plays the USA: (El burlador de Sevilla and tan largo me lo fiáis) for Twenty-First Century Performances in the United States*, Tallahassee: Florida State University, dissertation

Gutiérrez del Egido, Ernesto (1946) *¡Conquistemos el cine! Hacia una solución total y acertada del problema cinematográfico*, Ávila: Gloria

Hadfield, Duncan (2001) 'Don Giovanni: London Coliseum', *What's On*, 6 June, p. 25

Hall, Lesley A. (2001) *Sex, Sin and Suffering: Venereal Disease and European Society since 1870*, London: Routledge

Hansen, Miriam (1991) *Babel and Babylon: Spectatorship in American Silent Film*, Cambridge, MA: Harvard University Press

Harari, Roberto (2001) *Lacan's Seminar on 'Anxiety': An Introduction*, translated by Jane C. Lamb-Ruiz, New York: Other Pren, pp. 154–5

Haro Tecglen, Eduardo (2004) 'Rescoldo de una emoción', in César Oliva (ed.) *Seis caminos hacia el mito de Don Juan*, Madrid: Compañía Nacional de Teatro Clásico, pp. 178–9

Bibliography

Haslett, Moyra (1997) *Byron's Don Juan and the Don Juan Legend*, Oxford: Clarendon Press

Hayward, Susan (1996) *Key Concepts in Cinema Studies*, London: Routledge

Hera, Alberto de la (2003) 'El Tenorio de Dalí, una resurrección', *Guía del ocio*, 16

Hernández Ruiz, Javier (2004) 'La Celestina, don Juan y el Quijote en las pantallas: luces y sombras de sus recreaciones audiovisuales', in *Ties Mitos españoles: La Celestina, Don Quijote, Don Juan*, Madrid: Sociedad estatal de commemoraciones culturales

Holmlund, Chris (1993) 'Masculinity as multiple masquerade: the "mature" stallone and the stallone clone', in Steve Cohan and Ina Rae Hark (eds) *Screening the Male: Exploring Masculinities in Hollywood Cinema*, London: Routledge, pp. 213–29

Hooper, Kirsty (2003) 'Extranjera en mi patria: gender and nation in the pre-1914 writings of Sofía Casanova (1861–1958)', University of Oxford dissertation

Hoyle, Martin (2001) 'Turn of the screw: why Don Giovanni's critics have missed the point', *Time Out*, 10 June, p. 10

Huertas, Rafael (1992) 'Madness and degeneration, I. From "fallen angel" to "mentally ill"', *History of Psychiatry*, 3, pp. 391–411

Hutcheon, Linda (1985) *A Theory of Parody: The Teachings of Twentieth-Century Art Forms*, New York: Methuen

Hutcheon, Peter and Linda Hutcheon (1996) *Opera: Desire, Disease, Death*, Lincoln: University of Nebraska

Irvine, Ian (2001) 'Director Booed After Ibizan *Don Giovanni*', *Independent*, 1 June, p. 10

Jameson, Frederic (1991) *Postmodernism, or the Cultural Logic of Late Capitalism*, London: Verso

Jiménez Placer, Fernando, Francisco Cervera y Jiménez Alfaro and Antonio Sierra Corella (1944) *Centenario del estreno de 'Don Juan Tenorio' (1844–1944)*, Madrid: Instituto Nacional del Libro Español

Johnson, Roberta (2003) 'The domestication of a modernist Don Juan', in Roberta Johnson, *Gender and Nation in the Spanish Modernist Novel*, Nashville: Vanderbilt University Press, pp. 111–44

Jouve, Pierre Jean (1940) *Le Don Juan de Mozart*, Paris: Egloff

Juanes, José de (1964) 'Tercer "Tenorio" de Dalí, en el Español', *Arriba*, 31 October, p. 22

Kachur, Lewis (2003) *Displaying the Marvellous: Marcel Duchamp, Salvador Dalí and Surrealist Exhibition*, Cambridge, MA: MIT Press

Keller, Gary D. (1977) *The Significance and Impact of Gregorio Marañón: Literary Criticism, Biographies and Historiography*, New York: Bilingual Press

Kelly-Holmes, Helen (2000) 'Bier, parfum, kaas: language fetish in European advertising', *European Journal of Cultural Studies*, 3 (1) pp. 67–82

Kennedy, Michael (2001) 'Mozart plumbs new depths', *The Sunday Telegraph*, 3 June, p. 8

Kernan, Joseph (1990) 'Reading Don Giovanni', in Jonathan Miller, *Don Giovanni: Myths of Seduction and Betrayal*, New York: Schocken Books, pp. 108–25

Kierkegaard, Søren (1987) *Either/Or*, Princeton: Princeton University Press

King, C. Richard (1996) 'The siren screams of telesex: speech, seduction and simulation', *Journal of Popular Culture*, 30 (3) pp. 91–101

King, Jennifer (1990) 'Eco-Barbie: Barbie's latest accessory is a social conscience', *Utne Reader*, 39, p. 112

Koestenbaum, Wayne (1993) *The Queen's Throat: Opera, Homosexuality, and the Mystery of Desire*, London: Gay Men's Press

Koh, Stella (2002) 'The real in the virtual: speech, self and sex in the realm of pure text', *Asian Journal of Social Science*, 30 (2) pp. 221–38

Kraniauskas, John (1998) 'Cronos and the political economy of vampirism: notes of a historical constellation', in Francis Barker, Peter Hulme and Margaret Iversen (eds) *Cannibalism and the Colonial World*, Cambridge: Cambridge University Press, pp. 142–57

Kretschmer, Ernst (1925) *Physique and Character: An Investigation of the Nature of Constitution and of the Theory of Temperament*, London: Kegan Paul

Kristeva, Julia (1979) 'Ellipsis on dread and the specular seduction', *Wide Angle*, 3 (3) pp. 42–7

(1987) 'Don Juan, or loving to be able to', in Julia Kristeva (ed.)

Tales of Love, New York: Columbia University Press, pp. 191–208
(1990) 'The adolescent novel', in John Fletcher and Andrew Benjamin, *Abjection, Melancholia and Love*, London: Routledge, pp. 8–23

Labanyi, Jo (2000) 'Feminizing the nation: women, subordination and subversion in post-Civil War Spain', in Ulrike Sieglohr (ed.) *Heroines Without Heroes: Reconstructing Female Identities in European Cinema, 1945–51*, London: Cassell, pp. 163–84

— (2001) 'Internalisations of empire: colonial ambivalence and the early Francoist missionary film', *Discourse*, 23 (1) pp. 25–42

— (2003) 'Impossible love and Spanishness: adventures of Don Juan (Sherman, 1949) and Don Juan (Sáenz De Heredia, 1950)', in Federico Bonaddio and Xon de Ros (eds) *Crossing Fields in Modern Spanish Culture*, Oxford: Legenda, pp. 146–54

— (2007) 'Political readings of Don Juan and romantic love in Spain from the 1920s to the 1940s', in Luisa Passerini, Liliana Ellena and Alexander C. T. Geppert (eds) *New Dangerous Liaisons: Discourses on Europe and Love in the Twentieth Century*, Oxford: Berghahn Books

Lacan, Jacques (1998) *On Feminine Sexuality: The Limits of Love and Knowledge. Book XX: Encore, 1972–1973*, New York: Norton

Lasa, Juan Francisco de (1975) *Los hermanos Baños*, Madrid: Filmoteca Nacional de España

LaTorre, Gonzalo (1935) 'La plasmatoria', *La Nación*, 19 December, p. 14

Lázaro, Reyes (2000) 'El "Don Juan" de Blanca de los Ríos y el nacional-romanticismo español de principios de siglo', *Letras Peninsulares*, XIII (part 2), pp. 467–83

Leane, Elizabeth (2001) 'Popular cosmology as mythic narrative: a site for interdisciplinary exchange', in Julie Scanlon and Amy Waste (eds) *Crossing Boundaries: Thinking Through Literature*, Sheffield: Sheffield Academic Press, pp. 84–97

Léger, Fernand (1973) 'A critical essay on the plastic qualities of Abel Gance's film The Wheel', in Edward Fry (ed.) *Functions of Painting*, London: Thames & Hudson, pp. 20–3

Leitch, Luke (2001) 'Uproar as Mozart gets "Tarantino" treatment', *Evening Standard*, 1 June, p. 56

Leppert, Richard (2002) 'Commentary: culture, listening and

technology', in Theodor W. Adorno, *Essays on Music*, Berkeley: University of California Press, pp. 213–50

Lombroso, Cesare (1911) *Los criminales*, Barcelona: Centro Editorial Presa

London, John (1998) 'Twentieth-century Spanish stage design', *Contemporary Theatre Review*, 7 (5) pp. 25–56

Long Hall, Diana (1973) 'Biology, sex hormones and sexism in the 1920s', *Philosophical Forum*, 1 (2) pp. 81–96

López, Ignacio-Javier (1986) *Caballero de novela: ensayo sobre el donjuanismo en la novela española moderna 1880–1930*, Barcelona: Puvill Libros

López Rosell, C. and M. Cervera (2002) 'Bieito divide al público del Liceu con "Don Giovanni"', *El Periódico*, 1 December, p. 52

Losada, José Manuel (1997) *Bibliography of the Myth of Don Juan in Literary History*, Lewiston: The Edwin Mellen Press

Lozano Marco, Miguel Ángel (1990) 'Introducción', in Ramón Pérez de Ayala (ed.) *Tigre Juan: el curandero de su honra*, Madrid: Espasa-Calpe, pp. 9–44

Lyotard, Jean-François (1989) *The Postmodern Condition: A Report on Knowledge*, Manchester: Manchester University Press

M. H., P. (2002) 'El "Don Giovanni" de Bieito llega para cuestionar la moral de la sociedad actual', *ABC*, 27 November, p. 60

McClary, Susan (1991) *Feminine Endings: Music, Gender and Sexuality*, Minneapolis: University of Minnesota Press

McClintock, Anne (1995) *Imperial Leather: Race, Gender and Sexuality in the Colonial Contest*, London: Routledge

Madariaga, Salvador de (1983) 'La don-juanía o seis don Juanes y una dama', in Salvador de Madariaga (ed.) *Teatro en prosa y verso*, Madrid: Espasa-Calpe, pp. 419–48

Maeztu, Ramiro de (1925) *Don Quijote, Don Juan y la Celestina: ensayos en simpatía*, Madrid: Espasa-Calpe

—— (1926) *Don Quijote, Don Juan y la Celestina: ensayos en simpatía*, Madrid: Espasa-Calpe

Mandolini, Hernani (1926) 'Psicopatología del Don Juan', *Revista de Criminología, Psiquiatría y Medicina Legal*, May–June, pp. 332–30

Mandrell, James (1987) 'Don Juan Tenorio as refundicion: the question of repetition and doubling', *Hispania*, 70 (1) pp. 22–30

(1991) 'Nostalgia and the popularity of Don Juan Tenorio: reading Zorrilla through Clarín', *Hispanic Review*, 59 (1) pp. 37–55

(1992) *Don Juan and the Point of Honour: Seduction, Patriarchal Society and Literary Tradition*, Pennsylvania: Penn State University Press

Marañón, Gregorio (1924) 'Notas para una biología de Don Juan', *Revista de Occidente*, Año 11, vol. VII (January) pp. 15–53

(1928–9) 'Sesión de 6 de octubre de 1928', *Anales del Servicio de Patología Médica del Hospital General de Madrid*, Madrid: Compañía Ibero-Americana de Publicaciones, vol. 4, pp. 3–4

(1932) *The Evolution of Sex and Intersexual Conditions*, translated by Warre B. Wells, London: George Allen & Unwin Ltd

(1942) *Don Juan: ensayos sobre el origen de su leyenda*, Madrid: Espasa-Calpe

(1968) *Obras completas*, Madrid: Espasa-Calpe, 10 vols, Madrid: Espasa-Calpe

Marchetti, Gina (1989) 'Action-adventure as ideology', in Ian Angus and Sut Jhally (eds), *Cultural Politics in Contemporary America*, New York: Routledge, pp. 182–97

Marqueríe, Alfredo (1949) 'En el María Guerrero se estrenó una versión escenográfica del "Tenorio"', *ABC*, p. 19

Martín Gaite, Carmen (1987) *Usos amorosos de la postguerra española*, Barcelona: Editorial Anagrama

(1988) 'Prólogo', in Tirso de Molina, *El burlador de Sevilla y convidado de piedra*, Teatro Municipal General, pp. 1–7

(2000) *The Back Room*, San Francisco: City Lights Books

Martín Márquez, Susan (1999) *Feminist Discourse and Spanish Cinema: Sight Unseen*, Oxford: Oxford University Press

Mattauch, Hans (1995) 'La implantación del rito del Tenorio en Madrid (1844–1877)', *Actas del Congreso sobre José Zorrilla, Una nueva lectura*, Universidad de Valladolid, Universidad de Valladolid, pp. 409–15

Memba, Javier (1992) 'José Luis Sáenz de Heredia: El Leni Riefhsteald de Franco', *El Mundo*, 5 November, p. 10

Menéndez Pidal, Ramón (1968) 'Sobre los orígenes del "convidado de piedra" (1906)', *Estudios Literarios*, Buenos Aires: Espasa-Calpe, pp. 81–107

Bibliography

Mitchell, Juliet (2000) *Mad Men and Medusas: Reclaiming Hysteria and the Effects of Sibling Relations on the Human Condition*, London: Allen Lane and Penguin Books

Mitchell, Timothy (1988) *Violence and Piety in Spanish Folklore*, Philadelphia: University of Pennsylvania Press

Mitry, Jean (1967) *Histoire du cinéma*, Paris: Editions Universitaires

Molero Asenjo, Antonio (1910) *Observaciones antropológicas de las anomalías en los criminales*, Guadalajara: Daniel Ramirez

Monleón, José (1998) 'La realidad del teatro: *La sombra del Tenorio* (1994), de José Luis Alonso de Santos', in Ana Sofía Pérez Bustamante (ed.) *Don Juan Tenorio en la España del siglo XX*, Madrid: Cátedra, pp. 289–310

Montaner, Joaquín (1927) *El hijo del diablo*, Barcelona: A. López Llausás

Morgades, Lourdes (2002) 'Aplausos y broncas para Bieito en el estreno de "Don Giovanni"', *El País*, 1 June, p. 9

Mortimore, Roger (1975) 'Buñuel, Sáenz de Heredia and filmófono', *Sight and Sound*, 44, pp. 180–2

Mullan, John (2003) 'Diamond geezers: word of the week: bling bling', *Guardian*, 23 May, p. 23

Mulligan, James (2001) 'Sorted for e's, opera and mozart' *Sx Magazine*, 13 June, p. 5

Muñoz Seca, Pedro (1927) *Las inyecciones o el doctor Cleofás Uthof vale más que Voronoff*, Madrid: Zaballos

Muñoz Seca, Pedro and Pedro Pérez Fernández (1936) *La plasmatoria: farsa cómica en tres actos*, Madrid: La Farsa

Nash, Mary (1992) 'Social eugenics and nationalist race hygiene in early twentieth century Spain', *History of European Ideas*, 15 (4–6) pp. 741–8

(1999) 'Un/contested identities: motherhood, sex reform and the modernization of gender identity in early twentieth-century Spain', in Victoria Loree Enders and Pamela Beth Radcliffe (eds) *Constructing Spanish Womanhood: Female Identity in Modern Spain*, Albany: State University of New York Press, pp. 25–49

Nelken, Margarita (1931) *La mujer ante las cortes constituyentes*, Madrid: Castro

Nieva, Francisco (ed.) (1995) 'Introducción', in José Zorrilla, *Don Juan Tenorio*, Madrid: Espasa-Calpe, pp. 9–27

Nieva de la Paz, Pilar (1993) *Autoras dramáticas españolas entre 1918 y 1936*, Madrid: Consejo superior de investigaciones científicas

—— (1997) 'El teatro de Maria Teresa Borragán: una contribución al feminismo reformista de preguerra', *Estreno*, 23 (2) pp. 27–41

Nordau, Max (1993) *Degeneration*, Lincoln: University of Nebraska Press

Nozick, Martin (1950) 'Some parodies of Don Juan Tenorio', *Hispania*, 33 (2) pp. 105–12

Oliva, César (1998) 'Trayectoria escénica del Tenorio', in Ana Sofía Pérez-Bustamante (ed.) *Don Juan Tenorio en la España del siglo XX*, Madrid: Cátedra, pp. 27–38

—— (2004) 'Ángel Fernández Montesinos, director de escena: entrevista', in César Oliva (ed.) *Seis caminos hacia el mito de Don Juan*, Madrid: Compañía Nacional de Teatro Clásico, pp. 169–73

Ortega y Gasset, José (1921) 'Introducción a un Don Juan', in José Ortega y Gasset (ed.) *Obras completas*, Madrid: Revista de Occidente, vol. 6, pp. 121–37

—— (1926) 'Amor en Stendhal', *El sol*, 24 August, p. 6

—— (1935) 'La estrangulación de Don Juan', in José Ortega y Gasset, *Obras completas*, Madrid: Revista de Occidente, vol. 5, pp. 238–46

—— (1987) 'Para una psicología del hombre interesante', in José Ortega y Gasset (ed.) *Obras completas*, Madrid: Revista de Occidente, vol. 4

Otis, Laura (1994) *Organic Memory: History and the Body in Late Nineteenth and Early Twentieth Centuries*, Lincoln: University of Nebraska Press

—— (1999) *Membranes: Metaphors of Invasion in Nineteenth-Century Literature, Science, and Politics*, Baltimore: The Johns Hopkins University Press

Oudart, Jean-Pierre (1977) 'Cinema and suture', *Screen*, 18 (1) pp. 35–47

Oudshoorn, Nelly (1994) *Beyond the Natural Body: An Archaeology of Sex Hormones*, London: Routledge

P., A. (1950) 'Don Juan, el personaje español famoso en todo el mundo, en una grandiosa superproducción nacional', *Cámara*, 187, pp. 44–5

Pantorba, Bernadino de (1948) *El pintor Salaverría: ensayo biográfico y crítico*, Madrid: Espasa-Calpe

Bibliography

Pardo Bazán, Emilia (2004) 'La última ilusión de Don Juan', in Emilia Pardo Bazán (ed.) *Obras completas*, Madrid: Biblioteca Castro, vol. 8, pp. 379–94

Parr, James (2004) 'El burlador de Sevilla: authorship and authenticity', in James Parr (ed.) *Don Quijote, Don Juan and Related Subjects: Form and Tradition in Spanish Literature, 1330–1630*, Selinsgrove: Susquehanna University Press, pp. 138–63

Parra, Eduardo (2004) 'Primero es el objeto y luego la fotografía', 30 May http://www.quesabesde.com/noticias/1-1278 Accessed 30 July 2005

Paso Cano, Antonio and Carlos Servet y Fortuny (1907) *Tenorio feminista: Parodia lírica mujeriega en un acto, dividido en tres cuadros, original hasta cierto punto*, Madrid: Sociedad de autores españoles

Pavlov, I. P. (1929) *Los reflejos condicionados*, Madrid: Morata

Paz, Marga (2000) *El teatro de los pintores en la Europa de las vanguardias*, Madrid: Aldeasa

Pearsell, Ronald (1977) *Conan Doyle: A Biographical Solution*, London: Weidenfeld & Nicholson

Pedrola, Luis de (1950) 'La legendaria figura de Don Juan en una magnífica película española', *Cámara*, 186, pp. 10–11

Peláez Martín, Andrés (1993) *Historia de los Teatros Nacionales (1939–62)*, Madrid: Centro de Documentación Teatral

—— (2004a) 'Breve álbum de recuerdos del Tenorio', in César Oliva, *Seis caminos hacia el mito de Don Juan*, Madrid: Compañía Nacional de Teatro Clásico, pp. 241–8

—— (2004b) 'Tres personajes en los escenarios españoles en el último siglo: La Celestina, don Quijote y don Juan', in José Luis Díez, *Tres mitos españoles: La Celestina, don Quijote, don Juan*, Madrid: Sociedad Estatal de Conmemoraciones Culturales, pp. 93–108

Pérez-Bustamante, Ana Sofía (1998) *Don Juan Tenorio en la España del siglo XX*, Madrid: Cátedra

Pérez de Ayala, Ramón (1919) *Las máscaras*, Madrid: Calleja

Pérez Firmat, Gustavo (1986) *Literature and Liminality: Festive Readings in the Hispanic Tradition*, Durham, NC: Duke University Press

Piedra, Antonio (2001) 'Don Juan, ¿el fin de un mito?' in Gonzalo Santoja (ed.) *Don Juan, genio y figura*, Madrid: España Nuevo Milenio, pp. 89–101

Pike, Frederick B. (1971) *Hispanismo 1898–1936: Spanish Conservatives and Liberals and their Relations with Spanish America*, Notre Dame: University of Notre Dame Press

Porter, Roy (1990) 'Libertinism and promiscuity', in Jonathan Miller, *Don Giovanni: Myths of Seduction and Betrayal* (New York: Schocken Books) pp. 1–20.

Pratt, Dale (2001) *Signs of Science: Literature, Science and Spanish Modernity Since 1868*, West Lafayette: Purdue University Press

Radin, Paul (1956) *The Trickster: A Study in American Indian Mythology*, New York: Schocken Books

Rank, Otto (1913) *Don Juan et le double*, Paris: Payot

(1914) 'Der Doppelgänger', *Imago: A Journal for the Application of Psychoanalysis to the Human Sciences*, 3, pp. 97–164

(1975) *The Don Juan Legend*, Princeton: Princeton University Press

Resina, Joan Ramón (2000) 'The time of the king: gift and exchange in Zorrilla's *Don Juan Tenorio*', *Diacritics*, 30 (1) pp. 49–77

Richardson, Angelique (2003) *Love and Eugenics in the Late Nineteenth Century: Rational Reproduction and the New Woman*, Oxford: Oxford University Press

Ríos, Blanca de los (1889) 'Don Juan en la literatura y en la música', *La España Moderna*, 12, n.p.

(1909) *De la mística y la novela contemporánea*, Madrid: Imprenta Ibérica

(1911) *Afirmación de la Raza: porvenir Hispanoamericano*, Madrid: Imprenta de Bernardo Rodríguez

(1913) *Influjo de la mística, de Santa Teresa singularmente, sobre nuestro grande arte nacional*, Madrid: Imprenta de los Hijos de M. G. Hernández

(1916) *Los grandes mitos de la edad moderna: Don Quijote, Don Juan, Segismundo, Hamlet, Fausto*, Madrid: Oficinas del Centro de Cultura Hispanoamericana

(1926) 'Hispanismo', in Blanca de los Ríos de Lampérez (ed.) *Nuestra raza es española (ni Latina ni Ibera)*, Madrid: Imprenta E. Maestre, pp. 14–17

(1948) 'Don Juan y sus avatares', *Revista Nacional de Educación*, 77 (8) pp. 37–41

(1989) 'Las hijas de don Juan', in Ángela Ena Bordonada (ed.) *Novelas breves de escritoras españolas (1900–1936)*, Madrid: Castalia/Instituto de la Mujer, pp. 67–125

Rivière, Joan (1986) 'Womanliness and the masquerade (1929)', in Victor Burgin, J. Donald and Cora Kaplan (eds) *Formations of Fantasy*, London: Routledge, pp. 35–44

Robinson, Michael F. (1997) 'The alternative endings of Mozart's Don Giovanni', in Mary Hunter and James Wester (eds) *Opera Buffa in Mozart's Vienna*, Cambridge: Cambridge University Press, pp. 261–85

Rodgers, Eamonn (2000) 'Zorrilla's Don Juan Tenorio as cultural paradigm', in Andrew Ginger, Huw Lewis and John Hobbs (eds) *Selected Interdisciplinary Essays on the Representation of the Don Juan Archetype in Myth and Culture*, Lewiston: Edwin Mellen Press, pp. 149–67

Rodríguez Lafora, Gonzalo (1927) *Don Juan, los milagros y otros ensayos*, Madrid: Biblioteca Nueva

(1930) *Don Juan and Other Psychological Studies*, London: Thornton Butterworth

Rodríguez, Mariano (2002a) 'Un estreno con poca discordia', *La Vanguardia*, 1 December, p. 39

Rojek, Chris (2001) *Celebrity*, London: Reaktion Books

Ros, Samuel (1939) 'Un auto de Calderón en los jardines del retiro y en el año de la victoria', *Vértice*, 25, pp. 205–14

Rougement, Denis de (1965) *Love in the Western World*, translated by Montgomery Belgion, New York: Pantheon

Royo-Villanova Morales, Ricardo (1930) *Los médicos donjuanes: el nuevo donjuanismo*, Madrid: Imprenta Castellana

(1931a) 'La medicina y los médicos a la cabecera de Don Juan', *Revista Española de Medicina y Cirugía*, 14 (June) pp. 281–4

(1931b) 'Notas para una nueva biología de Don Juan', *Revista Española de Medicina y Cirugía*, 14 (November) pp. 570–9

Rubio Jiménez, Jesús (1989) 'Don Juan Tenorio: drama de espectáculo, plasticidad y fantasía', *Cuadernos de Investigación Filológica*, XV (1–2) pp. 5–25

(2001) 'Don Juan Tenorio en versión de Luis Escobar y Salvador Dalí', in Andrés Peláez Martín (ed.) *Luis Escobar y la vanguardia*, Madrid: Comunidad de Madrid, pp. 55–94

Rushton, Julian (1981) *W. A. Mozart: Don Giovanni*, Cambridge: Cambridge University Press

Saíd Armesto, Victor (1908) *La leyenda de Don Juan: orígenes poéticos de 'El burlador de Sevilla y convidado de piedra'*, Madrid: Espasa-Calpe

Sánchez Romeralo, Antonio (1989) 'Un Tenorio de Buñuel ("Libreto" para una representación en la Residencia de Estudiantes)', *La Torre*, 3 (10) April–June, pp. 357–79

Sánchez Vidal, Agustín (1988) *Buñuel, Lorca, Dalí: El enigma sin fin*, Barcelona: Planeta

Sans Rivière, Fernando (2002) 'Libertinaje marca Calixto Bieito', *La Razón*, 2 December, p. 58

Santa Ana, Rafael de (1919) *Manual del perfecto mujeriego*, Madrid: Imprenta helénica

Schmidt-Nowara, Christopher (2006) *The Conquest of History: Spanish Colonialism and National Histories in the Nineteenth Century*, Pittsburgh: University of Pittsburgh Press

Sengoopta, Chandak (1998) 'Glandular politics: experimental biology, clinical medicine, and homosexual emancipation in fin-de-siècle central Europe', *Isis*, 89, pp. 445–73

Serrano, Carlos (1996) *Carnaval en noviembre: parodias teatrales españolas de Don Juan Tenorio*, Alicante: Instituto de cultura Juan Gil-Albert

(1998) 'Don Juan y la inversion paródica: el caso de las Doña Juana', in Ana Sofía Pérez-Bustamante (ed.) *Don Juan Tenorio en la España del siglo XX*, Madrid: Cátedra, pp. 55–69

(1999) *El nacimiento de Carmen: símbolos, mitos y nación*, Madrid: Taurus

Serrano, Francisco (1927) *El Tenorio Sarasa*, Barcelona

Shaw, Donald L. (1978) *Historia de la literatura española*, Barcelona: Ariel

Siguan, Miguel (1956) *El cine, el amor y otros ensayos*, Madrid: Editora Nacional

Silver, Philip W. (1997) *Ruin and Restitution: Reinterpreting Romanticism in Spain*, Nashville: Vanderbilt University Press

Bibliography

Sinclair, Alison (forthcoming) 'Love, again: crisis and the search for consolation: the *Revista de Occidente* and the creation of a culture, 1923–1936', in Luisa Passerini, Liliana Ellena and Alexander C. T. Geppert (eds) *New Dangerous Liaisons: Discourses on Europe and Love in the Twentieth Century*, Oxford: Berghahn Books

Sinfield, Alan (1994) *The Wilde Century: Effeminacy, Oscar Wilde and the Queer Moment*, London: Cassell

Smith, Paul Julian (1998) *The Theatre of García Lorca: Text, Performance, Psychoanalysis*, Cambridge: Cambridge University Press

Smith, Terry Donovan (1996) 'Shifting through space–time: a chronotopic analysis of Peter Sellars' Don Giovanni', *Modern Drama*, 34 (4) pp. 668–79

Solano, María Luisa (1930) 'Una gran escritora española: Doña Blanca de los Ríos de Lampérez', *Hispania*, XIII, pp. 389–98

Sontag, Susan (1977) *Illness as Metaphor*, Harmondsworth: Penguin

Soriano, Elena (2000) *El donjuanismo femenino*, Barcelona: Ediciones Península

Soufas, C. Christopher (1995) 'The sublime, the beautiful and the imagination in Zorrilla's Don Juan Tenorio', *MLN*, 110 (2) pp. 302–19

Spinks, C. W. (1991) *Semiosis, Marginal Signs and Trickster*, London: Macmillan

(2001) *Trickster and Ambivalence: The Dance of Differentiation*, Madison: Atwood Publishing

Springer, Claudia (1996) *Electronic Eros: Bodies and Desire in the Postindustrial Age*, London: Athlone

Stewart, Susan (1993) *On Longing: Narratives of the Miniature, the Gigantic, the Souvenir, the Collection*, Durham: Duke University Press

Storm, Eric (2004) 'The problems of the Spanish nation-building process around 1900', *National Identities*, 6 (2) pp. 143–56

Studlar, Gaylin (1996) *This Mad Masquerade: Stardom and Masculinity in the Jazz Age*, New York: Columbia University Press

Talbot, Eugene (1898) *Degeneracy: Its Causes, Signs and Results*, London: Walter Scott Ltd

Tanner, Michael (2001) 'Lust without love', *The Spectator*, 9 June, p. 49

Ter Horst, Robert (1996) 'Epic descent: the filiations of Don Juan', *MLN*, 111 (2) pp. 255–74
Teruel, Barco (1961) *Elogio y nostalgia de Gregorio Marañón*, Barcelona: Barca
Till, Nicholas (1992) *Mozart and the Enlightenment: Truth, Virtune and Beauty in Mozart's Operas*, London: Faber & Faber
Tirso de Molina (1978) *El burlador de Sevilla y convidado de piedra*, edited by Joaquín Casalduvo, Madrid: Cátedia
Torrente Ballester, Gonzalo (1960) 'Don Juan, los españoles y el doctor', *Índice*, May–June, pp. 8
Triana-Toribio, Núria (2003) *Spanish National Cinema*, London: Routledge
Tydeman, William and Steven Price (1996) *Wilde: Salome*, Cambridge: Cambridge University Press
Unamuno y Jugo, Miguel de (1904) 'La raza ibero-americana en la gran raza latina', *Unión Ibero-Americana* (special issue)
— (1913) *Del sentimiento trágico de la vida en los hombres y en los pueblos*, Madrid: Prudencio Pérez de Velasco
— (1986) *En torno al casticismo*, Madrid: Alianza
Valentí Vivó, I. (1910) *La sanidad nacional: eugenesia y biometría*, Barcelona: La neotipia
Valis, Noël (2005) *Reading the Nineteenth Century Spanish Novel: Selected Essays*, Newark: Juan de la Cuesta
Vázquez, Luis (1988) '"El burlador" de Tirso, refundido por Carmen Martín Gaite', *Ya*, 15 October, p. 11
Vázquez Recio, Nieves (1998) 'Las hijas de don Juan (1907) de Blanca de los Ríos: fin de siglo y una mirada femenina', in Ana Sofía Pérez Bustamante (ed.) *Don Juan Tenorio en la España del siglo XX*, Madrid: Cátedra, pp. 379–403
Veblen, Thorstein (1899) *The Theory of the Leisure Class: An Economic Study of Institutions*, London: George & Unwin
Villán, Javier (2002) 'Don Juan Tenorio, historia de un mito', *El Mundo*, 30 October http://www.elmundo.ex/papel/2002/10/30/Madrid/1260334.ntml Accessed 12 December 2006
— (2004) 'La sombra de Dalí', in César Oliva (ed.) *Seis caminos hacia el mito de Don Juan*, Madrid: Compañía Nacional de Teatro Clásico, pp. 177–8
Vivanco, José Manuel (1952) *Moral y pedagogía del cine*, Madrid: Ediciones Fax

Waldoff, Jessica (1997) 'Don Giovanni: recognition denied', in Mary Hunter and James Wester (eds) *Opera Buffa in Mozart's Vienna*, Cambridge: Cambridge University Press, pp. 287–307

Watt, Ian (1996) *Myths of Modern Individualism: Faust, Don Quixote, Don Juan, Robinson Crusoe*, Cambridge: Cambridge University Press

Weber, Alison (1996) *Teresa of Avila and the Rhetoric of Femininity*, Princeton: Princeton University Press

Weinstein, Leo (1959) *The Metamorphosis of Don Juan*, Stanford: Stanford University Press

Wilson-Bareau, Juliet and Manuela Mena Marqués, (1994) *Goya: Truth and Fantasy: The Small Paintings*, New Haven: Yale University Press

Wirth, Andrzej (1993) 'The Don Juan myth radiantly transformed', *Performing Arts Journal*, 15 (1) pp. 42–58

Wright, Elizabeth (1992) *Feminism and Psychoanalysis: A Critical Dictionary*, Oxford: Blackwell

Wright, Sarah (2004) 'Ethical seductions: a comparative reading of Unamuno's *El Hermano Juan* and Kierkegaard's *Either/Or*', *Anales de la Literatura Española Contemporánea*, 29 (2) pp. 119–34

(2007) 'The reluctant Don Juans: Lorca, Amiel, Marañón', *Anales de la Literatura Española Contemporánea*, 32 (2) pp. 447–61

Yarza, Alejandro (2004) 'The petrified tears of General Franco: kitsch and fascism in José Luis Sáenz de Heredia's *Raza*', *Journal of Spanish Cultural Studies*, 5 (1) pp. 41–55

Yokota-Murakami, Takayuki (1998) *Don Juan East West: On the Problematics of Comparative Literature*, Albany: State University of New York Press

Zeiss, Laurel Elizabeth (2001) 'Permeable boundaries in Mozart's Don Giovanni', *Cambridge Opera Journal*, 13 (2) pp. 115–39

INDEX

1898, generation of, 24, 202, n.8; loss of colonies, 19, 20, 23
Abel, Sam, 180
absorption, 98, 101–2, 114–16, 119
accoutrements, 66, 84, 92, 105–6
Adorno, Theodor, 159, 164–5, 177, 182, 244 n.86
Adventures of Don Juan, The (Vincent Sherman film), 85, 96
advertising, 165, 172, 177, 180, 241 n.29
afterlife, 9, 91, 133, 224, n.19
Alcalá de Henares, 25, 132
alcoholism, 28, 32
All Souls, Feast of, 122–3, 133, 135; *día de difuntos*, 123, 135, 140
Allen, Woody, 13
Almodóvar, Pedro, 122, 236 n.82; *Hable con ella*, 122; *La flor de mi secreto*, 122; *Mujeres al borde de un ataque de nervios*, 224 n.21
Alonso Cortés, Narciso, 129
Alonso de Santos, José Luis, 142
Álvarez, Carlos, 246 n.99
Álvarez, Rafael, 142
Álvarez Quintero, Serafín and Joaquín, 128

Amar y morir en Sevilla (Víctor Barrera), 92
amor de Don Juan, El (John Berry), 93
amores de Don Juan, Los (Al Bradley, 92
androgyny, 190
Annabella, 113, 120
Aramburu, José, 139
Arias, Imanol, 122, 130
Arques y Escriña, Joaquín, 137
As You Like It (William Shakespeare), 148
Asamblea de Trabajadores del Espectáculo de Cataluña, 130
Aserejé (Las Ketchup), 181
atavism, 30, 204 n.31, 214 n.34
Atché, Rafael, 229 n.96
Augé, Marc, 170
Avrial y Flores, José María, 153
Aznar, José María, 131
Aznar, Tomás, 92
Azorín, José Martín, 83

Baker, Malcolm, 174
Bambú (José Luis Sáenz de Heredia), 95

275

Index

Baños, Ramón de, 86, 91
Baños, Ricardo de, 21, 86, 91
Barbie, 171–2, 177, 180
Barcelona, 118, 124, 131, 145, 160, 165, 170, 177, 183–4, 192
Bardot, Brigitte, 85
Barga, Corpus, 61
Barrera, Víctor, 92
Barry Lyndon (Stanley Kubrick), 181
Barrymore, John, 85
Barthes, Roland, 248 n.5
Batista, Aurora, 119
Baudelaire, Charles, 26, 207 n.72
Baudrillard, Jean, 18, 247 n.3, n.4
Belbel, Sergi, 131
Belén, Ana, 129
Benavente, Jacinto, 238 n.100
Benet i Jornet, Josep M., 131
Benjamin, Walter, 110, 175
Bennett, Susan, 233 n.46
Berger, John, 10
Bergman, Ingmar, 94
Berry, John, 93, 225 n.23
Bersett, Jeffrey T., 136–7
Bieito, Calixto, 21, 158–60, 163, 165–6, 169–72, 174–5, 177, 180, 182–5, 192, 194
bisexuality, 53, 67
Blanco, Carlos, 104
blood, 11, 26, 30, 34, 42, 47, 60–1, 64, 67, 72, 81, 160, 164, 174–5, 204, 207 n.72, 221 n.104; bad, 54, 55, 209 n.82, 213 n.11; bloodline, 20, 24, 28, 38, 80, 193; miscegenation, 44, 46–7, 49–50
body, 3, 4, 5, 10, 18, 31, 39, 60, 61, 63, 64, 66, 68, 71, 75, 81, 89, 120, 168, 175, 190, 191, 196 n.13, 196 n.15, 209 n.82, 214 n.30, 216 n.38, 222 n.113, 248 n.4, n.5
Bohème, La, 169

Bonilla, E., 70
Borragán, María Teresa, 204 n.24
Botticelli, Sandro (*The Birth of Venus*), 110
Bourdieu, Pierre, 21, 158, 159, 164, 165, 166, 180, 182
Bowlby, Rachel, 172
Brachfeld, F. Oliver, 62, 82
Bradley, Al, 92
Brando, Marlon, 85
Braque, Georges, 237 n.100
Brecht, Bertolt, 169
Brieux, Eugène, 209 n.81
Brígido, 139
Britt Arredondo, Christopher, 23, 44, 202 n.8
Brook, Peter, 148
Brown-Séquard, Charles Edouard, 55
Buero Vallejo, Antonio, 129
Buñuel, Luis, 94, 141, 186
Burgos, Carmen de, 83
burlador de Sevilla, El (Tirso de Molina), 8, 9, 10, 25, 124, 129, 130, 136, 195 n.7, 198 n.36, 238 n.100, 242 n.55
Burmann, Siegfried, 129, 153, 155, 238 n.100
Burmann, Wolfgang, 153, 236 n.82
Busato, Georgio, 153
Byron, Lord, 10, 26, 43

Calderón de la Barca, Pedro, 150, 160, 161, 171
canas de Don Juan, Las (Juan Ignacio Luca de Tena), 69, 128
cannibalism, 159, 175, 176
Cardenal, León, 68, 69
Cardwell, Richard, 17, 29
Caro Baroja, Julio, 141
Carrasquer Llopis, Onofre, 139
Casademunt, Joan Manuel, 137

Index

Casanova, Giacomo, 93, 131, 149
casticismo, 39, 42
Castile, 185
Castillo, Naia del, 188, 190–2, 247 n.3, 248 n.5
Catalan, 21, 185, 192
Catholicism, 41, 44, 47; Christian redemption, 96, 98, 112; national Catholicism, 19, 49, 94–5, 118, 192
Cebón, Vespasiano, 83
Celestina, 10, 23, 43, 187
cena del Rey Balthasar, La (Calderón de la Barça), 150
Cernuda, Segundo, 137
Certeau, Michel de, 144, 168
Cervantes, Miguel de, 23, 37, 125
Cervera Barat, Rafael, 32
Charcot, Jean-Martin, 59
Chardin, Jean-Baptiste-Siméon, 115
Cincuenta voces para don Juan (Mario Gas), 122
Cine Avenida, 95, 110, 225 n.31
Ciutti, 90, 102, 104, 117, 121, 143, 228 n.93
class, 5, 6, 31, 37, 40, 41, 159, 163, 165–7, 171, 180, 209 n.86, 210 n.104
Clément, Catherine, 158, 167, 169
Cleminson, Richard, 77
colonies, 19, 20, 24, 28, 29, 40, 42, 43, 45, 47, 66, 192, 193, 201 n.6
Columbus, Christopher, 95, 118
Commendatore, 160, 162, 174, 175, 181
Compañía Nacional de Teatro Clásico, 130
Companyia T de Teatre, 131
Conan Doyle, Sir Arthur, 72
conquistador, 24, 44, 49, 50, 244 n.77

consumption, 6, 37, 97, 158–60, 165, 169–70, 172–3, 175–7, 181, 182, 186; consumerism, 6, 17, 159–60, 164, 170, 172–3, 176, 180; cultural consumption, 159; disease, 28, 39
contagion, 36, 39, 45, 50, 209 n.82, n.84, 221 n.105
costume, 91, 93, 95, 105, 106, 161
Crawford, Joan, 100
Crosland, Alan, 85
Crystal, David, 2
Cuatro películas sobre el mito (Mario Gas), 122
Cueva, Jorge de la, 72, 146, 147
cult of sex, 57, 58, 59, 65, 66
Curtis, Liane, 167

Da Ponte, Lorenzo, 21, 130, 158, 167, 174, 176, 181
Dalí, Salvador, 21, 129, 136, 141, 143, 145–7, 149–53, 155, 187, 193, 238 n.100
Darwin, Charles, 28, 175
Davies, Ann, 13, 17
degeneration, 6, 20, 28–31, 38, 50, 80
Delgado, María, 144, 181
Delgado, Pedro, 126
Depp, Johnny, 85
destape, 92, 224 n.20
día de la bestia, El (Alex de la Iglesia, film), 181
Diaghilev, Sergei, 237 n.100
Diderot, Denis, 114
disguise, 4, 5, 80, 121, 161, 177
divorce, 19, 52, 72, 100
¡Dixtos Tenorio! (Ramón Muntané, play), 137
Doane, Mary Ann, 84
Don Giovanni, 161; as Calixto Bieito opera, 159, 169–2, 176,

Index

177, 185, 186, 247 n.118; Lluís Pasqual opera, 130, 246 n.99; Mozart/Da Ponte opera, 21, 158, 160, 167, 173, 197 n.33
Don Gonzalo de Ulloa (Guillermo Perín, play), 137
Don Joan, as Adrià Gual play, 137
Don Juan as Alan Crosland film, 85; Jacques Weber film, 92; José Luis García-Berlanga TV adaptation, 92; Molière, 2, 197 n.33; Sáenz de Heredia film, 94; Salvador Toscano Barragán film, 85
Don Juan de España, as Gregorio and María Martínez Sierra play, 128, 203 n.23, 232 n.27
Don Juan de Marco (Jeremy Leven film), 85
Don Juan en los infiernos (Gonzalo Suárez, film), 92
Don Juan en los ruedos (Salvador Távora, stage show), 131
Don Juan no existe (Condesa de San Luis, play), 128, 202 n.9, 232 n.28
Don Juan Notorio, burdel en cinco actos y 2000 escándalos (Anon., play), 136
Don Juan Tenorio as Alejandro Perla, film, 145; José Zorrilla play, 122–56, 197 n.28; Luis Escobar and Salvador Dalí, theatre, 21, 143, 145, 148, 149; Ricardo de Baños film, 21
Don Juan Tenorio en el panteón (Elí, 188
Don Juan último (Vicente Molina Foix, play), 130
Don Juan, buena persona (Serafín and Joaquín Álvarez Quintero, play), 128

Don Juan, mi querido fantasma (Antonio Mercero, film), 93
Don Quixote, 10, 23, 34, 43, 188
Doña Inés, 12, 88, 90, 103, 112–14, 116–17, 119–20, 122, 126, 129, 138–9, 142, 147–9, 228 n.93
Doña Juana, 188
Doña Juana Tenorio (Rafael María Liern play), 13, 137, 138
Donna Giovanna, 245 n.99
Dora, 28, 31, 33, 35, 39
Doty, William G., 7
duelling, 107
Dumas, Alexandre, 10

Echegaray, José, 28, 54, 238 n.100
Edinburgh Festival, 186
Edison, Thomas Alva, 72
effeminacy, 76, 77, 80, 105, 188, 219 n.85, n.89
Eisenstein, Sergei, 84
electronic eros, 2, 5
Elvira, Donna, 160, 164, 167, 171, 185
empire, 24, 46, 48–50, 66, 95–6, 188
endocrinology, 66, 67; *see also* hormones
energy (will), 5, 43, 49, 65, 121, 189, 198 n.33
English National Opera (ENO), 183
Ernst, Max, 237 n.100
erotic novels, 36
Eryximachus, 61
Escobar, Luis, 21, 129, 136, 143, 145, 148, 149, 153, 236 n.79
españolada, 97, 226 n.39
Espert, Nuria, 122
Espronceda, José de, 26
eugenics, 6, 28, 52

Fairbanks, Douglas, 80, 85, 93

Index

Falange, 120, 150
Falla, Manuel de, 232 n.27
Farinelli, Arturo, 24
Feal, Carlos, 16
Felman, Shoshana, 2, 3, 196 n13, n.15
feminism, 5, 52
femme fatale, 13, 84, 112–88, 227 n.65, 232 n.27, 248 n.4
Fernández, Amalio, 153
Fernández, Luis Miguel, 16
Fernández Montesinos, Ángel, 143, 155
Fernando de Igoa, Luis, 129
First World War, 56
firstness, 132, 135, 136, 143, 146, 147, 155
flamenquismo, 35
Fleck, Ludwik, 213 n.11
Fliess, Wilhelm, 229 n.1, 244 n.77
Flynn, Errol, 85, 96, 105
Foucault, Michel, 54, 64, 199 n.52
Fox, Inman, 40
Fragonard, Jean-Honoré, 115
Franco, Francisco, 19, 21–2, 50, 94, 97, 99, 128, 149; Francoism, 19, 50, 95, 130, 144–5, 246 n.99
Franco, José, 129
Freud, Sigmund, 18, 56–9, 63, 159, 174, 176, 213, 200 n.68, 229 n.1
Fried, Michael, 98, 114–15, 117
Frigerio, Ezio, 246 n.99
Frisch, Max, 10
Fuentes, José, 139

Galton, Francis, 28
Gàmiz, Rosa, 131
Gance, Abel, 86
García, Nemesio, 68
García Escudero, José Luis, 100
García Garzón, Juan Ignacio, 155
García Lorca, Federico, 77, 83, 141, 238 n.100
García Yagüe, Juan, 100
Garmendía de Otaola, A., 101
Garnivet, Angel, 24
Gas, Mario, 122, 130
Gaudreault, André, 91
gaze, 90, 108–9, 112, 116, 119–20, 191, 248 n.5
Gies, David T., 13, 125, 136, 231 n.21
Giménez Caballero, Ernesto, 48, 99, 221 n113
Giner, Ramón, 117
Ginger, Andrew, 16, 89
Glenn, Kathleen, 28, 38
Glick, Tom, 63, 68
Glyndebourne, 237 n.100
Goldoni, Carlo, 10
Gómez, José Luis, 122
Gone with the Wind (Victor Fleming, film), 108
González Álvarez, B., 32
González López, María Antonieta, 25, 50
Gould, Glenn, 186
Goya, Francisco de, 12, 198 n.37
Greuze, Jean-Baptiste, 115
Gris, Juan, 237 n.100
Gual, Adrià, 137
Gual, Adrià, 238 n.100
Guerrero, María, 129, 148, 155
Guerrero, Mercedes, 129
Guillén, Fernando, 92
Guitart, Enrique, 129
Gunning, Tom, 91, 224 n.19
Gutiérrez del Egido, Ernesto, 99
Gyenes, Juan, 145
Gyenes, Juan, 236 n.81

Han matado a Don Juan (Federico Oliver, play), 128
Hanover, 183

Index

Hansen, Miriam, 97
haptic, 6, 248 n.5
Haro Tecglen, Eduardo, 144–6, 148, 154–5, 236 n.79
Haslett, Moyra, 14
Hayworth, Rita, 100
herencia del Tenorio, La (Adelaida Muñiz, play), 137
heritage, 6, 24, 29, 96, 104, 125, 132–3, 156, 186, 188, 191
hermano Juan, El (Miguel de Unamuno, play), 12, 128
Hernández Ruiz, Javier, 93
Higueras, Modesto, 129
hijas de don Juan, Las (Blanca de los Ríos, short novel), 20, 25, 26, 27, 29, 34, 39, 44, 45, 50, 54, 202 n.9
hijo de don Juan, El (José Echegaray play), 28, 54
hijo del Diablo, El (Joaquín Montaner), 141
Hirschfeld, Magnus, 70
hirsutism, 65
hispanidad, 44, 49
Historia de una escalera (Antonio Buero Vallejo, play), 129
Hitchcock, Alfred, 84
Hobbs, John, 16
Hockney, David, 237 n.100
Hoffman, E. T. A., 10
Hollywood, 85, 96, 98, 108, 112
¡Hombres! (Companyia T de Teatre, play), 131
homosexuality, 21, 53, 71, 75, 77–80, 150
Hope, Bob, 93
hormones, 17, 61, 64–7; *see also* endocrinology
Hutcheon, Linda, 140, 169
Hynes, William J., 7

hysteria, 28, 31; female, 59, 167; male, 56

Ibsen, Henrik, 28, 38
If Don Juan Were a Woman (Roger Vadim, film), 85
Iglesia, Alex de la, 181, 182
infidelity, 6
Inquisition, 125
Internet, 6, 9, 197 n.29; chat, 1–5, 196 n.13, n.15; cyber-flirting, 1, 4; cybersex, 3, 10
intersexuality, 67, 79, 227
Íscla, Miriam, 131

James Bond, 37
Jarmusch, Jim, 85
Jiménez Placer, Fernando, 129
Johnny Tenorio (Morton play), 230 n.3
Johnson, Roberta, 17, 35, 232 n.27
jouissance, 9, 121, 168
Jung, Carl, 14

Kapoor, Anish, 237n.100
Keller, Gary, 219 n.89
Kelly-Holmes, Helen, 165, 241 n.29
Kennedy, Michael, 164
Kernan, Joseph, 167
Kierkegaard, Søren, 10, 168, 183
Kircher, Athaneseus, 93
Koch, Robert, 207 n.65
Korda, Alexander, 85, 93
Kristeva, Julia, on Don Juan, 13; on film spectator, 229 n.99; on music, 168; on nameless dread, 84, 91, 119; on perfect film, 84
Kruif, Paul de, 65
Kubrick, Stanley, 181–2, 184

Labanyi, Jo, 17, 40, 48

Index

Lacan, Jacques, 206 n.47, 227 n.68; on Don Juan, 222 n.2
LaMadrid, Bárbara, 126
LaMadrid, Teodora, 126
language, discourse, 2–4, 14, 16–18, 28, 52, 64, 80, 104, 109–10, 133, 145, 185, 199
Lasa, Juan Francisco de, 88
law, 9, 12, 15, 18–19, 28, 32, 47, 52, 54, 72, 84, 95, 140
Lázaro, Reyes, 28, 29, 37, 39
Léger, Fernand, 86, 90
Lejárraga, María, 128, 232 n.27
Lenau, Nikolaus, 10, 43
leona de Castilla, La (Juan de Orduña, film), 95, 106
Leporello, 160–2, 167, 171, 175, 181
Lévi-Strauss, Claude, 14
Liceu, Gran Teatre del, 158, 177, 184
Liern, Rafael María, 13, 137, 138
lies, 2, 58, 100, 103, 114, 117, 213 n.15
Lillie, Frank, 64
Llaneces, José, 187
Locura de amor (Juan de Orduña, film), 95, 106
Lola se va a los puertos, La (Juan de Orduña, film), 119
Lombroso, Cesare, 29
London, John, 150, 237 n.100
Long Hall, Diana, 66
López, Ignacio-Javier, 16
Losada, José Manuel, 10
Lourdes, 57
Luca de Tena, Cayetano, 129
Luca de Tena, Juan Ignacio, 69, 128

Lyotard, Jean-François, 79, 220 n.97

McClary, Susan, 169
McClintock, Anne, 209 n.82, 212 n.118
Machado, Manuel y Antonio, 128
McMaster, Sir Brian, 186, 247 n.118
Madariaga, Salvador de, 211 n.114
Maeztu, Ramiro de, 10, 24, 43, 44, 48, 210 n.90
Magee, Garry, 177
Mampasso, Manuel, 153
Mañara, Miguel de, 24
Mandrell, James, 13, 16, 18, 133, 198 n.36
Marañón, Gregorio, 18, 20, 22, 53–5, 57–61, 63–4, 66–71, 75–82, 104, 128, 150, 192–3, 212 n.2, 213 n.10, 214 n.31, n.34, 216 n.40, 217 n.57, 218 n.84, 219 n.86, n.89, 221 n.107, 227 n.67, n.69
Marianism, 126
Marín, Guillermo, 128, 129
Mark of Zorro, The (Fred Niblo, film), 80
Marquerie, Alfredo, 146, 148, 236 n.79
Marshall, Mary, 72
Martín Gaite, Carmen, 112, 120, 130
Martínez Sierra, Gregorio, 128, 232 n.27, 238 n.100
Marx, Karl, 176
Masetto, 161, 171, 185
maternity, 44, 53, 65, 212 n.118
Mattauch, Hans, 124
melodrama, 97, 98, 114, 117
Menéndez Pidal, Ramón, 24
Mercero, Antonio, 93, 94
Miró, Joan, 237 n.100

281

Index

Mitchell, Juliet, 18, 56, 57, 59, 170
Mitchell, Timothy, 123, 125
Molgosa Valls, José, 137
Molière, 10, 26, 43
Molina Foix, Vicente, 130
Montaner, Joaquín, 141
Montián, Niní, 128
Morales, Isaac, 69
Morales, Saturnino, 142
Morboria Teatro, 122
Morel, Bénédict, 28, 30
Morocco, 92
morphology, 56, 61, 62
Mozart, Amadeus, 10, 21, 26, 130, 158, 160, 167, 170, 173, 180
Munilla, Ortega, 27
Muñiz, Adelaida, 137
Muñoz Degrain, Antonio, 134
Muñoz Peña, Pedro, 26
Muñoz Seca, Pedro, 68, 71, 72, 73
Muntané, Ramón, 137
Murray, Bill, 86
Musset, Alfred de, 26
myth, 5–6, 14, 16–18, 20, 22, 26–7, 31, 43–4, 57–8, 61, 64, 73, 75, 78, 93–4, 97, 125, 142, 159, 165, 174, 175, 186, 193, 195 n.7

Naples, 11, 137
Narros, Miguel, 129, 153
nationhood (Spain), 6, 19, 192
Navarre, 39
New World, 40, 42, 47
Nietzsche, Friedrich, 48, 131
Nieva de la Paz, Pilar, 232 n.28
Nieva, Francisco, 125, 153
Nin, Carlos, 105
No hay deuda que no se pague ni plazo que no se cumpla (Antonio de Zamora play), 136
noblezas de Don Juan, Las (Enrique Pelayo play), 137

Nogués, José María, 137
Nordau, Max, 28, 31, 34, 35

Oliva, César, 127, 129
Oliver, Federico, 128
Olympic Games, 170
onanism, 55
Ontañón, Santiago, 238 n.100
Ontiveros, Lady, 102, 108, 112, 114, 120, 188
Orduña, Juan de, 95, 106, 118
Ortega y Gasset, José, 81–2, 127–8, 166
Oudshoorn, Nelly, 64

Pardo Bazán, Emilia, 27
Parellada, Pablo, 138
Paso Cano, Antonio, 138
Paso Díaz, Antonio, 139
Pasqual, Lluís, 130, 246 n.99
paternity, 55, 135
Patinir, Joachim, 93
Pelayo y Menéndez, Enrique, 137
Pellicena, José Luis, 129
Pereira, Francesc, 131
Pérez de Ayala, Ramón, 16, 54, 83, 132
Pérez de la Ossa, Huberto, 129, 236 n.79
Pérez Galdós, Benito, 16, 27
Pérez Puig, Gustavo, 130
performative, 2–6, 58, 153, 196 n.15
Perín, Guillermo, 137
Perla, Alejandro, 145
Philippines, 23
Picasso, Pablo, 237 n.100
Piedra, Antonio, 2
Pike, Frederick, 42
Plá, Carmen, 131

Index

plasmatoria, La (Pedro Muñoz Seca, play), 71–2, 75–7, 79–80, 219, 220 n.99
Plato, 61
Popular Party, 131
Potter, Sally, 169
Pratt, Dale, 217 n.53
Price, Leontyne, 245 n.99
primal horde, 175, 176
Primo de Rivera, General Miguel, 76
Private Life of Don Juan, The (Alexander Korda), 85–6, 93
promise, 2, 4, 5, 45, 128, 170
prostitution, 28, 30–2, 35, 39, 52, 54, 215 n.35
psychoanalysis, 6, 18, 56, 57, 59, 63
Puerto Rico, 23
Pushkin, Alexander, 211 n.114

race, 23, 27–8, 30–2, 39, 42, 46, 48–9, 53, 55, 193, 204 n.31, 206 n.45, 211 n.118
Ramón y Cajal, Santiago, 60, 78
Rank, Otto, 18, 123, 159, 174
rape, 105, 167, 169, 170
Regio, 138
Reina Sofía Museum, 145
rejuvenation, 70
Restoration, 20, 27, 32, 40
Riefenstahl, Leni, 94
Ríos, Blanca de los, 20, 22, 24–7, 31–2, 35, 37–9, 42, 44, 46, 48–9, 54, 192–3, 202 n.14
Rivas, Duque de, 25
Rivelles, Amparo, 119
Rivière, Joan, 227 n.68
Roca, Ágata, 131
Rodgers, Eamonn, 125
Rodríguez Lafora, Gonzalo, 56
Rome, 123, 148
Rose, Jacqueline, 60

Royo-Villanova Morales, Ricardo, 81, 221 n.107
Rubio Jiménez, Jesús, 13, 126, 135, 145, 150, 155

Sade, Marquis de, 131
Sáenz de Heredia, José Luis, 21, 94–6, 104, 118, 187–8, 192–3
Sáenz de Tejada, Carlos, 129
Saíd Armesto, Víctor, 24, 123
Salaverría, Elías, 73, 76, 188
Salgado, María Rosa, 116–17, 120
Salmerón, Nicolás, 29
Salpêtrière asylum, 60
San Luis, Condesa de, 128
Sánchez Gijón, Aitana, 122
Santa Teresa de Ávila, 31, 33
Santpere, Josep, 137
Saussure, Ferdinand de, 14
scapegoat, 6, 177
Scene from 'El convidado de piedra' (Francisco de Goya, painting), 198 n.37
scenography, 21, 129, 136, 150, 153
Scorsese, Martin, 174, 181
Segura, Santiago, 181
Sellars, Peter, 186, 237 n.100, 245 n.99
Serrano, Carlos, 136–7, 139–40, 210 n.90
Serrano, Francisco, 139
Servet y Fortuny, Carlos, 138
Seville, 8, 11, 24, 40, 46, 96, 102
sexual continence, 55
Shakespeare, William, 131, 148
Shaw, Donald, 125
Shaw, George Bernard, 10, 209 n.81
Sherman, Vincent, 96
Siguan, Miguel, 99
Silver, Philip W., 40
Sinfield, Alan, 77

283

Index

Smith, Paul Julian, 77
Smith, Terry Donovan, 245 n.99
sombra del Tenorio, La (José Luis Alonso de Santos play), 142
Somoza, Rafael, 71
Soriano, Elena, 17
Spain, 9, 12, 18–24, 27–8, 32, 34, 39, 42, 44, 46–8, 52–3, 57, 66, 72, 76, 83, 91, 94–5, 102, 112, 118, 123–4, 126, 128, 133, 139, 144, 149, 172, 184–5, 187, 192–3
Spanish Civil War, 73, 128
speech-act, 2, 3
star system, 21, 98, 101, 110, 112
Starling, Ernest, 56
Steinach, Eugen, 68, 70
Stekel, Wilhelm, 78
sterility (male), 55
Stewart, Susan, 133
Stone Guest, 8, 11, 12, 124, 133, 174
Stravinksy, Igor, 237 n.100
Student of Prague, The, 224 n.14
Studlar, Gaylin, 80
Suárez, Emma, 122
Suárez, Gonzalo, 92
Suero, Pablo, 69
suture, 107, 117, 118, 228 n.77
syphilis, 28, 38, 209 n.81, 213 n.11

tableaux vivant, 103, 151
Tamayo, José, 129
Tanner, Michael, 163
Tarantino, Quentin, 163, 181, 182, 184
taste, 21, 31, 40–1, 148, 159, 164, 166, 182, 185, 186, 210 n.104, 247 n.118
Távora, Salvador, 131

Teatro Eslava, 138
Teatro Español, 122, 126, 128, 129, 138, 155
Teatro Lara, 138
Teatro María Guerrero, 129, 149
Teatro San Martín, 130
Tenorio cosmopolita (Joseph Santpere play), 137
Tenorio en Nápoles Joaquí, 137
Tenorio feminista (Antonio Paso Cano play), 138, 140, 188
Tenorio 'inocentada' (José Molgosa Valls play), 137
Tenorio modernista (Pablo Parellada play), 138
Tenorio moderno, Un (José María Nogués, play), 137
Tenorio Sarasa, El (Francisco Serrano, play), 139, 140
Tenorios y castañillas (Joan Manuel Casademunt, play), 137
theatricality (in cinema), 21, 86, 88, 93, 94, 98, 103, 105, 114
Thriller (Sally Potter, film), 169, 243 n.57
Tigre Juan (Pérez de Ayala, novel), 83
Tirso de Molina, 8, 10–13, 24–7, 32, 44, 54, 96, 104, 124–5, 128–9, 133, 136
Toledo, 25
Trampas y seducción (exhibition), 188
Trent, Council of, 12
Tres mitos españoles: La Celestina, Don Quijote, Don Juan (exhibition), 187, 188, 233 n.41, 247 n.1
Tres noches con don Juan (Mario Gas, theatrical event), 122

trick-shot, 21, 91, 224 n.17
trickster, 5, 7, 8, 15, 43, 44, 192

Última escena de Don Juan (Antonio Muñoz Degrain, painting), 134
última ilusión de Don Juan, La (Emilia Pardo Bazán, short story), 27
Unamuno, Miguel de, 12, 16, 23, 29, 34, 42, 83, 128, 210 n.90
United States, 23, 42

Vadim, Roger, 85
Valis, Noël, 33
Valladolid, 26
Valle-Inclán, Ramón María del, 16, 141, 166, 186, 203 n.23, 232 n.27, 235 n.73; *Las galas del difunto*, 142; *Sonatas*, 142
Vasco, Eduardo, 130
Veblen, Thorstein, 165
Velasco, Concha, 122, 129
Velázquez, Diego, 62, 93, 186
Venice Biennale, 113
Vera, Gerardo, 153
vergonzoso en palacio, El (Tirso de Molina, play), 8
Vilar, Antonio, 103, 105, 109, 116, 118
Villamediana, Conde de, 78
Villán, Javier, 127, 154

violence, 163, 167, 181–2, 185, 241, 245, 255
Visconti, Luchino, 148
Vivanco, José Manuel, 100
Voronoff, Serge, 68

Wagner, Richard, 180
waste, 170, 172, 173
Watling, Leonor, 122
Watt, Ian, 11, 14
Weininger, Otto, 65
Weinstein, Leo, 10
Whale, Andy, 177
Wilde, Oscar, 219 n.85
Wilson, Robert, 130
Wright, Elizabeth, 176

Xirgu, Margarita, 141, 238 n.100

Yarza, Alejandro, 229 n.98
Yokota-Murakami, Takayuki, 10, 16

Zamora, Antonio de, 12, 124, 126, 128, 133, 136
Zorrilla, José, 9, 12–13, 17–18, 21, 26–7, 32, 37, 44, 54, 73, 86, 92, 94, 96, 104, 122, 124–5, 127, 129, 132, 133, 135–7, 140, 143, 146, 149, 156, 187
Zurro, Alfonso, 131

www.ingramcontent.com/pod-product-compliance
Lightning Source LLC
Chambersburg PA
CBHW071235230426
43668CB00011B/1453